Behind the Wall

A Season on the NASCAR Circuit

Richard M. Huff

Bonus Books, Inc., Chicago

96 95 94 93 92   5 4 3 2 1

Library of Congress Catalog Card Number: 91-77009

International Standard Book Number: 0-929387-66-X

Bonus Books, Inc.
160 East Illinois Street
Chicago, Illinois 60611

Printed in the United States of America

*To Michelle, my wife, for spending a year alone
while I went racing*

Contents

Contents

Acknowledgments

One never truly understands how much help is needed from others when embarking on an endeavor like this until the project starts. I know I sure didn't.

However not two minutes within the gates of Daytona International Speedway did I realize there was no way I could attempt this trip without the help and confidence of the people at Sun Refining and Marketing Company and the Hagan Racing Team.

Before Daytona I hadn't met any of my partners for this journey and to them I was this guy from New York, a Yankee, there to write a book about racing. During the ten months I spent following this team across the country and back, I grew to know them and respect their talents as mechanics, technicians of sort, and one as a race car driver. To each and everyone of them I offer my heartfelt thanks.

Throughout this journey they allowed me to look over their shoulders as they went about their business. I am confident there were times when they were tired of bumping into me or sick of my constant questions, however, not once did they complain.

To Bryan Robertson, Kelly Hunt, and Donnie Crumley, thanks for adding some humor to often depressing situations. Steve Loyd and Dewey Livengood, by allowing me to perform what seemed like menial tasks in the pits, they permitted a grown man to fulfill little boy dreams. Greg McElreath, Steve Wilson, Johnny Siler, Billy Siler, Dan Gatewood, Danny Culler,

Mark Metcalfe, Jesse Coke and Jim Coltrane, these guys are professionals of the highest order. To Harold Hughes, a special thanks for the occasional warnings there could be laxative laced brownies on the way. There's a whole bunch of other Hagan employees who rarely came to the raceway, they should be thanked also. So here goes. Gary Wagoner, Bill Carter, Frank Routh Tony Barker, Rick Potter, Craig Griffitts, Jeff McBride, Aaron Dudley and Nancy Keith, thank you.

On a trip like this some constants develop and Herb Hupperich was certainly one of them. Despite the events around him, Herb took time to answer my questions, honestly and openly. On days he wasn't talking to others he talked to me, and I appreciate that. No one made me feel as much a part of the team as he did.

This entire project hinged on the approval of Billy Hagan and for that go ahead I am grateful and will always be indebted. While Sunoco pressured him for performance on one side, and Hupperich pressured him about team problems, Hagan never once dismissed one of my questions. I always felt welcome in his presence. Whether it was talking about racing or Cajun cooking, Hagan did it with vigor and a sense of compassion not held by many.

If there was a person who could have been most offended by my notebook it was Terry Labonte. When he was standing by the car, I was right there. When he got out of the car after a few hours of racing, I was there. When things went wrong, I was there. Labonte's moods changed like his performance on the track. When he was in the right mood we talked like old friends, other times I got my answers and that's all. It's all understandable, though. Being the driver is like being a quarterback in football. The team rides and falls on his shoulders. Throughout the season, he may have been angered by my presence, but not once did he tell me to move on. I thank Labonte for his help and honest answers, and I know there are more wins to come for this former champion.

My odyssey with the Sunoco Ultra racing team started by my faxing the proposal for this book to Dennis Byrne, the company's public relations executive, working with the team. After being rejected by others, Byrne picked up the idea and forwarded my proposal to the racing committee, which later approved the idea. I thank Dennis for his enthusiasm with the project and for not throwing my letter in the garbage. Those same words of thanks go to the committee members, Dr. Bob Burtner, Geoff Plazer, Charles Chace, Kirk Chandler, Al Contino, Jim McCallister, Jim Meisner, Doug Plyler, William Salmon, and Harold Vaughn, who approved having me along for the ride and offered help when they were at the track.

Of the committee members two deserve special mention. Chairman Bud Campbell and public relations representative Paul Mecca.

Paul was there day in and day out answering my questions and showing me the ropes. I learned more about the inside workings of stock car racing in the first few weeks than I could have hoped for in a full season without him. Though some of his tales don't stand up to cross-examination, they were fun to listen to anyway. No one knows how to work the system better than he, and, perhaps, no one knows better how to use a racing hat for his own benefit. In racing, team caps are a premium, and with a handful, Mecca was king.

There are not enough kind words for Bud Campbell. From the moment we met outside the team transporter on a chilly February morning in Daytona, he opened his world to me. I am confident he would have offered the shirt off his back if I had asked. I didn't, but his help was never ending. However, I place a greater value on his friendship. I also want to thank his wife for letting Bud get so involved, which in turn allowed me to have so much fun. Moreover, because of Marilyn Campbell I now have some nice photographs to remember this experience.

Over the ten month period I trailed Hagan's team, I met more people than I could ever remember; however, there were a few who stick out and are in need of mention. Associated Press motorsports writer Mike Harris was gracious enough to take some time from his schedule to talk about the business. Eli Gold and the rest of the crew at Motor Racing Network, nobody calls a game better. And thanks to Bob Jenkins of ESPN's "Speedweek," who having met me only five minutes before offered me a ride to Florence, South Carolina, when our plane was canceled in Charlotte.

Over and over again during the ten months I was involved with this team they talked frequently about the NASCAR family. I thank them for allowing me to become part of that family, if just for a short time.

I also couldn't have done this without the support of my wife, Michelle, who spent a year essentially living alone while I was off following my dreams. And to my mother for her financial and emotional contributions to the project, thank you.

Larry Razbadouski and the people of Bonus Books, without your belief in me none of this would have happened.

In addition there were a bunch of friends behind the scenes offering help and support when the project seemed a distant dream. I will name only one, Alison Begany, who offered her knowledge of the book business which made it possible for me to move forward.

In all I would like to thank the teams that declined my request to follow them for the year. Without them, I never would have met the people who work for Hagan Racing. They are all winners.

one

Troubled Vibrations

"It's like bringin' a mule to a horse race."
Billy Siler

On July 7, 1991, stock car driver Terry Labonte did exactly what he had said he would do. Days before he was angry, very angry. And to some of those around him, he laid out exactly how he would do it.

It was a typical July day in Florida. The sun was high in the sky, the temperature almost unbearable by mid-morning. The hard asphalt surface of the Daytona International Speedway started baking shortly after sunrise. So did the people who jammed the steel bleachers bordering the 2.5-mile-long superspeedway. This day the race would start earlier than most professional stock car events, 11 A.M., instead of noon, an attempt by the sport's sanctioning body, the National Association for Stock Car Auto Racing, to make everybody comfortable.

Minutes after eleven, the 358-cubic-inch engines of forty-one highly modified stock cars roared to life. Waiting on pit road, the drivers pumped their gas pedals sending high octane racing gasoline through fuel lines like a heart feeding blood to a marathon runner. A few moments later, the drivers and their cars snaked around the speedway in two lines, jerking side to side to warm their tires. After two laps the driver of the pace car leading them around the speedway turned off the revolving yellow lights mounted on top. This was a signal to the drivers. When they hit the front stretch, the race would be on. The two lines of cars came out of turn four moving close together. As the cars approached the front stretch, NASCAR flagman Doyle Ford unfurled the green flag, starting the Pepsi 400.

Together the lines dove into turn one, getting lost in the waves of heat dancing on the surface of the track. The engines released a low rumble and the ground vibrated as the cars bounced around for position.

Terry Labonte piloted the last car on the speedway. At full speed the blue and yellow Oldsmobile could barely keep up with the cars in front of it — the slowest of the race qualifiers. For seven laps Labonte raced in last place. Then, as he passed the front stretch, starting his eighth lap, Labonte pressed the small button on the right side of the steering wheel, activating the microphone in his helmet.

"Steve it feels like something's vibrating," Terry radios from the car to crew chief Steve Loyd, standing in the pits.

"You want to come in and change the tires, maybe something's equalizing?" Loyd responds.

"No, it feels like something else, it feels like something's locking up."

As Labonte headed into turn four, team members climbed on top of the small cement wall separating them from pit road. They prepared for Labonte to pit and give them a chance to see what may be wrong with the car. Instead, Labonte made a sharp left as he entered pit road. He drove the car through a small opening in the pit wall and straight to the garages.

Less than ten minutes after the start of the race, it was over for the Billy Hagan/Sunoco racing team. The race day crew had only moments before completed setting up their pit area for this, the fifteenth race and the halfway point of the twenty-nine-race NASCAR season. Now they would have to pack the equipment and haul it back to the race car transporter parked on the opposite end of the speedway.

It was over. The team was through in Daytona and would head back to North Carolina to prepare for the next race. Labonte finished forty-first, right where he started the race, because of a "vibration."

The team regrouped and started to pack up the equipment. At the other end of the speedway Labonte reached the garage and quickly undid the safety net that was covering the driver's side window. He climbed out. By the time the first crew members made their way to the garage, Terry was gone. His fireproof racing uniform lay rolled in a ball on the floor of the team transporter.

Crew chief Loyd was one of the first crew members back. He found the car right were Labonte left it. Alone. With the help of a few of the others, Loyd pushed the car back into the garage to get a better look at the vehicle. The engine was still hot. The tires hardly worn. Loyd's eyes darted nervously around at the collection of people who had gathered. He then leaned into the car looking for a problem. He flipped the power switch and then the ignition to start the engine. The motor started without hesitation.

Loyd knew it wouldn't be long before team owner Billy Hagan made his way back to the car. He would expect answers. Loyd unfortunately did not have them.

Again Loyd fired the engine looking for some audible signals of distress from the machinery. Nothing. Visibly, there were no problems with the car either. Without the driver it would be hard to pinpoint any problems. Hagan, hampered by an ailing back that slows his walk, was now looming over Loyd's shoulders. Hagan started the car. Its engine roared as the fifty-nine-year-old Louisiana native, and occasional race car driver, jammed his twisted wooden cane on the accelerator. The motor responded as any engine would receiving a rush of fuel. He tried it again with the same results.

Team members stood quietly, waiting for an explosion. Privately, they knew nothing was mechanically wrong with the car. Instead, they knew all along that it was the wrong car for a superspeedway like Daytona. The high speeds and long straights of Daytona demand an aerodynamically efficient car. The car that Labonte started the race with is better suited for an intermediate track like Charlotte or Richmond.

Yet, despite having the wrong car, and knowing full well it was the wrong car, the team members were angry. It wasn't their decision to bring the car. They were just workers. They wanted to win. To them, Labonte quit, leaving them to fend for themselves.

Hagan stood dumbfounded, his face turning red with anger. He had already had enough questions from his primary sponsor, Sunoco, about the performance of the team. This would only make matters worse.

Knowing there were no problems, tireman Billy Siler, a twenty-two-year racing veteran, checked all four wheels looking for a tire that may have been losing air or may have equalized. Something to blame the vibration on. Stock cars use a tire that actually has a smaller tire inside. When the inner and outer tires are equal in pressure it causes a terrible vibration at high speeds. When he reached the last tire, he looked up at his brother Johnny and shook his head no. As with the rest of the car, there was nothing wrong.

From the moment the car rolled off the transporter Wednesday morning the team members knew they were in for a long week. The back-up car on board created for speedway use was a troublesome piece of equipment. Though the fastest car during winter testing, it had not been right since. Terry had complained about it when he drove it in the Daytona 500 in February. In two testing sessions after, the car handled terribly. The better superspeedway car Hagan owned had been destroyed at Talladega in May and not replaced.

Theoretically, a speedway car in bad shape should be able to cut the wind better and faster than the intermediate car. Combined with the restrictor plates NASCAR requires on all engines run at Daytona to cut horsepower, and ultimately speed, the intermediate car labored against the wind. They, however, would never know how the troubled speedway car would work.

With speeds climbing near 200 mph at the superspeedways like Daytona and Talladega, NASCAR decided it would be wise to cut the speeds down. As the mechanics found new ways to increase speeds the cars were more likely to become airborne during crashes and possibly fly into the bleachers injuring fans. NASCAR's latest attempt at slowing the cars would be put into effect at the Pepsi 400. The new rules involved adding thin strips of metal to the rear windows and along the edges of the trunk lid. Because of the new additions, NASCAR offered all teams an extra day at the track for testing before the weekend's events would get underway.

This free day was important because, it was just that, free. During the season, teams can test just seven times. Typically, a team rents a track for a day at a cost of $2,500 to $3,000 for a speedway like Daytona or around a couple hundred bucks for a short track like North Wilkesboro. All totalled, a team will spend about $250,000 each season on testing between rental fees, tires and the expenses incurred on shipping a car and crew to a test site. When testing, teams try cars with different set-ups. The idea behind testing is that the teams will be better prepared when the actual race day arrives. The extra day at Daytona gave teams a chance to experience the effects of the new designs and refine their vehicles before the race. Somehow, news of the free test day never reached the Thomasville, North Carolina, location of Hagan Racing.

The week before the Pepsi 400, NASCAR gathered one driver representing each of the auto manufacturers, Oldsmobile, Ford, Chevrolet, Pontiac and Buick, for a couple of days of testing at Talladega, Daytona's sister superspeedway on the circuit. These tests would provide a reasonable sample of how the changes would affect the cars. Testing was on an invitation-only basis. Bill Elliott, Harry Gant, Brett Bodine, Dale Earnhardt and Bobby Hillin, Jr., were the drivers selected.

The goal was to test the new configurations on the types of vehicles teams used, before NASCAR actually instituted the rules on all. Unfortunately, the test was shortened because of rain. Initially, NASCAR was going to resume the five-team test at Daytona on Tuesday, a day before the track was scheduled to open for all teams. But, NASCAR officials felt it would be fairer to open the test day to all teams wishing to participate, a fact reported in the June 29 edition of the *Charlotte Observer*, three days before the test. Apparently, news of the testing change never reached Loyd and no plans were made to attend.

"I went into the engine shop Monday [before the race] and asked about the test. They were like 'what test?'" Terry said later. "I said the same thing to Steve and he didn't know either."

Missing the test was a costly mistake. Other teams struggling with temperamental speedway cars considered running an intermediate car. However, the free test day proved them wrong.

The mid-season visit to Daytona has traditionally been a family week for the Hagan team members. Often they would have the week off and bring their families to Florida for the few days leading up to the race. Instead, this year the family portion was scrapped. Hagan team members arrived at the track on Wednesday, a full day after the free test. After a long and disappointing day at the track, team members retired to the hotel pool for a Fourth of July barbecue on Thursday.

After two days of practice at Daytona, Terry was unhappy with the team's performance and the vehicle he had to drive in Sunday's race. He remained indoors for most of the pool party, only coming down after being asked several times. It was a difficult situation. Two doors down from Labonte's hotel room was Sterling Marlin, the fastest qualifying driver for the race and the former driver of the Hagan Oldsmobile. Marlin was liked by many on the team and he would garner a lot of attention during the party. Moreover, Terry's grandfather, a man he had a close relationship with, was seriously ill, and weighed heavy on his mind.

Qualifying was horrible. The car did not handle well. With Labonte behind the wheel it limped along like it had a parachute dangling from the back slowing it down. Having one of the slowest vehicles on the track, Labonte was forced to rely on a provisional starting spot to get into the race. Without it the team would have had to pack up and go home.

Labonte fell back on the rule that gives former Winston Cup champions an additional chance to enter a race they may not have qualified for. Labonte was champion in 1984. When the sport's best known driver, Richard Petty, did not make a series of races a few years back, NASCAR adopted the rule. Petty's sponsor, STP, and the media got behind the cause and convinced NASCAR to create the rule. Regardless of his qualifying efforts, NASCAR believed Richard Petty should start every race. This time Labonte needed NASCAR's benevolence.

Despite a guaranteed starting position, Terry knew the car was hopeless. He would not be competitive even under the best of circumstances. Being some five miles per hour slower than the leaders in qualifying, he was destined to remain in the back of the pack. Privately, he told some on the team that he would rather park the car early and fake a problem than spend the day in last place.

"If this was the best we had I wouldn't feel so bad," Terry said on race day as he sat in the transporter. "If we had come down ... we had a free f_ _ _ing day, and now they say we're going to Talladega to test [three days later] ...."

"If they're not going to give me 100 percent, I'm not either," he said later.

Exactly how the team missed the all important free test date remains a mystery. Who decided to rely on the slower intermediate car and why remains a larger question. Team manager H.L. "Herb" Hupperich said a decision had to be made about the car. Terry was not happy with the speedway car and the decision to use the other car was made with the full cooperation of Terry and crew chief Steve Loyd.

"Terry wasn't comfortable with the speedway car," Herb said before the race as he prepared the radios the pit crew would use. "In this business you're either a hero or a zero. I made the call. Someone had to make a decision. Terry wasn't comfortable."

"It's like bringin' a mule to a horse race," said tireman Billy Siler as he prepared tires for the race. He suspected something would happen during the race. "Terry, he's hot. It was Herb and Billy's decision. We should have come down here on Tuesday and tried both. Some other teams did it and found out it [using an intermediate car] was wrong. I wouldn't be surprised if he parked it."

Others on the team expressed similar opinions about the car, and predicted the same outcome.

With the engines started, pace car driver Elmo Langley guided the field down pit road and onto the track. Driving past the pits, where the team was standing, Terry shot up his middle finger. It was a silent gesture, not caught by those standing there.

At the drop of the green flag starting the race, it was clear Labonte's car lacked the power other cars in the field had. He couldn't compete. He said it himself before the race. "All the guys I could run with went home yesterday," he said. Those cars did not have provisional spots to fall back on.

Terry pressed the accelerator to the floor. Still his car was the slowest of NASCAR's regular starters. Running in the back of the pack with absolutely no chance to move forward was embarrassing for the former champion. It was more upsetting to the team's sponsor, Sun Refining and Marketing, which had invested millions in the team to carry its advertising when on the track.

On lap 8, Terry reached his boiling point. He simply had enough. He quit. Blame the car and save the embarrassment he thought. It would also send a message to Hagan and to Sunoco that something was really wrong with the team. More than 100,000 people would watch the race from the stands and another couple million from home on CBS-TV. Being last in front of that many people is uncomfortable. "I wasn't going to run around in last place," he would say later.

After telling Steve Loyd it was over, Terry drove the car "behind the wall."

When the engine fired normally and the tires checked out okay, Hagan stood leaning on the car. His eyes scanned the garages for another driver to take the car out onto the track. Hagan, like the rest, didn't believe there was a vibration. The absence of his driver to explain the problem enraged him. With Labonte out so early in the race there were only a few drivers available. Greg Sacks, who had wrecked moments after Terry parked the car, had already left the track. Hagan told Loyd to ask Lake Speed, also involved in a wreck. Speed said no and waved his hands to make it clear he would not get in the car. Brett Bodine, involved in the same crash that sent Sacks and Speed to the garage, also declined. Bodine and Speed were bad choices anyway. Both drove cars sponsored by oil companies that compete with Sun Refining and Marketing Company and its Sunoco brand.

Neither driver was about to get into the car. If there really was a vibration than they could be at risk behind the wheel. More important, if one decided to take the ride and it turned out there was no vibration, it would prove Labonte was lying. Racing is a cutthroat business, but no driver wanted to be the one to prove wrong Labonte's claims of a vibration.

Hagan's anger grew. Terry was gone without a word, distancing himself from the fiasco. Sunoco's race committee representative, Bill Salmon, was as frustrated, except he had some idea of what was going on. He also wanted answers. The company was in this business for exposure and eight laps on the track was not the kind of exposure the company expected for its money. When it was clear no driver could be found, including Terry, the team loaded the car onto the transporter. There would be no trip to victory lane, no celebration on pit road. Instead, there would be a lot of questions without answers.

"I'm going up to watch the race and regain my composure," Hagan said as he prepared to climb the ladder leading to the roof of the transporter. The rest of the team headed to the beach.

two

Building, and Rebuilding, a Team

"Next year, we'll be sitting at the head table."
Billy Hagan

Midway through the 1990 Winston Cup Awards dinner Billy Hagan was holding court at a table near the rear of the Waldorf-Astoria's Grand Ballroom. Held annually on the first Friday of December, this is the night the top drivers are toasted. At the front of the room sat Dale Earnhardt, there to pick up a check for more than one million dollars, for winning his fourth Winston Cup Championship. The battle came down to the last race of the season, with Earnhardt winning the title by a slim margin over Mark Martin.

In the back of the room, at a table so far away from the stage that someone joked next year's table would be in the hallway, Hagan sat and predicted success for his race team. He was talking about a team that had not broken into the top ten since 1988.

At the table with Hagan were Sun Refining and Marketing president David Knoll and his wife, race committee chairman Bud Campbell and his wife, Marilyn, outgoing chairman Edwin Neithercott and his wife, team manager Herb Hupperich and Terry and Kim Labonte. Hagan was in his glory. While inconsequential to the evening's events he was important to those around him.

"Next year, we'll be sitting at the head table," Hagan said to those at the table. He was referring to the table where the points champion sat.

While Hagan's team finished fourteenth overall, it seemed a better year was on the horizon. Hagan was cocksure, and why not? Several weeks before he signed a new deal with Sun guaranteeing him $2.1 million for the 1991 and 1992 seasons before bonuses. Should the owner-sponsor relationship flourish, and there was no reason to think it wouldn't, there was an option year.

Moreover, Hagan had reunited with Terry Labonte, a thirty-four-year-old Texas native who Hagan befriended and nurtured in the late seventies. Hagan was responsible for Labonte getting started in Winston Cup racing. The two burst onto the racing scene in the early eighties with a string of top ten points finishes culminating with Labonte winning the championship in 1984. The two have a long history together. And they have had their best racing years when they were a team. Nonetheless, they parted ways in 1986 under strained conditions. This night, they were a team again and that's all that mattered.

Hagan believed that his remarriage with Labonte would put the team at the front table when the 1991 Winston Cup Banquet rolled around. What made the pitch more believable was Hagan's track record in making such predictions. He had done it before. In 1980, Hagan predicted a championship in five years. With Labonte behind the wheel they did it in four.

More important, the season that just ended, while disappointing in the overall finish, left several areas of hope. Driver Sterling Marlin raced with the front of the pack at times. Although there were no wins, he did come close. There were, however, too many times when luck wasn't with them. For example, at Bristol International Raceway in Bristol, Tennessee, Marlin was leading the race when he came in for a pit stop under caution. The stop was quick and he headed back out onto the track to take his position in the starting grid. As he approached the end of pit road entering the turn, the left side tires fell off. The lug nuts on that side were not tightened. Johnny Carson thought the episode was so funny he showed the clip on "The Tonight Show." On other occasions the car was simply not good enough. Whatever the problems, Hagan assured the Sun executives the problems were behind the team and that Labonte was the missing link.

Labonte's boyish good looks and endearing Texas drawl make him instantly likeable. He's a good spokesman for a sponsor's product. In the years leading up to 1984, Labonte, driving Hagan's cars, was in the hunt for the top prize until the end. In 1984, Hagan and Labonte did sit at the Waldorf-Astoria's head table, thanks to a series of top ten finishes.

Hagan was able to point to his last championship prediction as an example of the team's potential. He hadn't boasted like that since, and now here he was again. In 1980, moments after Terry won his first race, the Southern 500 at Darlington International Raceway, Hagan and Labonte went into the pressroom for the post race press conference. For a moment, Labonte would be the darling of the media and Hagan would give the reporters something to talk about.

"We will win the points championship within five years," Hagan told the reporters that had gathered. His boasting was met with skepticism by a jaded press corps. Who could blame them for not jumping on Hagan's bandwagon at the time? Standing before them was a team owner who, at best, was marginally successful and his driver, a young one, had only been behind the wheel of a Winston Cup car for a little more than a year and a half. In the previous ten years Hagan's team had only five top ten finishes in this sport. For many in attendance that day it was a hard prediction to swallow.

Hagan had confidence in his newfound driver. Besides, Hagan was and still is a helluva salesman, who knew how to get people motivated. Terry's driving prowess impressed Hagan on their first meeting. He knew given the right equipment, the two could be contenders.

Cars have pretty much been Labonte's life. Born in Corpus Christi, Texas, on November 16, 1956, Labonte was the oldest of two boys born to Robert Labonte and his wife Martha. He grew up in a house that sat in front of a two car garage. The garage served as a workshop for his father and his friend's part-time racing operation. His house sat seven to eight miles away from the bay, one of the deepest ports on the gulf, and fifteen miles away from the Texas beaches.

When Terry was seven his father took him to see a friend's son run quarter-midget race cars. The cars are popular in the South. The eighth of a mile dirt tracks dot the landscape in Texas and the Southeast, attracting large crowds of parents and kids. Young Terry watched and enjoyed the races. As he did, his father leaned over and asked if he too wanted to drive the car. He did, though he didn't want to do it in front of a crowd. Instead, he told his father he didn't want to drive. On the way home it was different story.

"I wouldn't drive it because there were too many people," Terry says looking back. "I didn't want to drive in front of people. I was afraid of messing up."

His father understood. A couple of weeks later, the friend was going to the track to practice. This time there would be people there but not as many as would be there on race night. Terry was asked if he would like to drive. This time he said yes. A few laps around the track and he was hooked. His father could see it.

On his next birthday, Terry received his own midget racer with his name written in script letters on the front cowl.

Terry's midget experience was his first in a race car, but not his first around race cars. His father and two friends had been racing for years and built their cars in the garage that sat behind the house where the Labonte's lived. Bob and his friends would work on the car, driven by another friend. They had been doing this since the mid-1950s. The partners had a few good years together, then, in 1963, the guy who drove the car quit racing. He gave the car to the remaining friends. They got out of racing and the car sat untouched in the garage until 1969 when the friends got together and started racing again.

"They built a Ford while everyone else ran Chevrolets," recalls Terry. "They ran good and then they quit again."

With that experience behind him, Terry's father turned to building a car for his oldest son, Terry. Almost sixteen, Terry would soon be able to get a driver's license, allowing him to race cars at the local short track. His father's friends also turned their attention to building cars for their sons, about the same age as Terry.

Terry attended high school during the day, like most sixteen-year-olds, and then rushed home to help his father, who worked at the local Army base, with the car. On weekends, they loaded the car onto a trailer and headed to an asphalt short track located in town. Competing with men twice his age or older, Terry was somewhat successful at first. Soon he was a regular on the circuit, and a winner at a handful of tracks within driving distance from home.

By the time he was seventeen, he and his father were spending weekends on the road racing. They would load the car and drive 150 miles to San Antonio to race on a quarter-mile asphalt track at night. Then provided the car wasn't damaged, they would pack it up and head 150 miles east to Houston and Meyer Speedway, another half-mile asphalt race track. Following a weekend of racing, the father and son team loaded the #44

Chevrolet Camero and returned home. Monday morning the routine would start up all over. It was a system that would last twenty-plus weekends a year.

"Dad built the car," he says. "I bet the project didn't have $3,500 in the whole car, except maybe $6,000 for the engine."

Terry's youth and driving skills quickly made him popular in the Texas short track racing scene. Labonte was making his mark on some of the same tracks that helped launch the careers of such racing greats as A.J. Foyt and Johnny Rutherford. It was not unusual for Terry to race with men who had once competed on the higher levels of the sport.

"Terry was, I think, the best short track driver I had at Meyer," says Ed Hamblen, the former lease holder and promoter for the now defunct Meyer Speedway. "His driving ability and his personality made him stand out. It was something else to watch him."

By the time he was twenty, Terry had notched track championships in Corpus Christi, San Antonio and Houston. He was also making trips to Shreveport, Louisiana, and other tracks within driving distance.

"I had a lot of fans because I kept going to so many tracks," he remembers.

Terry became a star in the declining years of Texas short track racing. Yet, the late seventies presented some of the toughest competition the area had ever seen according to those who watched and participated. For decades the southeastern portion of the state had been a hotbed for stock car racing and racing of any type. Local tracks regularly did bang up business on Saturday nights as people searched for entertainment. In the Houston area professional football was yet to take hold and racing provided an alternative to baseball. Meyer Speedway usually attracted 7,000 to 8,000 fans each night.

Competition was strong. During one stretch, Labonte finished second six consecutive weeks. Each time there was a different winner. "That's how competitive short track racing was back then," he says.

Located near the corner of South Main and Hillcroft in Houston, Meyer opened in 1960 and started having regular racing events in 1961. The track was situated in one of the less desirable areas of town, yet it was a good enough setting for a raceway. Terry raced there in the track's last two seasons of existence, earning track championships in 1976 and 1977. However, as the area around the track became more populated, the sounds of night racing became unwanted. Hamblen closed the place in 1978, because of public apathy and money.

"The area's now a slum," says Royce Rogers, president of Battleground Speedway, a local track that has taken the place of Meyer Speedway. "There's a driving range there now, but if you walk out into the weeds you can see part of the track."

Racing became more of a money sport and finances started becoming more of a problem for Terry's home-based racing operation. By his own estimates it cost between $600 and $800 a night just for tires. A feature win would pay only $1,200. Factor in any damage done during the race and the costs soared. Most of the parts on his race car came from a local junk yard, but, still, there were times when he and his father did not have the money to race.

"I didn't go to the races one night and the promoter called me the next day and asked why. I told him I couldn't afford it. I'd blown my engine the week before," says Terry.

The promoter, Hamblen, already feeling the financial squeeze that would eventually force him out of business, was concerned with Labonte's absence. Hamblen knew that Terry brought out at least some of the fans to the track and a prolonged absence could affect his pocketbook. Meanwhile, Hamblen knew that a lot of other drivers were spending considerably more money on their cars than Terry. Still, Terry was competitive. Other drivers in the same position couldn't compete with racers that had money to spend. Hamblen couldn't afford another draw to leave. He also knew that without some form of financial relief, Terry could follow the crowd.

Following his conversation with Labonte, Hamblen turned to a friend and business associate, Billy Hagan. Hagan, a Louisiana native and a self-made businessman, was riding high on profits he had made in the oil business. As the sole owner of Stratagraph, Inc., a firm that electronically monitors oil wells when drilled, Hagan had money and enjoyed spending it.

Hagan has a deep appreciation for racing. "After all this time I still get chills when those cars come up for the start," he said once.

Hagan bought his own car in 1960 and immediately started road racing. He acquired his first machine by trading a Cadillac and $2,500 for a used Porsche. Road racing success came early and often for Hagan, despite some nearly career-ending accidents. Nonetheless, he quickly realized there was more money in the ranks of NASCAR.

Three years after his first race he made the move to stock car racing. His stock car, like his road racer, was used. Though unprepared, Hagan jumped into stock car racing with the same determination he had shown in road racing. This was an era in professional racing when many people would run what they drove to the track. Hagan was no different. He ran those early races with street tires and used duct tape to put the numbers on the car. On his way back home from buying his stock car in Philadelphia, Hagan stopped by Atlanta Raceway. Without a racing license, he couldn't get in. While peering through the garage fence he spotted someone who knew him from his road racing efforts. Quick on his feet, Hagan convinced the officials to give him a driving test on the spot. If he passed, he could race. Two laps around the track with an official and he was entered in his first stock car event.

During the next few years, the oilman would alternate between road racing and stock car racing, with his best performances coming on the road courses. His stock car abilities were overshadowed by the regulars of the series, who had committed to the sport full time.

Occasionally, Hagan would race at Meyer Speedway. It was there he became friends with promoter Ed Hamblen. Hamblen was struggling then, and asked Hagan for a loan of $25,000. In return, Hagan would get 15 percent of the gate receipts. Not a bad deal because Meyer was still a pretty hot attraction for the locals.

When Hamblen realized that Terry was having problems he again turned to Hagan. Terry had a sponsor, a local business, which supplied him and his father with a motorhome for the races. Yet the financial aspects were becoming a problem. The sponsorship provided little in real money, and certainly not enough to fix Terry's expired motor. It might have been weeks before Terry could race again.

Hamblen related Terry's financial woes to Hagan. Not only was a talented racer missing events, but Hamblen was losing a competitor who contributed to his bottom line. He could not afford to lose another racer.

"I called Billy and asked him to sponsor Terry," says Hamblen. "He said, 'If you think that he's good enough, certainly I'll sponsor him.'"

The deal wasn't worth much, maybe $300 a week or so, but it served as the seed to start a new relationship between a car owner and driver. Hagan hadn't met Terry, yet he contributed to his racing efforts. In return, Terry put the name of Hagan's company on the side of his car. Promoter Hamblen also took the unusual route of creating a side financial deal to keep Terry racing. If he didn't make enough to keep racing, Hamblen would subsidize his efforts.

"I set it up myself," says Hamblen. "It never came to pass. He always made enough. I wanted to see him race."

Two weeks after Hamblen put them in touch, Hagan traveled to Meyer to watch Labonte. It would be their first face-to-face meeting. "He seemed like a real nice guy ... he seemed like he really wanted to help us," Terry says of that first meeting.

Hagan was impressed with his new partner. Sitting in the stands on a hot Texas evening, Hagan watched Labonte battle to a second place finish in the feature race. In short track racing, drivers need to place in heat races in order to make it into the feature. Placing in the feature would pay money. That night Terry put on a show that won Billy as a fan. Terry was eventually awarded the first place prize when it was determined that the guy who finished first was running illegal parts.

"I was impressed. I watched as he kept a faster guy behind him," recalls Hagan of their first meeting.

That visit and later trips to watch Terry stuck in Hagan's mind. He thought a lot about Labonte and his own modest racing operation, then in Charlotte, North Carolina, the hub of the stock car racing community. Hagan's three-year-old team had yet to taste victory in the big leagues of NASCAR. His driver, Skip Manning, was considered mediocre. Hagan and Manning occasionally shared the driving duties and were about equal, neither a standout.

"Billy had a guy, Skip Manning," Hamblen said. "He was alright, but he wasn't Terry Labonte."

Manning had been behind the wheel of Hagan's cars for a little more than two years. In that time he could only put together a couple of top ten finishes.

"I realized he wasn't going any further," said Hagan of Manning. "He had reached a plateau." From time to time, Hagan would actually qualify better than Manning, making for an unsteady relationship between the two.

Months after Hagan and Terry met, Labonte continued to burn the Texas tracks, as Hagan and Manning struggled in Winston Cup. Terry was doing so well that one night a man came down from the stands wanting to buy his car. Terry's father put a deal together with the man, Lee Adams, with just eight races left in the season.

"This guy comes out of the stands and wants to buy the car. And, he wants us to run it," Terry says. "He'll buy it and pay all the bills."

"He would meet us at the track. If we needed tires, he would strap them on the back of his Lincoln and drive them to the track. He was a great guy and we had a blast. He paid for everything and he paid my dad for the car."

Terry raced for Adams, but kept the name of Billy's company painted on the side of the car. During this time, Terry told Hagan he might like to get into Winston Cup racing, but he was not 100 percent sure that it was for him. As the season end neared Billy called and asked Terry to move to North Carolina. He wanted him to become part of the team, and possibly drive a couple races. Replacing Manning was never part of the equation, according to Labonte. Just the chance at a few races.

"I didn't want to go at first. I was having fun doing what I was doing and I didn't know if I wanted to do this [racing] or not," Terry says. "It took me a month to decide. Then I called my dad. I called my girlfriend, Kim, and she started crying. I called Billy and told him I can't go right now. I wanted to go up at the start of the season."

By then Hamblen closed Meyer, and did not make good on his loan from Billy. Hagan to this day refers to the $10,000 he lost from the loan as an "employment fee" for getting Labonte.

Terry moved to North Carolina in January 1978, and went to work as a mechanic for Billy's team. Shortly before he left, his father called Lee Adams and gave him the news. Terry wouldn't race for him anymore, he was moving away.

"He's going to move?" Adams said. "Then ya'll just keep the car, don't worry about the car." His father soon after sold the car to another man.

Because of a prior engagement, Terry could not be with the team for the first race of the 1978 season held at Riverside, California. He was, however, able to make the trip for the first race at Daytona. His parents and some friends went along for the trip. One evening after a day at the track, Terry and his parents went out to dinner. On their way back to the hotel, they passed a restaurant where Hagan and his wife, and Skip Manning and his wife were having dinner. When Terry passed outside the window, Billy's wife turned and pointed. "There's Terry," she said. "He's won a lot of races in Texas." Billy gave her a quick nudge to stop but the damage had been done.

"From there on Skip hated my guts," Terry says.

During the next couple of months, Hagan's racing operation started to fall apart. They were not performing on the track and people were quitting. Terry's relationship with Skip rapidly deteriorated. Infighting amongst team members became standard operating procedure. Terry considered leaving. He called his father, crying, and asked about going back to Corpus Christi. He had his taste of NASCAR and decided if this was what the big leagues were like, he wanted out. Manning's behavior toward Terry was intolerable.

"I said screw this guy. I called my dad and said I believe I'm gonna come home. Besides, I'm outta money."

"With all this stuff going on why don't you stay there another month," his father said. He reminded his son that this might be his only shot at NASCAR racing.

Terry stayed. Then, one night in the last week of August 1978, he got a call from Billy. Hagan's request was simple. He wanted Terry's address. He wanted Terry to stay away from the shop for awhile, until the situation was settled. Billy would pay him for staying home. Then he asked if Terry would drive the car at the upcoming Southern 500, at Darlington Raceway, about two weeks away. Terry agreed to all of Billy's requests. The idea of getting paid to stay home wasn't that bad, and he would be away from Manning. He did, however, question Billy's decision to let him run Darlington. The track is one of the series' most demanding. More important, Terry had never raced on anything longer than a half-mile and never run more than 100 laps. The Southern's 367 laps seemed endless to him.

"Couldn't it be Martinsville or one of the smaller tracks," Terry asked. Hagan assured him everything would be all right. He'd be in touch as soon as everything at the shop was complete.

A few days later Terry's phone rang. "Go down to the shop and make sure everything is all right," Hagan said. Manning was leaving and Hagan wanted Terry to make sure he didn't leave with something that wasn't his.

"I knew he kept a gun down there. So, I called my girl-friend and told her to call me in a little bit to make sure I hadn't got shot," Terry said.

Terry then drove to the shop, not far from his home. Pulling into the driveway he noticed Manning standing in the doorway preparing to leave . . . They met at the door.

"I hope you have fun," Manning said, handing Terry the keys to the shop. Manning drove off without another word.

In the short period Terry was away from the shop, the situation there had gotten worse. Only a handful of the original staff remained, and the cars had to be ready for the Labor Day weekend race in Darlington. Terry and the remaining guys prepared the car to run at Darlington, and loaded it onto the truck.

Having never participated in a NASCAR event, Terry was prohibited from entering first round qualifying, which would set the top twenty starting positions. The remaining cars would get a second chance a day later when the rest of the field would be set. Terry had the fastest car in second round qualifying and secured the twenty-first starting position—eleventh row on the inside.

Darlington is the oldest speedway on the NASCAR circuit, and the demands the track places on drivers are legendary. Darlington's narrow straights and banked turns are deceiving. The track has been called "The Black Lady" because many a racer has appeared to have a win all sewn up only to have a mistake on the track take it away. Terry realized the demands almost from the start of the race, when several wrecks damaged a bunch of the cars in the field.

"I was going along, just staying out of trouble," he remembers. "I'm thinking damn, I got tires, I made pit stops, I got water ... It's hot." He knew the length of the race was almost three times longer than any he had run before. He mentally kept track of the laps that had gone by and tried to stay out of trouble.

"I'm going along, 320, 340 ... checking the scoreboard, cause I knew how many laps there were ... I never thought to look for my number. I finished fourth."

Labonte and Hagan continued as a team for four of the remaining races of the 1978 season. His fourth at Darlington would be his best for the year, though he did manage two other top ten finishes. The next season would be tougher. Labonte ran the entire year competing for the rookie of the year title. Normally the rookie race was only important for those involved; the 1979 rookie race was slightly different. According to some race observers, the 1979 rookie competition may have been the toughest in history. Labonte battled Harry Gant, Dale Earnhardt and Ricky Rudd for the title. All have since gone on to become top competitors in NASCAR.

Terry lost out to Earnhardt for the title, although, in the process he would notch six top ten finishes in thirty-one races. He earned $130,057 in prize money that season.

Between 1980 and 1983, Labonte posted a decent record on the track and placed in the top ten each season. Paced by engines built by the newly hired Dewey Livengood, a veteran engine craftsman, Labonte grew stronger on the track.

During those seasons he would earn a total of seventy-four top ten finishes and place in the top five forty-two times. On the downside, his record would also show thirty-five DNFs (did not finish). Nonetheless, he ended 1980 fifth in the points race. In 1981 he would lead the field going into June, only to end up fourth. He improved to third in 1983.

Hagan and Labonte had their best year together in 1984, when Labonte would go on to win two races and finish in the top ten twenty-two times to capture the championship.

Labonte, with veteran crew chief Dale Inman, took the points lead with nine races remaining in the season. After a win at Bristol, Terry led Dale Earnhardt by just 15 points. Harry Gant, who finished the Bristol race in fifth, was 129 points behind Labonte.

Gant pressured Labonte, scoring wins in the Southern 500 at Darlington and at Dover Downs International Speedway. Labonte finished second at Dover to maintain an 81-point lead over Gant. However, Gant pulled to within 42 points of Labonte going into the last race of the season at Riverside.

Labonte excelled on road courses, such as Riverside, which required more driving skill than the normal Winston Cup ovals. Yet, some extra precaution was taken with Gant so close in the points race. Hagan fielded a second car for the race driven by Joe Millikan. He would be the enforcer. If another driver pressured Labonte, Millikan would step in. If Labonte spun off the track, Millikan was to push him back onto the track, and to the pits if necessary. A track the size of Riverside posed problems for the wrecking crews as they maneuvered the roadway. A car off the track could be stuck there for a few laps losing valuable time. Hagan did not want to take the chance.

Hagan's insurance policy didn't last long though as Millikan was forced out of the race early. Labonte was on his own, but, fortunately, no problems arose. Labonte finished third even though he felt his car was strong enough to win. But third was all he needed to secure the championship; Gant finished eighth. Driving a white and blue Chevrolet Monte Carlo SS sponsored by Piedmont Airlines, Terry, at twenty-eight, became the youngest driver to win the championship since Richard Petty did it at twenty-seven, in 1964. Terry, his family and his friends started their celebration right after the race and did not stop until sometime the next evening.

For the season, Terry earned, on paper, $713,010, of which roughly $150,000 was from Winston for winning the championship. Combined with various NASCAR sponsor bonuses, Terry would pick up a check for over $200,000. For comparison, the 1991 champion's prize was $1 million before all of the other bonuses kicked in.

"We went out and did the best we could at every race and it worked out pretty good," he would say later. While winning the championship was exciting, the off-season was hectic. Terry welcomed the start of the 1985 season, and a return to racing.

"All that traveling around was nice," he told reporters, "but it was getting a little old." After his annual trip to Corpus Christi for deer hunting and family visits, Labonte would travel to New York for the Winston Cup banquet, to Chicago for a Boy's Club benefit and to Long Beach for another banquet.

Labonte started the 1985 season off right with a victory in the Busch Clash, a short race held as a warm up for the Daytona 500. The race pitted the pole winners of the season before against each other. Starting eleventh out of twelve cars, Labonte dashed for the lead and held on to win the $65,000 purse. Despite the confidence that the Clash victory brought, Terry knew the upcoming season would be tough. He was well aware of the struggles of past champions the year after winning the gold.

"It felt good to win the first race of the year," he told reporters. "And, as consistent as we were last year we've still got some room for improvement. But I don't really feel any more pressure from the outside. The only real pressure is what you put on yourself. We all know this sport is extremely fickle. I'm sure Bobby [Allison] felt like we do, that the year after was going to be even better. But it didn't happen that way."

Allison had won the championship in 1983 and struggled through the 1984 campaign.

Labonte got through the 1985 season in fine shape, finishing seventh in the points race. He earned $694,510 in prize money. Although he was on the front row seven times that season, he would not finish in eight of twenty-eight races. Yet, without a win, he was the points leader through the first eleven races.

Ironically, at the same point in the season, the eventual runner up, Bill Elliott, had already won five races.

While Labonte's performance on the track remained consistent, Hagan's racing operation was crumbling. Behind the masks of former champions were the faces of unhappy crew members. Hagan's team was in trouble. Dissension and morale problems among team members were taking a toll. Some left. The usually outgoing Hagan distanced himself from the team as he attended to personal problems. His business was limping along, and he was also having problems with his marriage.

Hagan had yet to pay Labonte a dime of his Winston Cup Champion's payout, leaving Labonte with just the trophy and the memories.

"Things really changed," Labonte says. "We had a lot of good people, a good team. People started leaving. Billy was going through a bankruptcy."

Hagan's financial problems extended to the team. Equipment wasn't replaced. The cars were getting old. Then, Hagan leased the team to a man named J. Wayne King, as a way to raise cash and relieve himself of some of the responsibilities. It was possible that Hagan could lose his team altogether if his financial situation worsened. King wanted to be in racing, Hagan was his in. According to some who were on the team at the time, the move was a disaster. Morale slipped further. Turnover increased. And for the first time since he came into racing, Labonte was out of the top ten at the end of 1986.

Labonte was angry about money he was owed. Team owners receive race winning checks immediately after the event and the Winston Cup payout was no different. Yet, two years after winning the championship, he was still out more than $150,000. Terry called owner and racing legend Junior Johnson about a job driving. Johnson was looking for someone to replace Darrell Waltrip, who was leaving the Johnson stable to work elsewhere.

"The oil business went away, I was going through a divorce, Budweiser came in and offered Terry a tremendous sum of money to drive for them," Hagan says. "The future of my operation was in question. It was an offer he couldn't refuse."

It was also an offer Hagan couldn't refuse. Because he still owed Labonte money, essentially the driver's paycheck, their contract was void. Labonte's leaving further hurt the team.

"I had to do it. I don't regret it." Labonte says now.

Labonte signed a three-year deal with Johnson. When the deal was done he called Hagan to say he was leaving.

"Will ya come back when it's all over?" Hagan asked.

"Yeah," Labonte replied.

Notwithstanding Labonte's departure, Hagan was able to keep his racing team operating. King and Hagan hired Sterling Marlin, the son of former Winston Cup driver Coo Coo Marlin, to replace Terry. Marlin, who fancies himself as a trackside playboy, was winless after 74 sporadic starts. His background was in short track racing around his Columbia, Tennessee, home.

During three years with Johnson, Labonte earned five wins and forty-seven top ten finishes. In replacing Waltrip, Labonte was replacing a three-time Winston Cup champion. Ironically, before leaving, Waltrip had often cited Labonte as one of the best young drivers.

"No one saw Cale's (Yarborough) or Darrell's (Waltrip) potential fulfilled before they came to me," Johnson told a reporter before the 1987 Daytona 500. 'We're going to put Terry in a position to fulfill his. We're coming back for a championship."

Johnson immediately took a liking to Labonte. He often commented on Labonte's ability to speak well on his feet, and not having to send him for public relations training. He called Labonte "intelligently aggressive," although as the relationship grew Johnson would come to say that he wished Labonte was more aggressive on the track. Not as much with other drivers, but with the way he drove the car.

Terry is called "The Iceman" for his cool, emotionless demeanor and laid back driving style. He's outgoing, but only to those who know him. Fans will always get an autograph when they ask, but they're never encouraged to come back.

"Terry drives the race car the same way each time," says long-time Associated Press motorsports writer Mike Harris. "He drives the same way as his personality — low key.

"He's not the kind of guy who sticks his nose where he shouldn't, not like a Dale Earnhardt... Terry is a very good driver but I don't think he's Hall of Fame material. Terry is very capable, he gets a lot of good finishes."

Halfway through 1989, Labonte's final year under contract to Johnson, rumors started to circulate that Labonte wanted out. It had nothing to do with Johnson or the team. Instead, he wanted to become a team owner. He had long since started construction of his own shop, using land given to him by a friend. He had also started collecting equipment and had some cars built. Around July, he informed Johnson he was leaving at season's end.

Labonte wanted to be in control of his own future and the welfare of his family. Financially he was stable, and like most successful drivers, he yearned to own his own team. Moreover, his brother Bobby, who had entered racing through NASCAR's Busch Grand National series, would eventually make it to the Winston Cup level. Terry saw himself as Bobby's team owner down the road.

Soon after Labonte broke the news to Johnson, Johnson signed a deal with Geoff Bodine to take over the wheel of the red and white Budweiser sponsored Ford. There was no turning back for Labonte.

However, as the season end neared, Labonte's plans to start his own team fell apart. He believed he had a sponsor and partial financial backing from another individual. Both deals fell apart leaving Labonte looking for a ride for the 1990 season.

On January 16, 1990, Labonte announced he would drive for Precision Products Racing, a team owned by Richard Jackson and sponsored by U.S. Tobacco's Skoal brand chewing tobacco. They signed a one-year deal and agreed to put the No. 1 on the black, white and gold cars. It was the number that Terry had acquired from NASCAR to use on his own team. He replaced Phil Parsons behind the wheel of Jackson's cars.

"I announced in July of last year that I would be forming my own team, and those were my intentions," Labonte said in the news release sent out to the media. "However, I got behind in getting the shop built and at the time I didn't know I'd have this opportunity."

Like 1986, the 1990 season was a disappointment for the former champion. He ended the season in fifteenth place overall, one spot behind Marlin, and for the first time since he became a full-time driver he finished a year without a win.

Labonte liked the people at Jackson's Precision Racing, although he and Jackson disagreed over who should be crew chief. Labonte had his candidate and Jackson had his.

"Some of the guys I wanted they said didn't fit their image," Labonte said. "What kind of shit is that. They're selling shit [tobacco] that kills people and they're worried about an image?" The rift sent Labonte looking for other options.

Nonetheless, about halfway into the season, Labonte gave Jackson an oral agreement that he would return for at least one more year. But the trackside rumor mill had Labonte leaving.

Hagan's operation had long since rebounded from Terry's departure and the other assorted ailments that had affected its ability to be successful. Hagan had yet to shake a reputation for being frugal and slow in bill paying, but the atmosphere was positive. After two years with Sun Refining and Marketing, a major oil company, sponsoring the car, Hagan and his sponsor were on the eve of extending their relationship.

Nevertheless, before putting ink to a new contract with Sun, Hagan had to get his current driver, Sterling Marlin, to agree to a new deal. Marlin had become tired of the thrifty way Hagan ran his shop. He also had complained about dated equipment. In fact, after his motor blew just forty-five laps into the July race at Pocono International Raceway, Marlin said it was just as well. "It was a good thing," he told reporters, "it was nothing but junk anyhow. It wasn't holding a flip. Besides that, it wouldn't run a lick."

In September 1990 rumors surfaced that Marlin was going to jump ship. The "silly season" between August and September, when NASCAR participants take part in spreading rumors, had started. However, within this community a good percentage of the rumors become reality before the season ends.

Sterling Marlin's case was no different. Halfway through the season he started entertaining offers to drive elsewhere. One of those offers came from Junior Johnson's team via crew chief Tim Brewer, the same team Labonte left Hagan for in 1986. Brewer was vague when he called Marlin, but told him to wait a few days before making any decisions about the future. Hagan and officials from Sun had scheduled a meeting to finish their deal for the coming season.

Hagan had a feeling that Marlin was not going to show. Indeed, he bet the Sun people $100 that he wouldn't. Each time Hagan addressed the subject with Marlin, the driver refused to discuss it. Hagan, a seasoned veteran, could see what was ahead.

About a week before Sun and Hagan were to sign the new deal, Labonte spoke with Hagan crew chief and friend Steve Loyd about the atmosphere at Hagan's shop.

"Do you think Billy would let me drive his cars?" Labonte asked in passing.

"The only way to find out is to call the man and see," replied Loyd. Loyd also had the feeling that Marlin was not going to return. Labonte did not call, though he spoke to Loyd again a week later.

Hagan and two of Sun's racing committee members, Geoff Plazer and Edwin Neithercott, were to meet at 10:00 a.m., in Hagan's Thomasville, North Carolina, shop on the first Tuesday of September. Hagan and the committee members showed up but Marlin didn't. He didn't call either. Instead, Marlin was at Junior Johnson's shop in Ingle Hollow, North Carolina, about an hour and half away, with no intentions of coming back.

Once it was obvious that Marlin was a no-show, Hagan asked the committee members what they thought about having Terry Labonte drive the Sunoco-sponsored racer. They responded in favor of the idea, and Hagan called his former driver. Labonte, Hagan, Plazer and Neithercott met over lunch and by the end of their hastily called gathering, they had a verbal agreement to be a team for the 1991 season. Labonte told the men that he wanted to talk with his current team before signing a contract, but he made it clear to all involved that he wanted to drive for Hagan. Hagan and Labonte settled their money discrepancies, and Sunoco agreed to back the operation. The rehiring of Labonte was announced the next day. Under the terms of the deal, Labonte would earn more than $300,000 annually, plus 50 percent of his race winnings.

Labonte told reporters that the differences between he and Hagan had been settled and that those problems were behind them. Richard Jackson meanwhile was left to figure out what to do with his team.

"We weren't very consistent like we need to be," Labonte told Richard Dean of the *Houston Chronicle* in December 1990 of his stay with Jackson. "We had some good runs. I just felt like it wasn't going to get much better. When I had a chance to get with Billy's team I didn't hesitate."

Hagan and Labonte were together again. Bound by a three-year contract and backed by millions of dollars in sponsorship money from Sunoco, Hagan was bragging again.

three

The Super Bowl
of Racing

"The overall reaction was championship here
we come again."
  Billy Hagan

Terry Labonte climbed through the window of his blue and yellow Oldsmobile Cutlass race car and started his methodical practice of checking the safety harness and making sure radio connections were set. Like a pilot before takeoff, Labonte gives the car a quick inspection, looking for anything that makes his ride unsafe. Nothing is left to chance.

It was an overcast December 2, 1990. The day would mark the first time he would drive for Billy Hagan in competition since he had severed ties with him at the end of the 1986 season.

Two weeks before, after completing 493 of 500 laps on the season ending race at Atlanta, he stepped out of an Oldsmobile owned by Richard Jackson for the last time. It brought to a close what was a disappointing one-year relationship.

To some extent it was a homecoming, but one on foreign soil. Instead of sitting on pit road on one of the regular stops on the NASCAR tour, Labonte was getting ready to race in Keilor, Australia, just outside Melbourne, at the Calder Thunderdome. The weather that day was typical for that area. Warm like an American summer with a chance of rain. Melbourne doesn't get a lot of rain, but when it does it comes in constant intervals. December 2 was no different. As the start of the race neared, rain clouds moved in.

However, this was as close to NASCAR competition as the team would get before the new season got underway in February with the Daytona 500, in Daytona Beach, Florida. To get to this point, Hagan had shipped a skeleton crew on an expensive thirty-hour trip down under. One race car was shipped to the same place a month before. To help offset the costs, Sunoco kicked in $25,000 for the trip. It would cost some $5,000 to get the car to Australia.

Hagan wanted to travel to Australia for a couple of reasons. He had been there before and thought the racing was fun. Driver Sterling Marlin, who Labonte replaced, had finished second there in 1989. The trip would also give his team and new driver a chance to work together under race conditions before the season started. Also weighing on his mind would be unloading the race car to a native when the race was over.

Labonte started the race in third place and early on it was apparent the race was his to win. He dominated the field. On lap 105 of the 220-lap event it started pouring rain. Labonte was in the lead, as he had been for 79 of the laps run. Race officials put the race under caution and instructed the drivers to run 7 more laps, putting the race past the halfway point. Doing so would make the race official should the rain not let up before sundown. The rain continued and Labonte was declared the winner. He won $50,000 in Australian dollars, roughly $39,250 in American dollars. Hagan and the crew went home winners. The car remained in Australia, sold to a local racer.

The win gave a burst of energy to a struggling team. Morale was low, still suffering from the final days of Marlin's stay, yet there was hope with Labonte aboard. Not having won a race in a long time, they fed off Labonte's good luck. (Marlin did win the Winston Open, a non-points race in 1989.) Sunoco, Hagan's sponsor also saw the Australia win as a good sign. They also had not tasted victory as a team sponsor.

However, Labonte saw it differently. The car was fast, but it also wouldn't have been legal by NASCAR's racing standards. His car wasn't the only one slightly enhanced for this race. Most of the American entries were. In fact, second place finisher Ken Schrader remarked to some that Labonte's car was so fast that the only way anyone else would have won the race was if Labonte crashed or the engine blew up.

Nonetheless, Labonte saw it for what it was. "We should have won that race," he said. "Here we are, people who do this full time, going against a bunch of guys who basically do it on the weekends."

"I felt it was real important that the crew and I were able to work together under race conditions," Labonte said then. "It gave us all a real good idea of just how well we are all going to work together in the upcoming season."

Later in the month after a trip to Hawaii and attending the annual Winston Cup Banquet, Labonte, crew chief Steve Loyd, engine builder Dewey Livengood, and the pre-race crew headed to Daytona for three days of testing at Daytona International Speedway. Daytona is the season opener and one of the fastest tracks on the circuit. So much so, the car's carburetors are equipped with restrictors, limiting horsepower and keeping the cars below the 200 mph level. Before the restrictors were instituted by NASCAR, cars regularly traveled over 200 mph and were climbing higher. For example, during December testing seasons in 1986, Labonte tipped Daytona's race qualifying record with a lap of 206.422 mph, in a Chevrolet owned by Junior Johnson.

Daytona testing is an annual ritual. It marks the coming of the new season, the same way that leaves turning color mark the coming of fall. A pre-season of sorts for racing. When the checkered flag drops ending the last race of the season at Atlanta, teams immediately start working on car designs for the next year. Body styles are slightly modified to cut the wind and different engine combinations are tried. Each done in search of the fastest combination.

Teams are allowed only seven days of testing during the season. During December and January, testing is unlimited, though the teams usually restrict those tests to manufacturer supported days at Daytona. Normally, the auto manufacturers, General Motors and Ford, will rent the facility for a couple of days each month to test. During those periods any team running that manufacturers equipment is eligible to test. Often cars from both Winston Cup and the next level down, Busch Grand National, will show up for the tests.

Tests are held more like practices than races, though NASCAR officials are on hand. The only racing going on is against the clock.

Loyd, Labonte, Livengood and the crew spent three days testing under the cool December sun, and then headed back to Thomasville. There they would take the information culled in Florida and make some minor changes on the car. They returned for a second session a month later.

The conditions for the second session were near perfect for running a race car fast. It was cool, real cool. The air was still and the sun shone brightly.

Labonte's car had been fine tuned for the session. Painted Sunoco blue, the car only carried the #94 and a few decals. Nothing like the way it would look for the first race just a month away. With minor adjustments the car handled flawlessly, as Labonte guided the car around the track with his right foot mashed to the floor. Alone on the track, Terry was the fastest. When all the manufacturer sponsored testing was complete,

Labonte would go down as the quickest with an unofficial lap of 193.993 mphs. For comparison, a 737 airplane moves down the runway at about 187 mph when taking off. The results were encouraging. They were the fastest. The season ahead would be theirs.

Labonte took it for what it was worth. A fast lap around a superspeedway without traffic on a perfect day. This was a test he reasoned. Had any of the other manufacturers been there that day, maybe one of those cars would have gone as fast or faster. His day for testing was great. The other manufacturers may not have had the weather on their side. A few degrees warmer or cooler and the results may have been different. Also, with only one car on the track at a time, they could only test for speed. The effects of running with other cars, either in front or behind, could dramatically change the way the car handled.

"The overall reaction was championship here we come again," Hagan told the *Charlotte Observer*. Labonte, meanwhile, was playing the event down. "We ran good the whole time we were there," he told the *Charlotte Observer*. "And we're confident we're going to have a competitive car at Daytona and the other tracks." Yet, he continued with the conversation by saying that realistically it was hard to make a fair comparison to what the other teams did in testing because they all did it at different times.

"What I'm saying is I don't think being fastest in testing makes us the favorite for the Daytona 500 pole. I'd love to win the pole, sure, but I think that about all our speed shows is that we'll be strong and probably a top ten car at time trials."

Labonte went into the season confident, however, he did have some concerns that the season wouldn't add up to all the hype that Hagan was laying on. Being on the outside the season before, and for the previous few seasons, Labonte saw the team from another perspective. He could see the problems the team was facing that those inside couldn't see or failed to recognize.

After the testing session the team began to prepare for the Daytona 500. The 500, the sport's most famous attraction and its biggest spectacle, is racing's version of the National Football League's Super Bowl. It carries the same intrigue and media awareness, except while the Super Bowl comes at the end of the season, NASCAR holds it's biggest bash at the beginning.

Back at the shop, the cars to be used for the first weeks of the season were nearing completion. Normally, the teams start work on the car for the current race and the next one almost simultaneously. Providing the manpower is available, several cars could be in various stages of readiness, depending on the upcoming race schedule. Another deciding factor in how many cars are prepared is how long it's going to take the truck driver to return from the race the week before.

Before the first race of the season, Sun racing committee members Al Contino, Bud Campbell, Geoff Plazer and public relations representative Paul Mecca traveled to Thomasville to give a morale boosting seminar. Team members gathered in the main building of the Hagan facility, in a room that sports a black and white checkered floor. There they were given some ideas that would help pull them together as a team and then were instructed to break off into groups based on their duties. The engine room workers made up one group, the fabrication shop guys another and so on. Each team member wrote down suggestions and goals for the season. They then discussed the individual suggestions and worked out the group's overall goals. These ideas were then merged to be the team's goals.

The idea for the seminar was Contino's. He had given a version of the seminar to Sun's regional operations and had modified the message slightly for the team. The thinking behind the session was to get the team members to believe that they were as important a contributor to the team's success as was Labonte. As a committee member during previous seasons, Contino noticed that at times the fiber of the team was stretched and there was some dissension. He believed that to get the team in winning form they had to believe in each other. Contino returned to Pennsylvania with the team suggestions and commissioned T-shirts, plaques and small cards to be made including the teams goals. He distributed the items before the first race.

When the crew returned from the January test, the car was rolled off the transporter and pushed over to the race car preparation section of Hagan's facility. The Thomasville shop is made up of three butler type buildings housing various areas of race car development. Fabrication and paint shops are in one building, race car preparation in another, and the office and engine rooms in the main building.

While at the race car prep side, the engine was removed and the remaining shell pushed across the back lot to the fabrication shop. There the body was finished and final decals applied. For the first race the car would carry more than fifty decals in addition to the main set provided by Sunoco. Sunoco's large yellow diamond and red arrow logo was placed on the front hood and along the rear quarterpanels. Sunoco spelled out on big yellow letters would go on the rear of the car, just in case Terry was running in front of a car carrying a camera. If so, Sunoco's name would be plastered in front of millions of people watching the race at home.

Finally, NASCAR-supplied associate sponsor decals were mounted in positions mandated by NASCAR. Most of the NASCAR decals are mounted in a cluster just behind the right wheels in a panel that starts from the bottom of the car and extends upward.

NASCAR sells companies on the additional associate sponsorship deals with the assumption that the sponsor will have its decals on most if not all of the participating cars. In return, those companies, such as Right Guard, Gatorade, Goody's Headache Powders and Plasti-kote Spray Paint, offer additional race bonuses to the cars running those stickers. Right Guard, for example, gives a bonus to the driver leading the race at the halfway point in the race.

Teams are not forced by NASCAR to run the decals, however, if a driver is leading the race at the halfway point and is not carrying the Right Guard decal, the driver loses out on the money. In fact, some teams do not run all of the decals at the behest of their major sponsors. Those teams are reimbursed by their sponsors should they qualify to win a bonus and are not carrying the decal.

When the team returned to Daytona something had changed. Despite the conditions being nearly the same as they were for testing, Labonte's car was no longer the fastest. The car was now handling worse than in testing. Labonte complained the car was loose, meaning that when he gave the car more gas it felt like the rear end of the car would lose contact with the track. He could no longer drive the car as fast as he had before. Somewhere along the line, the car had changed.

Unfortunately, they had found the answers to the questions unanswerable during the winter tests. When running in packs at superspeedway speeds, the car would not perform as well as it did when alone.

The engine was fine, it seemed. The spring set up, which would control the way the car handled, was supposed to be identical to the set up used in testing. Yet, the car did not react the same.

Before the first round of qualifying, Loyd instructed Bryan to change the springs a handful of times in search of the right combination. They got close, but not close enough.

Daytona's Speedweeks got underway the first weekend of February, when the track played host to the twenty-four hours of Daytona, a sportscar race. Winston Cup racing moved into the spotlight on February 10, with the running of the Busch Clash. Labonte would not participate in the Clash, a race he had won before, because he failed to win a pole position in 1990.

The day before the Busch Clash, NASCAR held the first round of qualifying for the 500. Some sixty cars attempted to grab the top starting spot for the main race. Under NASCAR rules, only the top two were guaranteed starting positions. The remainder of the field would have to compete in one of two 125-mile races scheduled for Thursday. When all sixty cars had made their qualifying runs, Davey Allison earned the pole with a lap of 195.959. Ernie Irvan, driver of the Kodak Chevrolet Lumina was second with a lap of 195.639. Labonte finished fifteenth fastest overall traveling around the speedway at 193.228 mph for his qualifying lap.

After Allison and Irvan, the rest of the field was split into two groups on an odd and even basis. Labonte would start seventh in the second field of twenty-nine cars. The races were scheduled for midday Thursday, however, as race time neared, it started to rain. For awhile it looked like the rain wasn't going to stop. Fans headed for their cars, sure there would be no racing. But the rain finally stopped, and the races got underway, late.

Labonte finished his heat in eighteenth, good enough for a thirty-first starting position in the Daytona 500 three days away. Forty-two cars would make up the field.

Daytona Beach, Florida, is the home of NASCAR, the sport's sanctioning body. While racing started in the foothills of North Carolina in the 1930s and 1940s as something for moonshine runners to do in their free time, it was Daytona and the France family that put stock car racing on the map. The first races in the seaside resort were held in 1930. Daytona's long stretches of wide beach made for an excellent surface for speed. Nonetheless, until 1936, racing in Daytona had only been done in straight lines, sometimes for twenty miles or more.

In March 1936, using $5,000 put up by the city, promoters created a race and added curves to the surface. Using a stretch of beach and part of an adjacent highway joined by banked turns made of sand covered with clay, a speedway was born. Never mind that the race was a disaster, stopped short of its 250 miles because cars got stuck in the sand.

Bill France, who had moved to Florida from Washington, D.C., with his family, was one of the original racers that day.

Eventually, he started helping promote the event and then in 1947 became its only promoter. He founded NASCAR that same year. A dozen years later, France commissioned the construction of the Daytona International Speedway, which still stands today. France wanted a track that could compete with the Indianapolis Motor Speedway, the home of the Indianapolis 500. He got it. Some 135,000 fans would attend the running of the 1991 Daytona 500, and more than 7 million would watch at home on television.

From its humble beginnings, NASCAR has grown to become a multimillion dollar family-owned empire. In fact, recent consumer poles ranked NASCAR as the most popular motorsport in the United States, above all others including Championship Auto Racing Teams (CART), which oversees Indy-style racing.

During the past thirty-three years, the Daytona 500 has become a piece of Americana. The place is a museum for speed. The event is called "The Great American Race." It brings together all the aspects that have made professional stock car racing popular, from the death defying speeds to the good times had by infield campers, who will spend a week living it up inside the 2.5 mile long speedway. Americans love automobiles and the stock cars at Daytona give them something they can relate to. Sure the machines used on the raceway are nothing like those at the local dealer on the inside, but from the outside they look very much like the cars found on city streets and country roads. Fans can associate with a souped up Oldsmobile Cutlass Supreme or a Chevrolet Lumina like the ones driven in the Daytona 500. There are no comparisons to keep fans interested in Indy-style racing.

The 1991 running of the Daytona 500 would be slightly different from those held in the past. This year, for the first time ever, the event carried the name of a title sponsor through a multi-year deal with STP, one of the sport's oldest sponsors. All of NASCAR's other events have had title sponsors for years.

From the Valleydale Meats 500 at Bristol in April to the season ending Hardee's 500 in Atlanta, each has taken advantage of the promotional and money making opportunities that are present with a title sponsor. This year Daytona, the granddaddy of all stock car races, would become one of the pack. The Daytona 500 by STP was born.

While the weather for the Twin 125s was warm, in the seventies, the temperatures dropped suddenly on Friday afternoon, two days before the 500. A front moved in, bringing with it temperatures in the forties.

As part of a side deal Labonte had with Sun, he planned to drive his own Busch Grand National car in a 300-mile race held on Saturday. Labonte had sought full sponsorship, and was close to getting one with a tool manufacturer, but the deal fell apart before the season started. Instead, he signed a deal with Sun to carry the company's colors in five Busch series races. He would get $10,000 for each race. Labonte's younger brother Bobby, runner-up in the Busch series championship race a year before, was also in the race. However, a day earlier the younger Labonte wrecked his car in practice. Under Busch rules, Bobby could not go to a back-up car. Since he was running to accumulate points for the championship and Terry was not, Terry lent his car to Bobby.

The Busch race started at noon on a bright, but cool Florida day. In the first lap, Bobby got tangled in a multi-car wreck that caused the car to burst into flames. Terry's car was finished and Bobby was out of the race.

Rules which governed the pits were, perhaps, the most talked about event at the track as the Winston Cup teams planned strategies for the race. At the 1990 season-ending race in Atlanta, Mike Rich, a rear right side tire changer on former Winston Cup champion Bill Elliott's crew, died after a car driven by Ricky Rudd spun in the pits and struck him. During the off season, NASCAR vowed to make pit road safer for crew members. In the past, the pits became uncontrolled chaos when the caution flag was out. Depending on how many cars were on the lead lap, there could be as many as forty 3,500-pound vehicles streaming into the pits during caution periods. After the cars were serviced, the drivers raced out of the pits trying to gain some positioning on their toughest opponents. The death of Rich wasn't the first pit accident, it was only the latest.

NASCAR created new rules for 1991 that drastically changed the strategy for the 500. No longer were teams allowed to change tires during the cautions. Now they could come in for gas only. Drivers would have to wait until the race went back to green before changing tires. And pitting under those first green flag laps after the caution would be done on an odd and even basis depending on starting position. Odd numbered starters would pit on the second lap under green while evens would have to wait until the third green flag lap. A typical green flag stop for gas and four tires takes about 22.5 seconds for the better teams. At Daytona 22.5 seconds could put a driver behind half a lap or more.

"I think a lot of different people will be doing different things," said Labonte during practice on Saturday. "Some guys might pit for gas under caution, others might wait for green to get gas and tires. One thing, we'll go a long way on tires. Your car has to work good on hot tires. You've got to run good on used tires, not run over anything, get good fuel mileage and not screw up."

The Loyd-led team continued making changes to the car during Saturday practice sessions to get it right. In addition to not having the right set up, the winds and temperatures were taking a toll. Moreover, like Labonte, many of the drivers were used to running bias-ply tires on the superspeedway. This time out NASCAR wanted radial tires used. The change would affect the handling of the race cars.

"We're better than yesterday," Labonte said of practice. "We're not as good as we should be, but better."

Team members and "late coming" fans start arriving before dawn on race day. It is a cold morning, with temperatures in the high thirties. Thousands of fans from all over the country have camped out in the infield at the historic raceway for days. Some walk over to the fence surrounding the garages looking to catch a glimpse of one of the drivers. Better yet, some hope for autographs. Inside the chain link fence the garage doors remain shut as crew members continue to work on preparing the cars for the race. High powered kerosene heaters roar, warming each garage area. Hot coffee is the drink of the moment.

Sponsor colors are everywhere—hats, seat cushions, pens and pins. Just about anything that can be painted is carrying the name of the major sponsors. It's big business with companies spending anywhere from a few hundred thousand dollars to several millions to get their message out. Team marketing people run pit and garage tours for sponsor guests at the race. They come in bunches, each adorned with a team hat and sporting the team colors. Occasionally, they ask for autographs. Almost always they'll ask a friend to take a picture of them near the race car. This is racing, one of the only major sports where fans can visit the lockerrooms before the event. No other sport allows such access. NASCAR has been able to become a big business and yet keep its intimate relationship with the fans. They come in bus loads, ceremoniously taking a lap around the track.

Teams work closely together in the garages, although no secrets are shared. It's 8:30 a.m. The Sunoco car is on four jack stands, its wheels off. A checklist has been taped to the left rear of the car. The crew member completing the task checks the list and moves on. There are about thirty items on this checklist, ranging from waxing the car to tightening wheel lug nuts. Some concern appearance, others safety, and some performance. Each is as important as the other.

Once all the jobs on the list are complete, Bryan Robertson mounts the tires. One by one he works his way around the car, tightening the five lugs that hold the wheels on. When he's done, the car is taken off the jack stands. Truck driver Harold Hughes then checks each lug nut with a torque wrench to assure the wheels are on snug.

The team members then push the car to the inspection area. It passes easily, though the team was worried NASCAR inspectors would check the front air dam. It had been altered and may not have fit the NASCAR templates for the car. To off-set the change, the team did not continue a yellow stripe running along the bottom of the car over the dam. Once the car is pushed to the starting line, the team members return to the car transporter to eat lunch, change into their race uniforms and relax.

Following the introductions, the drivers move to their cars. There Labonte goes through his pre-race checks. He walks around the car looking for problems before he climbs inside. One by one he fastens and tightens his safety belts. With his helmet on, he tests his radio connections. This will be his lifeline to the pits should a problem develop during the race. He will also receive instructions via his radio. Crew chief Steve Loyd will tell him when to pit, and spotter Danny Culler, sitting above the front grandstands, will tell him when it's safe to move down on the track.

A loud cheer develops from the crowd as the grand marshall shouts the famous words, "Gentleman start your engines." At once forty-two souped up V-8 engines roar to life. Back at the pits, crews test the air wrenches. They rev the guns like motorcycle engines, bursts of noise sounding up and down pit road. As the cars pull out onto the track, camera crews stand between the two lines of race cars. Dust blows in their faces as the cars thunder past side by side.

Moments before the start the excitement level in the pits and the stands reaches a roaring crescendo. The fans are on their feet shouting and waving. Across the track, team members shift around in the pits trying to get a good view of the cars coming down the stretch to the start/finish line. So much can happen in those early moments as drivers nervously head for the start. The worst had occurred a day earlier. No one wanted a repeat performance.

The field takes two warm-up laps to loosen up. Now the drivers are deciding exactly when to hit the gas hard, hoping that the driver in front of them will do the same thing at the same time. Drivers position their cars close together, ready to make a move the moment the green flag falls. In some cases they are less than a few feet away from the car in front of them. Some touch. Their speed picks up as they come out of turn four heading for the green. The flag is out and the race is underway. There are no mistakes today.

Billy Hagan stands at the pit wall for the start. After the cars roll by, with the help of a team member, he moves to a seat atop the pit box. The box contains tools and equipment, and serves as a viewing point for Hagan. Team manager Herb Hupperich sits in an elevated chair to the right of the box. He will stay there for the entire race, tracking laps and pit stops. An unlit cigar is present in the corner of his mouth.

As with the practices before the race, the car is loose. During a caution period, Loyd bangs the rear spoiler up a bit to put more downward pressure on the rear wheels. The move will also slow the car. Nonetheless, Labonte runs in the top fifteen for most of the race, avoiding several accidents in the process.

Because of the new pit rules, the leaders are spread out throughout field. As a result, the early stages of the race are largely uneventful. However, the intensity picks up near the end. With three laps remaining, Davey Allison tries to pass Dale Earnhardt to take over second place. Earnhardt, a four-time champion, has never won the Daytona 500. The fans are going crazy as Allison and Earnhardt drive side-by-side behind Ernie Irvan. Then, as Allison makes his move, he and Earnhardt touch, causing both to spin. The 1991 Daytona 500 ends under caution, with Ernie Irvan taking the checkered flag.

The new pit rules proved tough for the racers and the fans. Limiting tire changes to under the green made the teams run longer on tires that in the past they would have changed. Moreover, for the fans it was difficult to watch. The green flag stops spread the field making it hard to know which car was running where.

Aside from the obvious benefits of making pit road safer for its inhabitants, the new rules had a positive benefit on the wallets of team owners. At $225 a tire, a four-tire change can be an expensive proposition. In the past, most teams would change tires on just about every caution. But, by limiting teams to green flag stops, teams cut down their tire use. In past Daytona 500s Hagan's team spent upwards of $5,000 on tires just for the race. Their race-day bill is about $1,000 this time out.

When the race is over, Labonte wheels the car back to the garage. He climbs out of the car and finds a seat on a nearby work bench. Paul Mecca hands him a Sunoco hat in case any camera crews or photographers come around. Despite the finish, Labonte is happy. Sitting on the work bench, he jokes that he should leave before anyone figures out where he finished — thirteenth, two laps down. The finish is good for $34,355. Labonte feels that he didn't deserve thirteenth; he didn't run that well. He signs a few autographs and speaks to the lone reporter that is interested in what he has to say. Finishing thirteenth does not attract a lot of media attention.

"This is the first race I've ever been in that I couldn't keep up with who was running where," Labonte said after the race. "I wasn't even sure where I was or who I was racing."

four

Racing the Sun

"We bought our way into a lot of races . . .
provisionals and stuff."
Geoff Plazer

"I suspect this is about the worst finish we'll see this season," said
Sunoco racing committee chairman George (Bud) Campbell three
days after the Daytona 500. While agreeing there would be blown
engines and accidents that would take Labonte out of races early,
Campbell believed in the team and believed the team was destined
to be at the top portion of the Winston Cup standings.

Campbell, fifty-three, stands a little over six feet tall. His
reddish hair surrounds a round face accented by wire frame
glasses and highlighted by an easy smile. A thirty-one-year employee of Sun Refining and Marketing, he was one race into his
first year as a member of the committee that oversees the company's involvement in motorsports. He truly believed that the
season before him would be a good one, if not great.

A year before, he and his wife, Marilyn, were regular fans, attending fourteen races. During the season, they became friends with team manger Herb Hupperich and team owner Billy Hagan. Through them, they gained access to the pits and garage areas at the races they attended. Other times they would purchase tickets and spend the day in the stands cheering on the Sunoco sponsored entry.

Campbell is easy with conversation and able to blend in with those around him. He had seen the previous season, and could see there was something to get excited about. Aside from Hagan's preaching, Campbell had watched the season before and the bad luck that the team had experienced. When Marlin was destined for a win, something would go wrong. Yet, Marlin would post ten top ten finishes, with his best finish being a third. Looking at the team from the outside there was some hope. With Labonte behind the wheel, and Hagan's increased excitement, Bud, and many others, thought the team's problems were solved.

Bud has been called a manager's manager by some that work with him. An outgoing guy with no ties to the racing program, he was hand selected by company president David E. Knoll to run the committee. The executive stopped by Campbell's office one day and asked if Campbell thought the company should remain in racing. Campbell said yes, provided that the company used the program more efficiently than it had of late.

"We should, not because I like racing or because you like racing," Campbell told Knoll, "but because there are benefits involved, if done right."

Campbell felt marketing of the racing program was an area being underutilized by the company. He thought there were some opportunities available the company could benefit from. He also told Knoll that if the company backed out of racing, the executive would have to find another device to build employee morale. Campbell knew that he found many people talking about racing on Monday mornings after race weekends, and that void would have to be filled.

Knoll needed someone to replace the current committee chairman, Edwin Neithercott, who was retiring. About a month after their impromptu talk, Knoll called with the offer. It took Campbell around twenty seconds to say yes.

In the previous year, the committee's members had grown independent. Each handled their own duties, although many had extended their reach beyond the boundaries set by the current leadership. Knoll wanted someone without an allegiance to any of the factions within the committee to take the reins. What ever Campbell wanted for the committee was fine, within reason, just get it in order.

Sun's racing committee consists of a hodgepodge of department managers from ten wings of the company. Committee member's racing knowledge spans from the neophyte to the experienced with a lot of them falling somewhere between. Like any group, there are some who want to lead, some who just follow and others who complain a lot without any real knowledge of the subject.

The 1991 season started Sun's third as a major NASCAR sponsor. Sun is the nation's largest independent refining and marketing company, with 5 refineries, 6,000 miles of crude oil pipeline and an employee population topping 13,000.

Sun had been involved successfully with racing on a national level before. Between 1967 and 1973 Sunoco backed team owner and Indy-style racing legend Roger Penske and his driver Mark Donohue. The investment in the Penske/Donohue racing program paid off for Sunoco by getting its product name to consumers. Penske/Donohue combined for the United States Road Racing Championship in 1967 and 1968, and reached a peak in 1972 with the winning of the Indianapolis 500. However, a few years later, Donohue died in a racing accident. Shortly after, Sunoco backed out of Indy racing and focused its attention on deals with local racers.

In 1986, Charlie Rudolph was a decent racer on the Northeastern DIRT circuit, a series of races run on clay surfaced ovals. Like many racers, Rudolph wanted to make the jump to NASCAR, where the money and the glamor was. He had acquired a Winston Cup car and was searching for sponsorship. Sunoco Racing Fuels, directed by gasolines manager Dr. Bob Burtner, partially subsidized Rudolph's dirt track efforts. Under gas and oil plans, supervised by Burtner, racers would get those products in return for the driver placing a Sunoco sticker on the car.

Rudolph contacted Burtner seeking sponsorship for his Winston Cup efforts. He wanted sponsorship for four races, all held in the North — Michigan, Pocono and Dover. All the race tracks were well within Sunoco's Northeast marketing area and were just short drives from the company's headquarters in Philadelphia. Burtner liked the idea, but told Rudolph to contact Kirk Chandler, the company's national sales manager for commercial and industrial lubricants. Chandler and Burtner had discussed NASCAR deals before and Burtner urged Chandler to move in that direction. A NASCAR-wide deal with Unocal to provide gasoline at the race tracks prohibited Sunoco or any other gasoline manufacturer from becoming a sponsor. But, by using the Sunoco Ultra Products' banner, Sunoco's non-gas offerings, the company could move into NASCAR headfirst.

Armed with the news there might be an opening, Rudolph turned to Paul Mecca, a friend who operated his own promotion and marketing firm in Buffalo. Mecca had helped Rudolph before with other sponsorship deals so it made sense to work together again. Mecca called Chandler representing Rudolph.

"Send me a proposal," Chandler said, having already received recommendations from Burtner. "I'll get back to you after I receive it." Days later, Mecca followed the conversation with a proposal asking for a $15,000 sponsorship for each of the four races. Chandler called almost immediately after receiving the deal, leaving three numbers where he could be reached.

By the time Mecca and Chandler made contact, Rudolph had committed to racing at the Pocono race in June, the first Winston Cup race at the track that season. Since he was racing, the team was allowed six sponsor passes permitting access to the garage and pit areas. Mecca invited Chandler to the track for the weekend, thinking it would be a good way to give the executive a taste for the sport.

Chandler took him up on the offer and made the hour-plus trip to the raceway. With the Winston Cup race on Sunday, Mecca and Chandler would have all day Saturday to talk racing. Mecca introduced Chandler to the team and the two headed to the bleachers to watch the support race that afternoon. Prior to all Winston Cup events "support races" are held and typically feature a lower caliber class car. For this race it would be an ARCA race, best compared to a AA farm team in baseball. Between breaks in the action, and during the race, the two talked about the proposal. Before the race was over, they had verbally agreed to a three-race deal with the first race under the deal being the next race at Michigan International Speedway.

Between the Pocono event and the Michigan race, Rudolph had his car repainted with the Sunoco colors. Sunoco unveiled its sponsorship at the track. According to Mecca, the car looked hideous; the colors were wild. Sunoco's blue, yellow and red logo was overshadowed by bright red and yellow. It looked like a clown.

"When they unloaded the car at Michigan, it was like a bomb went off," recalls Mecca. "All of a sudden this little guy's [Rudolph] got Sunoco on his car. Sun started getting calls from all over the place."

Almost immediately Sun started getting alternative proposals, each wanting to take the package away from Rudolph. Sun immediately formed a committee of eight to handle the influx of information and to consider other racing offers. After looking at the proposals, the committee realized they needed someone with an outside perspective to help wade through the information. They also needed someone with racing experience to help them ask the right questions. Company executives were happy with the exposure the Rudolph deal brought them, although his performance on the track was not enough to keep the sponsorship.

"Charlie didn't have the depth to run Winston Cup," says Geoff Plazer, a thirty-year Sun employee and vice chairman of the racing committee.

They turned to racing veteran Pat Patterson for the answers, even though Patterson had a candidate of his own for the sponsorship. Following a meeting with the committee, Patterson admitted what he was going to say could be considered unethical, but he recommended a team fielded by Mike Curb, the former lieutenant governor of California. Curb was based in Kannapolis, North Carolina, a town north of Charlotte. In addition to racing, Curb had ties to gas and oil drilling rights, which also interested Sun. He submitted a proposal and the company agreed to back his team for twenty races at about $500,000. The deal was later amended to include twenty-eight races for $750,000. The only race Curb was not to run was the road course in Riverside, California.

Sunoco hired Patterson to market the race team, and with great fanfare Sunoco marked its full-time return to racing with the running of the 1988 Daytona 500. Buicks prepared by Curb's team would carry the Sunoco yellow diamond logo. Fearing a car that would look like the one Rudolph presented, Sun hired the identity consulting firm of Lippincott & Margulies to design the graphics of the car. What L&M designer Karen Shinoda came up with was a blue base with the company logo on the hood and the two rear quarter panels. A graduated yellow line was placed along the bottom of the car to lead the eye from yellow to blue. The car would carry the number 94 representing the company's highest octane leveled gasoline.

Ed Pimm, a thirty-one-year-old rookie driver, was behind the wheel. His first NASCAR experience was less than a year behind him.

Pimm ran a few races for Curb and then was replaced by sprint car driver Brad Noffsinger. With the driver change, Sun also wanted a change in marketing. They turned to Mecca. Chandler asked Mecca if he could help out for three months until someone else could be found. Privately, he was told that the deal could be his provided he convinced company public relations executive Dennis Byrne that he knew what he was doing. Being from Buffalo, there was some trepidation that by not being in Charlotte, Mecca couldn't get the job done. He did and kept the job.

Meanwhile, Curb's performance on the track was dismal. The team had trouble making races and did not do well in the races they could make. Sun's deal was good for only a year, though there was an option. Failing to make races kept Sunoco's image away from the fans and the television viewers. Without the exposure, the deal was worthless.

"We bought our way into a lot of races . . . provisionals and stuff," says Plazer.

"Curb was taking the money and making all kinds of promises," remembers Mecca. Curb's team couldn't make the field for the September race at Martinsville, a half-mile track in Virginia. Mecca called Sun and told the executives that the team missed the race and he was going to head home. Doing this would save money, and without a car in the race there really wasn't any need for him to be there.

Instead, they told him to stay through Sunday and nose around to see if there was another team needing sponsorship. Sun was ready to talk. There were at least three regular teams in such a situation, along with a handful of smaller teams searching for a big sponsor. Kodak's commitment to the team it sponsored was shaky, driver Lake Speed needed sponsorship and a team owned by Billy Hagan was waiting to see if its deal with

Piedmont Airlines was going to continue. Mecca and Chandler approached Hagan a week later. They asked if he was interested in talking about sponsorship and he said yes, provided Piedmont backed out. It was almost certain the company would; it had just been acquired by USAir.

After some debate within the committee, they agreed to sponsor Hagan and his driver Sterling Marlin. The deal was worth $1.5 million in the first year and $1.7 in the second. And, despite receiving proposals from teams that had been more successful on the track than Hagan's, Sun signed a new deal with Hagan for the 1991 and 1992 season worth $2.1 million each year.

When Knoll selected Campbell to run the committee he wanted all of the various factions within the committee to answer to one person, Bud. In the past, the committee members would at times operate independently, each making demands on the team and Hagan. It made for an uncomfortable situation all around. When a committee member had what he perceived to be a problem with the team's performance, he would go straight to Hagan, or team manager Herb Hupperich. Often the conversations would include a veiled threat that the program would go elsewhere when the contract that bound them together expired.

"I'm not used to running by committee," Hagan would say later in the season. I think a lot of people not being as aware of what actually goes on in racing is part of the problem."

Both Hagan and Campbell expected their problems to be behind them when the 1991 season started. Campbell was expecting a top ten points finish.

five

The Eighth Man

"I don't know I just don't qualify well."
Terry Labonte

From the sunbaked shores of Daytona Beach the NASCAR circuit traveled 600 miles north to a chilly Richmond International
Raceway for the Pontiac Excitement 400. The race is the second
stop on the Winston Cup series, scheduled for the last week of
February. In the Northeast, biting cold associated with the tail
end of winter carries enough sting to make it almost uncomfortable to stay outdoors for any extended period, let alone to watch
a three-hour stock car race.

This February would be no different. Temperatures hov-
ered in the forties and the air was damp. Richmond's open garage area invites in the cold. Under a metal roof, teams work side
by side, their garage stalls draped with blue tarpaulins helping to
block blowing winds. Kerosene fumes fill the air as heaters roar,

their ends glowing bright orange. The heat is a comforting friend to the team members who have been at the raceway preparing for the day's events since the sun broke over the horizon. Garages are assigned by NASCAR, based on a performance order, with last year's champion picking first followed by the current points leader and so on down the line.

First round qualifying was held Friday morning at the three-quarter mile oval. One at a time the teams line up on pit road waiting for their shot at the pole. By mid-morning the first fifteen starters are set. Non-qualifiers will spend the remainder of the day tweaking their cars to milk out another tenth of a second for second round qualifying the next day.

Terry, by his own admission, didn't qualify well. His lap of 22.844 seconds or 118.193 mph was only good enough for the eighteenth starting position. Davey Allison, driving the Texaco/Havoline Ford Thunderbird, won the pole with a time of 22.420 seconds for 120.428 mph. A mere 2.23 mph separated the pole sitter and Terry.

"I don't know I just don't qualify well," he would say afterwards. "Do real good in practice, but just don't qualify well."

During early practice sessions, Terry complained that the car was loose. Going into the corners and coming out, the rear end of the car felt like it would swing out if he pushed it harder. Throughout Saturday practice sessions, crew chief Steve Loyd instructed chassis mechanic Bryan Robertson to change springs in the front and the rear of the car. The springs affect the handling of the car, hopefully tightening it up.

This would be the second race the team would be using a front-steer, rather than a rear-steer, equipped car. Labonte had decided before the season that the switch was needed. A majority of the top teams had already made the switch with success.

The difference in the two technologies was minimal from outward appearances, although drastic in how the car handled. If a straight line were drawn joining the center of the two front wheels, the steering gear in a rear-steer system is located to the rear of that imaginary line, off to the left. Front-steer cars use the same system, although the steering gear is forward of the center line and all of the other steering parts — idler arms and steering arms — are reversed.

In addition to affecting the handling, front-steer set-ups can have an effect on horsepower. The parts that connect a rear-steer mechanism run under the engine and directly impact the size of the oil pan that can be used. However, mechanics found that by moving the steering system forward, they were free to use whatever size oil pan they wanted. Other benefits of front-steer are the ability to lower the engine within the frame and use a taller intake manifold, in turn lowering the center of gravity of the car.

The design has been around for almost two decades, though it did not become popular until the late 1980s, when NASCAR started requiring the use of restrictor plates at Talladega and Daytona to keep speeds down. After finding their horsepower cut because of the restrictors, engine builders and chassis mechanics started to search for other means of beefing up performance. Front-steer cars then moved to the forefront. The trend of radial designed tires also helped fuel the use of front-steer cars among the NASCAR ranks. Radial tires are more durable than bias-ply tires, and have a more ridged side-wall. Teams have found that a car with radials handles better with the steering box slid forward. With Goodyear close to creating radials specifically designed for each track, it is only a matter of time before bias-ply tires are phased out.

The changeover came with built in problems. Neither Terry, Steve, nor any of the other members of the team had much experience with front-steer cars. Terry did not have much seat time with front-steer cars and as a result was not 100 percent sure how the cars were supposed to feel. Without a front-steer expert on the team, or even someone remotely familiar with the technology, everything they did was on a trial and error basis.

"Front steer was going to be a struggle." Labonte said. "It had to be done, I knew that. I would have brought in somebody, though, a front-steer chassis wizard."

During practice the team changed the car's set-up a number of times hoping to hit upon something that was comfortable to Labonte. With each change came another series of laps on the track. Armed with stopwatches, team members moved to a position near the track to watch Labonte test out their latest changes. The times were roughly the same throughout—nothing to write home about. After ten laps or less testing the last series of adjustments Labonte slowed his car and dropped down to the inside of the track to enter pit road. The team members headed back to the pits, waiting for Labonte's comments to crackle over their radio headsets. It was still not perfect, but better. Nonetheless, time had run out. The next time he could get into the car would be moments before the race.

A half-hour before the race is to begin, the drivers move to the rear of a podium set up in the front straight of the raceway. One by one they are introduced to the fans and then head for their cars, parked a couple hundred feet away. It's a ritual held before every race. A driver failing to make introductions can be fined by NASCAR. The announcer starts at the back of the pack and works his way forward. Depending on the popularity of the driver, the crowd reacts differently. Terry's introduction drew a response that was barely audible. Meanwhile, Dale Earnhardt, who qualified further to the front of the pack and always a crowd favorite, received the equivalent of a standing ovation.

Throughout his career, Labonte has been a consistent finisher, although, his on track performances carry little flair. While other drivers are more daring, willing to put it all on the line for a better position, Labonte rarely takes such gambles. As a result, his popularity with the fans is much lower than the more exciting drivers like Earnhardt. Those who have watched Labonte's career suggest that if he were a little more aggressive, the fans would follow. Perhaps sending Earnhardt into the wall, they said, would increase fan awareness of Labonte, which in turn would have a positive effect on the sale of Terry Labonte souvenirs at the various race venues. However, with his cool attitude, the fans offer little in return when his name is called during driver introductions.

The race starts and Terry moves up a few notches through the pack of cars in front of him. A year before he finished this race in thirty-second position, driving the Skoal Oldsmobile, in which the motor blew on lap 229 of the 400 scheduled. This year, however, the race went differently.

The first caution comes on lap 10 and lasts for one lap. Rick Mast, now driving the Skoal Oldsmobile owned by Richard Jackson, slammed into the wall in turn three to bring out the caution.

"That last lap was a 22.94," says Steve Loyd to Terry who continues around the track under caution. "How's the car?"

"It's pretty good," he replies.

The new pit rules put into effect at the Daytona 500 had been roundly panned after the race. Drivers maintained that they had to run on worn tires, which led to accidents. NASCAR adjusted the rules for the Pontiac Excitement 400.

The caution was the first chance to see round two of the new pit rules in use. Teams could now change tires damaged during spins or accidents under caution. This was significant because often tires would become "flat-spotted" after an accident where the driver locked up the brakes, causing the tires to wear flat in one area. During the Daytona 500, if a driver had a flat tire because of a spin, he was penalized if he changed tires under the caution, which often he was responsible for causing in the first place. The teams that did pit during the yellow flag would have to return to the pits to change two tires during the first lap of green flag racing.

Teams welcomed the additional changes, though the rules did take some of the fun out of racing. In the days after the Daytona 500, fans wrote letters to the racing newspapers complaining that the new rules made it difficult to watch races. No longer were the leaders battling it out, racing side-by-side for the checkered flag. Forcing the drivers to pit under the green flag spread the field out making the race confusing to watch, especially during long periods of green flag racing.

Terry stays on the track for the first caution to maintain track position. With each lap, spotter Danny Culler, sitting above the grandstands, calls out Terry's lap times. Doing so helps Labonte find the right line on the track. By hearing lap times, he might find that going deep into the corners and high on the straights makes the car a tenth of a second faster. Even the slightest variable can cut the time it takes going around the track.

By lap 20, Terry has moved up to fifteenth place, while pole sitter Davey Allison continues to hold the lead. Another twenty laps later Terry is running in seventeenth and forty laps after that he has fallen to nineteenth. The position changes are largely due to green flag pit stops. A lap around Richmond International Raceway takes little more than twenty-two seconds. A four tire pit stop by the best teams takes about as long. From the start, Loyd decided that the team would change just two tires each stop, which would take roughly fifteen seconds. However, just before the second caution of the day, and after a long stretch of green flag racing, Loyd decides to bring Labonte in for a four tire pit stop. Loyd holds up four fingers and radios to team members that they will change four tires. It will be their first four tire stop of the year.

Each member moves into position near the short wall separating him from the cars on pit road. Kelly Hunt, who serves as the jackman on race day, places the aluminum racing jack on the pit wall and waits. Bryan Robertson, left side tire changer, and Steve Wilson, front tire changer, each press the trigger on their high-speed air guns, letting loose a whirl of air. Donnie Crumley, a fabrication worker back at the shop, lifts the two right side tires he will carry onto the track.

"Here he comes," Culler says as Labonte reaches the entrance to pit road.

Labonte pulls in, and the team springs to action. Crumley, with a tire under each arm, runs to the outside of the car, stopping first at the right front to drop a tire and then the right rear for the second. Hunt has already pumped the jack two of the four times needed to lift the car, and Wilson has already loosened the lug nuts. The tires are on and the jack is dropped. But, before they would reach the other side of the car, Greg McElreath steps over the wall to clean the windows, becoming the eighth man over the wall. Eight men is one too many under NASCAR rules.

The NASCAR inspector responsible for overseeing the pits occupied by the Hagan team steps in front of Labonte's car. He counts off fifteen seconds and steps away. The penalty is costly, putting Terry a lap down.

Labonte pulls away. Immediately the team realizes they made a mistake during the stop that will impact Labonte's finish. They practiced pit stops in the weeks before the first race at Daytona, but when it counted they messed up. Pitting behind the shop is nothing like pitting on a speedway. On a speedway every second counts, and unlike practice behind the shop, there are no "do-overs."

Despite the setback, the team rebounds and each member replaces the tools used. Bryan and Steve recoil the fifty foot hoses leading to their airguns. Crumley places two new tires within arm's reach and the tall orange gas cans are refilled, ready for the next time Labonte pulls down pit road. One thing certain about being a pit crew member is that nothing is certain. Moments after sending their driver back onto the track, he may return, a victim of an accident or a faulty part. They must always be ready to go to work. Racing action changes in split seconds.

Terry makes his way from the back of the pack to the thirteenth position at the 300-lap point, although two laps behind the race leader Dale Earnhardt, driving the Goodwrench

Chevrolet Lumina. Terry finishes fourteenth overall, four laps off the lead pace. His winnings for the day: $7,200. The race, with only six cautions for twenty-three laps, took just two hours and fifty-two minutes, nearly twenty-three minutes shorter than the same race the year before.

"One of the guys went early," Hupperich said later about the pit stop that brought the fifteen-second penalty. "You know we practice that for two weeks, but in the heat of the moment they get a little bit ahead of themselves."

six

Accidents Will Happen

"I almost had it saved but we slid sideways into the wall."
Terry Labonte

A week separated the race in Richmond and the Goodwrench 500 held at the North Carolina Motor Speedway in Rockingham, North Carolina. Called "The Rock," the 1.017-mile-long speedway is a demanding track with an abrasive asphalt surface that is hard on tires. The track is about an hour and a half south of Hagan's Thomasville shop.

The pre-race crew arrived with the sun on Thursday morning. The gate to the garages is unchained by 6 a.m., with the drivers not due until 11 a.m. For most races a skeleton crew will go to the track three days before the race to help during practice and qualifying rounds. The remaining crew members involved on race day will arrive the night before or the morning of a race.

Bryan Robertson, a twenty-one-year-old rookie to the Winston Cup racing scene, Herb Hupperich, Steve Loyd, head engine builder Dewey Livengood and truck driver Harold Hughes made the trip to Rockingham for first round qualifying. Terry qualified twenty-fourth for the race, not good enough to be guaranteed a starting spot, but yet fast enough so the team would decide to stand on the time for second round qualifying.

Unlike a majority of the teams on the circuit, Hagan's operation did not use a qualifying motor. Engine builders design qualifying motors using lighter parts and make other adjustments to wring out just a little more horsepower. They advance the engine timing and tune the carburetor jetting. Qualifying motors are built to have an increased amount of high end power and as little friction as possible. High end power gives the car maximum strength through the straights. Thinner oil and a flat fan blade, to reduce drag, are also used on the motors. Teams install the qualifying motors before heading to the track. This allows them to spend their time working on the chassis for the right set-up during the short period of practice time available before qualifying. Once the teams qualify and are assured a starting spot, the motors are replaced with more durable race motors, with low end torque for passing.

By not using a qualifying motor the team sacrificed better starting positions. Instead, they focused on the race set-up, a combination of springs and shocks to give Labonte a better feel for the road. Springs of different sizes were switched in and out of the four housings located at each well to get the car handling properly. At Rockingham, Terry was driving a rear-steer leftover in the Hagan stable. Most of the cars Hagan owned were somewhat dated, some leftover from the last time Terry drove for him.

During Friday's early practice session, Terry fired up the car and headed onto the track. After a few slow laps, normal at the start of a practice session, Labonte turned the car loose. The car was running well, to the point where Terry thought the right set-up might be within reach, and then disaster struck.

Labonte drove the car deep into turn four and then headed down the front stretch. As he entered turn one, the engine exploded. The force drove a connecting rod through the engine wall, creating a gaping hole for the oil to leak out. In an instant, the surface under the car was slick, and Labonte lost control of the car. Before he could regain control, the 3,500-pound vehicle slammed into the wall.

"I was heading into the first corner and the engine let go," he said. "I really had no warning that anything was wrong. It just let go. Something came through the bottom of the engine and we lost all the oil. I almost had it saved but we slid sideways into the wall."

There was no damage to the frame of the car, although the impact bent the rear end housing and the truck arms. Truck arms are bars of steel that steady the rear suspension. While used on stock cars the arms are literally truck parts. NASCAR teams use a modified version of an arm used on Chevrolet trucks built in 1962. For comparison, today's passenger cars in most cases use MacPherson struts to handle the same chores. The right front ball joint and a few other suspension parts were also damaged in the wreck. In a matter of seconds, two days work at the track and a handful of days work back at the shop were wasted.

Safety crews at the track towed the car back to the garage where Loyd and his crew surveyed the damaged. They had three choices: work on the car in the garage area, bring it back to Thomasville, or unload the back-up car on the truck. They were uncomfortable with going to the back-up car and if they decided to work on the car in the garage there was a small chance it wouldn't get done in time. Choosing either the back-up or taking the car home for repairs would result in Terry having to start the race at the rear of the field. Only repairing the car at the track would maintain his twenty-fourth place starting position.

With noontime approaching and rain in the forecast for the next day, they decided to load the car onto the transporter and haul the mangled vehicle the ninety miles back to Thomasville. When most of the equipment was loaded back onto the transporter they headed home. Before leaving the track Herb Hupperich called the shop and said they were hauling the car back and everyone was needed. They were likely to have to work into the night. Ironically, this was the second consecutive year that the Hagan team's car had been wrecked during practice at Rockingham.

"We put two days work into a rear-steer car, so we wanted to stay with it," Hupperich said. "We had gotten it working real good. The other car on the truck was a front-steer."

Staying at the track to make the repairs would have also put a time limit on their work. It was already noon and NASCAR would close the garage at 5 p.m., no matter what state the car was in. That in itself would force them to do most of the work on Saturday, eating up valuable practice time. And with the threat of rain, the work would have to been done under tarpaulins. Fans would also want to watch, often getting in the way. Lastly, under the working conditions there was the risk of forgetting something important on the car.

"Because the car was working so well before the accident," Labonte said, "we decided to fix it rather than go to a back-up car. We figured we could repair the car and get it pretty close to what it was before we wrecked. We were worried that if we went to the back-up car and we didn't get any practice [Saturday] because of the weather we would wind up starting the race in an untested car, and we didn't want to do that."

Harold had to wait more than an hour before he was able to leave the raceway in the transporter. NASCAR was to have stopped practice at 1 p.m., however, the session was extended. Because of the layout of most raceways, Rockingham being no different, the transporters must use the raceway surface to exit the track. Harold sat in the cab facing out onto the track until it was time to go.

By the time that Harold reached the shop there were twelve team members waiting. When he opened the rear door to the blue and yellow trailer, a thin layer of brown baked beans covered the walkway inside. In their rush to get back to the shop, no one noticed the crock-pot full of the murky beans on the counter top inside the truck. Harold had left them stewing all morning and they would have been lunch had the mishap not happened.

Team members unloaded the car and quickly moved into the shop. Midway through the repairs the phone rang. It was Bud Campbell.

"Buy the team dinner," he told Hupperich, "and tell them it's from their sponsor."

Having the necessary tools within reach, the team got the car repaired and loaded back onto the transporter by 9:30 p.m. Harold would drive the rig back to the track Saturday morning.

"We did in six hours what would have taken ten hours at the track," Hupperich said.

"If we hadn't taken it back, we would still be working on it," Terry said early Saturday morning. "We wouldn't have been able to finish on time."

As predicted, the rains came. It rained for a portion of Friday afternoon and some of Saturday morning. When it stopped, emergency vehicles were dispatched to drive the track. Constant laps by the vehicles heated the surface, aiding the natural drying process. Once the track looked reasonably safe, NASCAR officials asked Terry and Davey Allison to take a few laps to see if practice could be started.

"God, why me?" Terry asked. He then headed onto the track for a few slow laps.

"Terry's considered one of the most conservative and cautious drivers," said Hupperich. "They know if it's wet he'll tell them."

The track proved to be unsafe. After a few laps Labonte and Allison returned to the garages, making way for the safety crews that would do more laps around the track. Again the rain returned.

NASCAR's weather information equipment indicated there would be a five hour window without rain Saturday afternoon and no window for Sunday. The information was partly correct. The rain eventually stopped allowing the teams to get some practice Saturday afternoon. After the practice session, Terry thought the car felt good. As is always the process, Harold and Bryan draped a blue canvas cover over the car. With the truck locked up, the garage area was cleared. The team headed back to a nearby hotel, only to return twelve hours later.

Sunday morning was a lot like Saturday. Skies were overcast and the threat of rain was present. The car sat underneath the garage, up on four jack stands, tires removed. The race day crew had arrived and started going through their pre-race rituals. Gone was the checklist that had been on the car for Daytona. What needed to be done was now a habit.

Like clockwork they move around the car going through their routines. Donnie Crumley and Greg McElreath wax the car, while Kelly and Bryan attend to the chassis checks. Dewey controls the front of the vehicle, checking the engine valves and spark plugs. Steve checks the rear end gear, pulled before each race to make sure there are no broken teeth on the main gear responsible for turning the rear wheels.

Out on the race track gasman Dan Gatewood prepares the pit area. Piece by piece he unloads a large pit box that carries the essentials needed for a race. The box will double as a platform on which Hagan will sit during the race.

Tireman Billy Siler is also in the pit area, gluing lug nuts to the tires for the race. Like most everyone, Billy's procedure varies little from race to race. One by one the tires are laid on the ground in sets. Air pressure and circumference are checked and then five lugs are placed on the outside. Using a strong adhesive, he and Steve Wilson glue the silver lug nuts to the holes on the wheels. This way, during the race, the lugs are in place and only need be tightened.

The race is to start at 12:30 p.m. However, by 10 a.m., it is raining hard. "We'll I looked at the radar and it's going to clear up around 12:30, one o'clock," Loyd said returning from the NASCAR trailer. "But, behind that it's not clear until west of Tennessee."

The car is ready an hour before race time. By then the rain has stopped and the winds have picked up, helping to dry the track. Kelly, Bryan, Donnie, Greg, Dewey, Danny Culler and Loyd push the car through inspection. There NASCAR officials check the body shape against factory templates, weigh it and perform various other checks of the vehicle. It is then pushed out to pit road, where it will sit until the start of the race.

After the rain stopped falling, the safety crews went onto the track. At about the same time the sun came out, giving all indications that there would be a race held this day.

Back at the truck, Terry, Herb, Billy and Steve go over the strategy for the race. Sitting in the lounge, located forward in the $150,000 vehicle, they compare charts from last year's event. With the new pit rules prohibiting caution flag tire changes, the face of racing has changed. The accident on Friday also had an impact. Terry would start from the rear.

"I will be at a disadvantage," says Terry, "because the guys up front will have a clear track while I will have to get through traffic. The guys up front will be able to run faster with the open race track in front of them. My biggest concern will be, because the lead cars will be running so much faster, to not get lapped."

If Terry got hung up in traffic, it wouldn't be long before the front of the pack was passing him. Without a caution to bunch the pack, a green flag pit stop was sure to put the team down a lap no matter how fast it was. "If we get some long stretches of green flag racing, we could be in for an even longer day."

During the meeting, everyone has something to say about pitting strategy. "When the tires are done, drop the car and go," Loyd suggests. "It doesn't matter if the gas is done."

"The car is a little faster when the tires are cool," says Herb, using his time charts from the past day's practice to back up his point. "It's three-tenths of a second faster the first couple laps after a pit stop. The whole goal we're lookin' at is to get from the start of the race to the end of the race in the least time possible. In the past we've been judging off what [the leader does], if he's slower, we're slower. We've got to look at changing our whole way."

"What they're doing is having the whole race under green," adds Labonte. "Whenever we pit early we are going to be a lap down . . . we'll lap and unlap ourselves all day, all the way to the end."

"Going an additional ten laps, you may drop a tenth or two-tenths," says Herb.

"If the leaders move out it's time to change," Hagan says. "If you're staying with them it might be time to stay out. Pick a point and when we get too loose then we'll come in."

"We look at it like this. The rule changes, we got to God dang change with it," Herb says.

"Cautions work in our favor. I need a couple of cautions early," Terry says. "When the fuel goes out of the car, it gets tighter. Of course, the weight moves to the front but by then the tires are looser so it balances out. There are going to be forty people out there doing different things."

"We've seen this picture show before," jokes Herb.

Terry and Steve must go to the drivers meeting so the im-promptu gathering breaks up. Before each race, NASCAR offi-cials gather the drivers and crew chiefs to go over any rule changes and to emphasize any other valid points before the race starts. With the pit rules changing each week, officials devoted most of the meeting to the latest wrinkle. This week teams can pit for tires under caution, although they will have to pit again on the first green flag lap.

While Terry and Steve are at the driver's meeting, the rest of the team members change into their race day uniforms and complete setting up the pit area. Then they wait. Bryan gives the air gun he will use to change the rear tires a few bursts and then sprays a graphite material on it to assure the lug nuts he takes off will shake free. Steve Wilson does the same with the gun he'll use on the front wheels.

Kelly Hunt, a thirty-two-year-old North Carolina native and an eleven-year veteran of Winston Cup racing, oils and checks the jack he will use to lift the car during pit stops. This racing jack can lift a car in four downstrokes. The normal garage jack takes twice as many and weighs twenty pounds more. Then he makes a large L-shape with white tape on the speedway sur-face in front of the pits. The line is a jack's length away from the pit wall and four feet long. Labonte uses the line as a marker when pitting. If he cuts it too close, Hunt won't be able to get the jack under the car.

Team members are staking out their areas in the pit, and trying to gain a few inches on either side of the pit area. When placing the tires he will use during the race on aluminum stands, Donnie Crumley tries to slide the stands a few inches into the next pit area. No one complains.

While the teams are preparing for the race, the safety crews dry the track. All totalled, the race would get underway just thirty-minutes late.

After driver introductions, Labonte heads for his car. Paul Mecca, Donnie Crumley and Harold are with him on pit road, as is Loyd. Once Labonte is strapped in and the drivers are given the command to start their engines, the remaining team members will return to the pits.

"All right Terry, you're pittin' right behind the 68 Country Time and right in front of Sterling [Marlin]," Steve says over the radio.

"10-4," Terry replies.

As the pack of cars, lined up two-by-two for twenty rows, nears turn four it tightens up, with each driver trying to position his car to get a good start. Then, when the pack reaches the end of the turn, the green flag is out and the race is on.

"Spin in turn four," Danny Culler shouts over the radio a few laps later. "Stay high, stay high. Take a high groove, Terry, the leaders are taking yellow."

"What kinda car you got," Steve asks Terry.

"Doesn't feel to bad."

"There'll be one to go when you get to the stripe," Steve says.

Again the green flag is out. Terry guides his car past some of the slower traffic ahead of him. It is one of the pitfalls he faces, starting behind cars that in some cases qualified six mph slower than he did. From his vantage point, each can be dangerous. Moving forward, passing slower cars, Terry finds himself racing with Jimmy Spencer, a thirty-four-year-old native of Pennsylvania, driving a Chevrolet sponsored by Banquet Foods and Planters Peanuts. In his short Winston Cup career, only forty-three races old at the start of the season, Spencer has won the nickname around the garages as "Mr. Excitement." They call him this for his erratic, wild driving style that has occasionally resulted in wrecks.

The two cars run side by side through turn three — the Sunoco Ultra Oldsmobile on the outside, Spencer's Lumina on the inside. As they come out of turn four Spencer starts spinning, catching the front of Labonte's car in the process. Labonte locks the brakes as the right side of the car slams into the wall.

The front of the car catches a small indentation in the surface and spins around in the front stretch, coming to a stop in a cloud of white tire smoke in front of the flag stand.

Spencer's car collides with the wall that separates the pits from the raceway.

"You alright," Steve asks.

"Yeah," Terry replies, sitting in the car, which is facing the wrong way on the front stretch.

"Stupid sonofabitch I knew he was going to do that," Steve says.

"Does it look like we can fix it?" asks Terry, hoping that with some work he can get back into the race.

"Nah, it's pretty tore up." Terry stays in the car for the ride back to the garage, behind the wall. When the wrecker drops the car off, Loyd and the rest of the crew inspect the damage. As first thought, it is too severe. The suspension is shot, as is much of the steering mechanism. The best they can do is fix the car enough to load it back on the truck.

"I was trying to pass Spencer, trying to get him out of four and he started spinning," Labonte says.

Later, referring to Spencer, Labonte says, "He's a nice guy and all, but when he puts on his helmet it cuts off the blood to his head and he gets stupid."

Despite being prodded by scorekeeper Doris Livengood to call home and tell Kim he is alright, Terry doesn't. Kim hadn't made the race because of the weather, but she later hears him on the radio and knows he is fine.

"I said if it was raining I wouldn't go," she said later. "It was fine for a while, but by the time I got dressed it was raining. When I went to go out later I thought wouldn't it be funny if the race was on. I flipped on the radio and there it was. The two times I didn't go to watch, he wrecked."

About an hour after the crash the team loads the car back onto the transporter. A pile of sheet metal that was removed from the car is being picked over by fans looking for a souvenir. Anything to prove to their friends back home that they were there. Most of the team leaves to beat the traffic out of the raceway. Terry retires to the driver's lounge to cool down. For the second time that weekend, Harold will have to wait for the racing to end to leave.

Terry finished thirty-ninth out of forty cars, winning $5,425 for the day. Spencer, who caused the crash, was able to complete five more laps before bringing his car behind the wall for good, finishing one spot above Labonte. Pole sitter Kyle Petty would go on to win the race, leading 380 of the 492 laps. Petty's take for the day would be $131,450, which included a $68,400 bonus from Unocal for winning the pole and the race.

seven

Rain Delay

"It's like being on drugs — you get hooked and
then you get obsessed by it."
Mark Metcalfe

After Labonte's wreck at Rockingham, the team returned to
Thomasville to regroup. Despite the accident being no fault of
Labonte's, some of the race committee members back at Sun's
Pennsylvania headquarters started to question the performance
of the team. Since the start of the season, Terry had dropped
from fifteenth position in the points race to twenty-seventh at
the close of Rockingham.

Moreover, some of those committee members could
not comprehend what was going on with the team. They had
listened to Hagan's pitch at the beginning of the season and
they had seen the results from Australia and the testing.
Either something was drastically wrong or Hagan had misled
them.

"Some of those guys on the committee ask, 'well if you can do so well in Australia or in testing, why can't you do that now?'" says Herb Hupperich. "Well it's different in Australia. That was the old technology, this is the new technology. We've got to work things out now so in the middle of the season we won't be groping for things."

While it was hard to believe for some, in reality the 1991 Billy Hagan race team was a new operation. Steve Loyd had only been crew chief for one full season and he had never worked with Labonte before in a racing situation. Sure they were friends, but those relationships change dramatically when placed in a work atmosphere.

The switch to front steer was having a bigger impact on the team than anyone had expected, including team owner Billy Hagan. The learn-as-you-go approach was resulting in more learning than going. Hagan had not taken that into consideration before he pumped up the Sun executives.

"Some of them ask 'why can't you do this and why can't you do that?'" Herb said about the committee. "I said to Bud [Campbell], 'how many refineries do you start up that are perfect from the start?' He said, 'none.'"

"You go through a learning curve when things are going to go wrong. We're in it," said Hupperich.

The results of the first four weeks were also taking a toll on the team. Their attitudes were tense, the fiber of the team stretched. There was a lack of respect for what crew chief Loyd was doing, and the way he treated some team members. Privately, they complained that he didn't know what he was doing. They were angry because he wouldn't consider any suggestions from team members on even the most minor issues. For example, one team member suggested there could possibly be a problem with the steering box itself causing part of the handling hassles. Loyd dismissed the idea. It later turned out there was a problem with the placement of the steering gear. Many were afraid to raise questions during the sporadic team meetings held

Monday mornings after races. They feared rocking the boat, and losing their jobs.

Racing is a funny business. Throughout the season team members will be allowed only a handful of days off. For twenty-nine weekends, scattered between February and November, they will work. On the non-race weekends it's likely they will have to work in the shop. During the ten-month season, team members will spend more time with their friends in racing than they will with their families.

"It's like an obsession," says showcar driver Mark Metcalfe about racing's attraction. "It's like being on drugs — you get hooked and then you get obsessed by it."

The hours in racing are long. Days start at the shop around 8 a.m., and often extend well into the evening. Race weekend days start before sun up. The pay, while not making many rich, is not terrible. The lowest shop worker makes around $20,000, with the scale moving upward for the more senior staff. However, for every one of those on a team, there is a whole list of others that would make the same sacrifices to be in racing. The racing teams, and those waiting to break into the business, are made up of predominately whites, with only a handful of minorities venturing into the racing world.

"Some of the guys are saying 'hey what's going on,'" racing committee member Al Contino says sitting in the back of the transporter. "If this was a new team, with a new driver, there would be some excuses, but not here. This is when the leadership must rally the troops and pull them together."

Contino himself was questioning the performance, although having more racing experience than some on the committee he had a little more patience. Meanwhile Campbell had mentally given the team seven races until he would question Hagan openly on the performance of the team. He, like Contino, had been asked questions by other executives and committee members who had not attended a race this season. Campbell was willing to give Hagan the benefit of the doubt.

The Atlanta Motor Speedway, located in Hampton, Georgia, is about thirty miles south of Atlanta alongside routes 19 and 41. It's a nice facility with plenty of infield parking for Winnebagos and Hertz rental trucks, converted to campers for the weekend. As with many of the stops on the circuits, Hampton relies on the race to increase revenue. Though the hotels, motels and restaurants are assured their cut, local organizations have to be a bit more industrious — collecting money from motorists stopped at stoplights.

Qualifying for the Motorcraft 500 at the 1.5-mile-long Atlanta Motor Speedway was held on Friday. For first round qualifying, Labonte complained the car was too tight, meaning it was hard to turn. His first attempt at making the forty-car field was poor, ending in twenty-first position overall. After spending Friday afternoon trying to fine tune the car, the team went home for the night. Unsponsored driver Alan Kulwicki won the pole with a lap of 31.415 seconds or 174.413 mphs. Terry was about three miles an hour slower.

The team returned to the raceway Saturday morning to overcast skies and cooler temperatures. With the track cooler than the day before the cars were sure to be faster. During the hour-long practice session preceding the 10:30 a.m. qualifying session, Terry complained the car was loose. Yet, he was turning laps faster than he had run during the initial qualifying attempt. They decided to try to requalify. Like Labonte, the other cars on the track were running faster. Without requalifying he risked moving further back in the starting grid.

For each race there are two rounds of qualifying. Depending on the size of the field — smaller tracks start fewer cars — the first round would either guarantee the top fifteen or twenty spots. Atlanta starts a forty-car field, so the first round would secure starting berths for the top twenty. The remaining cars can either stand on the lap time posted the day before or try to requalify. At best, Labonte could keep his twenty-first place starting spot.

The team pushed the car through inspection and then out to the line of cars forming on pit road. There, Harold Hughes stood with a small portable gas generator used to operate the oil heater. An orange cord snaked from the generator to a plug hanging from underneath the car in front of the left side rear wheel well. Hagan's team, like all the others, uses an oil heater before qualifying and before starting a race to warm the engine lubricant, located in a tank behind the driver's seat. Warming thins the substance, providing a smoother flow around moving parts at the start of any activity. Once the race starts, the oil temperature soars, and the on board oil *cooler* takes over.

With the car in place, Bryan Robertson turned and took a place on the pit wall, stopwatch in hand, waiting for Labonte's attempt. Steve did the same, a few feet away. The Sunoco Oldsmobile was third in line.

Terry moved quietly to the car, and slid in through the driver's side window. There are no doors in NASCAR. Hardly a word was spoken to the team members standing by.

"That's why they call him the Iceman," said Bryan of the snub.

Labonte's cool personality and conservative approach to racing won him the "Iceman" moniker early in his career. Off the track his personality was really starting to reflect his nickname. As the season started going wrong, he distanced himself from the team. Often Labonte stood off to the side, talking only to Steve. He turned his back on the rest of the team. If most of the guys were working on the rear of the vehicle, he was in the front. He had little confidence in Loyd as a crew chief, but they were friends. Labonte was responsible for Loyd being in this position, and he hoped somehow they would be able to hit upon the right combination. While his confidence in Loyd was low, it was practically nonexistent for most of the others on the team. He often commented he didn't trust some of the team members to carryout their duties properly. As a result, he built a buffer between the team and himself.

Joe Ruttman, a guy who has raced off and on since 1963, went out onto the track before Terry. Ruttman fired the engine on his Dinner Bell sponsored Oldsmobile and a NASCAR official standing at the end of pit road signaled him to go. After going around the track once, the green flag was waved, his qualifying attempt on the line. Ruttman guided his car into turn one, the engine emitting a high pitch as it was fed high-octane gasoline. When he got back to the start/finish line the checkered flag was out, his qualifying session over.

Labonte then received the go ahead from the same NASCAR official. He too got the green flag as he passed the flag stand for the first time. Then, as he dove down deep into turn one, the audible sound of the engine dropped, as if it was getting less gas. His time for the lap was 32.129 seconds or 170.538 mph. Instead of moving up, he would move down to the thirty-second starting spot. Had they stood on their time from the day before he would have started in twenty-sixth.

What was wrong with the car? Bryan was asked later.

"There wasn't nothing wrong, Terry just let off," he answered. Hagan shrugged off the poor starting spot, saying there was a lot of racing time available to move up. "You can do a lot in 500 miles, it's just getting past the first 100."

During practice, Loyd tried several combinations of springs and frame weights trying to get the car to where Labonte was comfortable driving it. Other drivers can do a lot with a loose car. Terry, on the other hand, would just drive the car in the middle of the pack if the car was not just right.

"The car has to be there. [Labonte] doesn't take a car that isn't there and take it to the front," says Mike Harris, AP motorsports writer. "There are guys who are willing to break off some sheet metal, he saves his car."

"Terry is a slow starter and at the end he finishes strong," Hupperich said once. "He's a lot smarter about strategy. He's always asking what can I do. Sterling would be like 'whatever ya'll think.' Terry will say 'let's do this.'"

First Loyd tried putting a piece of rubber in the right front spring. The rubber, a little more than an inch thick, helped stiffen the response of the right front. Then, long pieces of lead were taken out of the frame rails in an attempt to shift more of the weight to the left side of the car. Blocks of lead, some more than a foot long and weighing more than thirty pounds, were removed from the right side. Doing so shifted a majority of the weight to the driver's side of the car, which would have to be compensated for before the car went through inspections on race day. NASCAR rules stipulate that no more than 55 percent of the total weight be on the driver's side. The day ended with the car still not right, but about as good as they were going to get it for the race.

Steering is to a race car driver what a brush is to a painter. The user has to be comfortable with the device and willing to push it a little further to gain a competitive advantage. Steering and handling, inseparable as race cars go, are Terry's connection with the track. Without the proper tools, he is unable to extract anything from the car.

With daybreak Sunday morning it was raining. Yet, the teams started about their race day duties as they would if the sun was shining. Blue tarps hung off the back of the garages, helping keep the rain off the cars, and plastic covered stacks of tires. People moved about the garages using umbrellas or pulling their jackets up over their heads to keep dry.

As the guys stood around the car making the final preparations to ready the car for inspection, Loyd returned to the garage from a visit to the NASCAR trailer. The trailer, located in the garage area, was the headquarters for the sanctioning body at the raceway. Loyd lets everyone know that Winston Cup Director Dick Beaty is saying there's a window in the weather pattern that might allow the race to start on time.

"I ain't never heard him say there wasn't a window," says Hupperich. "He'll never admit it. I've been in this business too long to speculate. I've seen times when I thought we wouldn't race and we have. If Dick Beaty says we're going to run this race at 1 p.m., then maybe we are."

The rain did stop about forty minutes before the scheduled start of the race. Safety crews immediately went onto the track and ran in packs trying to dry the surface. The storm hadn't fully passed yet; dark clouds loomed heavy over the speedway. By 1 p.m., the track surface is dry enough to get the cars started under caution. Doyle Ford waves the green and yellow flags simultaneously, starting the race officially although keeping them at a safe speed until the track is race ready. Until then, the cars, spewing warm exhaust and throwing off heat from their engines, will circle the track slowly helping to further dry the speedway.

"Terry, they say they're going to run ten laps and then turn you loose," radios Steve. Five laps later, NASCAR decides to turn them loose. "All right Terry they're saying one to go, one to go, be careful."

There's a deep roar from the engines and the crowd is standing as the cars rumble toward the starting line.

"Green flag, go, go," says spotter Danny Culler, sitting atop the main grandstand.

During an early caution Steve asks, "How's your car, Terry?" "Car's pretty good," he says. "I might need a round of wedge."

"Okay, okay," Steve says.

A round of wedge would change the weight distribution of the car in turn affecting how each wheel grips the track. It's Donnie Crumley's job to change the wedge after dropping the two tires he carries during pit stops. Using a ratchet he keeps stuck in his belt, Donnie will turn the bars controlling the wedge set-up, accessible through two holes in the rear window.

Terry pits for tires, gas and the round of wedge a few laps after the race goes under green again.

"When you cut a good lap, it's in the [32.] 80s and 90s," Steve says. "That 22 car [race leader Sterling Marlin] is running in the 60s and 50s."

By lap 35, Terry has moved up to twentieth position. His car is loose coming off the corners, but otherwise all right. He has fallen back to twenty-fourth when the rain starts to fall on lap 45.

Two laps later the race is stopped because of rain. Doyle Ford, waving the red flag, signals the cars to return to pit road. There only two team members are allowed to go over to the car, and the drivers can get out of their vehicles. The rain is coming down in buckets. It's clear the race will not be completed today.

Team members work their way back to the transporters to wait out the rain. Some collect in various pockets in the garages, talking about the race ahead with friends who work for other teams. The once cluttered work benches serve as makeshift seats. The rain does not appear like it is going to let up; however, because of insurance clauses involved with the television contract for the race, NASCAR will have to wait until 5 p.m. to make a final decision. Meanwhile, the safety crews continue to circle the track.

"There are two things you can't predict," Loyd says. "NASCAR and the weather." Herb sits in the back of the transporter, checking the tire charts he has collected during the weekend. Two small bench seats with enough room for six provide for a meeting place and a platform to watch others in the garage area. A member of the Quaker State team walks up and sits down across from Herb. "How's your car?" he asks.

"It's just right," Hupperich answers, knowing it isn't.

Moments later Steve walks into the back of the transporter and sits down next to Herb. Steve is asked the same question.

"It's a little loose, but not bad," Steve says.

At 5 p.m., after four hours of a steady downpour, the race is officially cancelled. Under NASCAR rules, the race is to be held on the next raceable day, normally the next day on the calendar. Weather forecasts for Monday are favorable. Before leaving the raceway for the evening, the cars are covered up and left on pit road in the same position they came in. Sterling Marlin was leading the race in a car owned by Junior Johnson.

The race is rescheduled for 11 a.m., Monday. The teams wake to find fine racing weather. As can be expected, the stands are only 60 percent full for the make-up race. Many fans, some who had been in the area since Friday afternoon, had to return to work on Monday. They would miss the race they came to see.

Teams can only do minor work on the cars before the race begins. Air cleaners can be changed, because of the possibility that they got wet the day before, and tire pressure can be changed. Nothing else. There is some concern that the weather might have done some damage to the cars. One problem is that cool air stuck in the engines after they were turned off the day before may have distorted the engine valves.

"There wasn't much water," Kelly Hunt says Monday morning. "There may be some engine problems, but the track is as green as it was yesterday."

As a race weekend progresses, rubber from the tires collects on the surface of the speedway. The more rubber left on the track, the more it changes the handling of the car. All NASCAR races are preceded by a support race, held on Saturday. Weather providing, the Winston Cup cars will get a practice session on the surface after the support race. This helps them adjust to the track with the additional rubber imbedded in the surface. Sunday night's rain washed away Saturday's deposits of rubber. The race would start with a fresh surface, or "green" as the racers call it.

Before the race, team members scrounge around for whatever food is left from the weekend. There is little. Most of the crew sit on the back of the truck and watch a parade of young women go by. Most of the women, wearing a little more makeup than needed and leaning towards "tall" hairstyles, greet the team members with smiles and nods, nothing more.

Driver Mark Martin stops by and takes a seat in the back of the truck with Labonte and Loyd. He too is looking for food. Terry suggests he try the No. 1 car or the No. 33, both owned by the Jackson brothers.

"Hell, they took out some springs just to make a pantry," Terry says. "If you get there and they're all sleeping, it means they've eaten already."

Because of the late pit stop Labonte made on Sunday, he should have an advantage at the restart. Most of the other teams will have to come in for service after about ten laps, unless the caution flag comes out early, which would nullify the advantage. Labonte will be out of sequence, pitting later by himself, but the difference will allow him to gain valuable track position early while the others pit.

Consistent with the luck of the Hagan team so far this season, NASCAR starts the race under caution, waving both the green and yellow flag. Immediately, the leaders dive into the pits for gasoline. Terry moves up to fifth place when the caution is lifted, and is up all the way to second by lap 60. But by lap 87 he has slipped to fourth. Despite being in the top five, it does not appear the car has the strength of the other leaders. Terry radios to the pits that the car is not handling well. He is losing three-tenths of a second each lap because of worn tires.

"All right, we got another set of tires, we'll get ya fixed up," Steve says. He then signals the team that they will change four tires when Terry comes in.

Terry pits on lap 151. Waiting on the pit wall, the team springs into action. "Come on Donnie, come on," Loyd says as they start to move. Donnie Crumley must climb over the wall with two tires, help put them in the wheel wells and then turn the ratchet controlling the suspension. When the crew is done, twenty-three seconds later, Terry puts the car into gear and it stalls. The guys still over the wall push the car into starting.

"You can't push it, you can't push it," shouts Loyd. A few feet later the engine fires and Labonte rejoins the field.

In order to try and tighten the car up the team put on scuffed tires, ones that had been used for a couple laps in practice. Terry had said all weekend that the motor in the car was strong. In fact, once he joked that they shouldn't tell the guys in the motor room the engine was so strong because then they wouldn't try to make one stronger. However, the strongest motor in the world couldn't make the poor handling vehicle grip the road any better.

On lap 256 Terry radios back that something is wrong with the engine. He quickly pulls the car down pit road and into the garage area where the team can work on it. At first they thought, perhaps, the distributor had broken or that a plug wire was off. Livengood took the distributor cap off the distributor and told Labonte to start the engine. As the engine strained the distributor did not move, indicating the camshaft had broken. Labonte would not be able to finish the remaining laps of the race. NASCAR's record book shows Labonte finishing in thirty-fifth position, taking home $6,385 in prize money. Ken Schrader, driving a Kodiak sponsored Chevrolet Lumina, won the race and the $69,250 that went with the top spot.

Labonte fell to twenty-ninth in the overall point standings.

eight

Last Minute Adjustments

"We need to do some minor things that ain't
necessarily legal."
Herb Hupperich

There were seventeen days between Atlanta and when the team
arrived at the Darlington Raceway, in South Carolina. Those
seventeen days were the last break the team would have for a
month. April kicked off a stretch of five consecutive racing weekends. Those team members who go to the track a few days early
wouldn't have a free weekend until the middle of May.

The time between races is welcome. Performance on
the track hasn't been what's expected and the extra time to
work on the cars is needed. In addition to working on the car for
Darlington, the team starts to prepare cars for the next few
races, when the NASCAR circuit moves to some of the short
tracks that served as the stepping stones for the growth of
the sport.

The down time would also allow the team to make some of the changes suggested after wind tunnel testing in Detroit the previous week. As part of Hagan's deal with Oldsmobile, which is worth a couple hundred thousand dollars a year to run the manufacturer's body style, the team had free use of the auto-maker's wind tunnel. There Oldsmobile technicians put three of Hagan's cars in the tunnel and checked for aerodynamic deficiencies. They found some.

"We learned a few things," said Hupperich during practice at Darlington. "It wasn't anything major, just fine tuning. We need to do some minor things that ain't necessarily legal."

What they found was that if they made the rear quarter panels slightly higher and wider, the car would cut the wind more efficiently. The predicted result was a faster car.

Darlington holds a special place in Labonte and Hagan's relationship. It was here, in 1978, that Terry took his first laps as a Winston Cup driver. He also got his first win at the track, dubbed "The Black Lady," back in 1980, when Hagan predicted a championship for the two.

However, the team's first trip to Darlington with Labonte on board did not start well. For the fourth straight week Labonte's qualifying effort was dismal. Qualifying was held Thursday. When it was over, Labonte's time was good enough for only the twenty-seventh starting position, thirteen rows behind the pole sitter Geoff Bodine, driving for the Junior Johnson-owned Budweiser Ford Thunderbird. Labonte's time of 31.198 seconds represented a speed of 157.625 mph around the raceway. Labonte complained that the car wasn't handling, nothing new, but he also complained privately that the motor wasn't strong enough.

The car was running tight during Friday practice sessions and Labonte decided to stand on his time posted during qualifying a day earlier. Most other teams would do the same.

Saturday was a near perfect racing day, with temperatures rising into the seventies and bright sunshine. Bryan

Robertson just shrugged his shoulders when asked how the car is running. It's a gesture that suggested nothing is going to change the way the car is running.

At 9 a.m., Terry fired up the engine of the Oldsmobile Cutlass and backed it out of the garage with the help of Harold Hughes, signalling as if he were guiding an airplane out of a hanger. After several laps around the 1.36-mile-long banked speedway, Terry returned to the garage. The car was pushing, he said. Pushing is the feeling that the front end is going to break away from the track before the rear. With each run, Terry returned for more changes with the car.

"Let's throw in that soft set," Labonte said to Loyd, "And that way we won't go back Monday and say we didn't try."

NASCAR teams use coil springs in the front and rear to adjust the ride of their cars. During a race weekend these springs are likely to be changed several times to get the handling smooth. Typically, teams use springs between 800 and 3,000 pounds per inch. The higher the number the stiffer the coil. For example, in a testing situation it would take 3,000 pounds of pressure to compress the spring one inch. Teams use the stiffer springs on speedways. For comparison, a street vehicle spring rate is about 400 pounds per inch. Labonte hoped that by using a lower rate spring the car might be a little more responsive.

Between practice runs Terry said the motor didn't have enough power. In past races the motor was fine. At the race in Atlanta, Labonte said the motor he used was actually stronger then the car they had it in. Now just a few weeks later while practicing for Darlington, Terry goes to Steve to express his displeasure with the motor that's in the car. It doesn't have the strength he wants.

Practice lasted for an hour or so and then the pre-race activities for the Busch Grand National series began. The break gave the team three hours to work on the car before the afternoon practice session. Steve talked with engine builder Dewey Livengood and the two decided to try another motor. There were two to choose from on the transporter. Hughes rolled one of the two from a front compartment in the transporter to the rear of the trailer where he hooked it to an engine stand. He then rolled the stand and engine to the garage where the team was removing the other engine. In two hours the motor was changed and the car was set up for practice. The two hour job could have been accomplished in one hour if time was of the essence.

Bobby Labonte finished second in the Busch race. When the race and the winner's circle ceremony were over, the Winston Cup cars returned to the track for the last practice before the race the following day. Terry took several slow laps around Darlington trying to break in the new engine before giving it the gas. Confident the engine was operating properly, he let loose. The first practice laps under full speed were actually slower than the ones he cut earlier that day with a motor he said was inferior.

"Terry, lookin' at the clock we're staying even . . . but you seemed to be takin' a lower line than others," said Hupperich over the radio. Hupperich had returned to the top of the transporter to monitor practice armed with a cup of black coffee, a cigar and a couple stopwatches to record lap times of Labonte and the other cars on the track. "If you stay down there it will give you room."

By the end of practice the team had made some progress in working out some of the bugs involved with the transition to front-steer cars, but not enough. The car was slow, not only according to Hupperich's stopwatch but to others. The team left the raceway Saturday night realizing they had a lot of work ahead as well as a lot of learning.

Labonte was still not happy with the car. As a result, he began to further distance himself from the team. During breaks in practice sessions, he often walked away and visited with other teams. Other drivers stay and talk to their crews as they work on the cars. Labonte's attitude could also be seen taking root in the team. It too was separating. Some members were doubting crew chief Loyd's knowledge. With the doubts came a lessening of respect for Loyd. The team needed Loyd to take charge, but he seemed to lack the confidence.

On the way home from the raceway, team public relations and marketing man Paul Mecca stopped by the lounge at the Ramada Inn that sat across the road from his hotel. Like most hotels within driving distance of a raceway on race weekends, the place was packed. Members of other teams, journalists, drivers and fans filled the hotel and some had also retired to the lounge.

Once there, Mecca found a few friends and acquaintances from the racing fraternity. Most had some comment or question about the Hagan operation and its spiral downward.

"That car was going so slow there was a dog pissing on his tires," said a veteran motorsports journalist about Labonte's late practice runs. Mecca laughed along at the joke, and had to agree that the car was embarrassingly slow.

"Dewey's [Livengood] one of the best engine builders out there," said a member of another team who had entered the bar. Dewey's supporter was familiar with the problems at Hagan's shop, having been parked next to the Sunoco team in the garage area. "He doesn't get enough credit. For [Labonte] to blame it on the engine is crazy. I'd hire Dewey in a heartbeat. You had something better and you let him go." Mecca was unsure what was meant by the final comment, although he suspected the man was talking about Sterling Marlin. Marlin's driving style is 180 degrees different from Labonte's. Where Marlin would take the car to the front early only to have the run evaporate toward the end of the race, Labonte tended to stay in the middle of the pack and work his way through, often ending the race near the front. There was no comparison, however, to overall statistics. Labonte, sixth on the all-time money list going into the season, had amassed ten wins and Marlin none.

Nonetheless, the NASCAR rumor mill had started to percolate with items about the Hagan team. Before Saturday was over there was a rumor that Labonte had contacted Cale Yarborough, who had fired his driver Dick Trickle following the Rockingham race, seeking a change of scenery. Terry said the rumor was just that. Rumors also started circulating that Hagan's racing operation was now on a cash on delivery basis with many of its suppliers. This was true, and surprising since he was being paid $2.1 million for the season, which breaks down to payments of between of $150,000 and $175,000 monthly before any bonuses kicked in.

Because of the team's performance throughout the first four races and the rumors, Hagan was scheduled to visit Pennsylvania the day after Darlington to meet with the Sunoco racing committee. They had heard the rumors and wanted answers. Hagan was hoping for a strong performance at Darlington.

Labonte has done well at the 1.36-mile speedway, located just west of Florence, South Carolina, in the past. During his career he has placed in the top five eight times, including the win in 1980. The track, built in 1950 and the home of the first 500-mile superspeedway event, has earned the reputation as being "to tough to tame." Its egg-like shape and very narrow straights have caused many drivers problems. Turns one and two are longer than three and four, making the setting up of the car a nightmare for teams. Drivers talk about the "Black Lady" as if it's haunted. They say things look differently then they really are. Is that oil ahead or just the sun reflecting off the pavement? The track's deceiving nature has been the cause of more than one freak accident over the years.

Despite Terry's success at the speedway, he has had his share of unnatural events occur there. A couple of years ago he was involved in a three-car crash during a caution period. "It was like an invisible hand reached out from the backstretch wall and slapped us into each other," he said then. If that wasn't enough, when he got back onto the track after the collision his in-car fire extinguisher went off, filling the car with foam and almost sending him into the wall for a second time.

Terry would start this TranSouth 500 from the twenty-seventh spot, forcing the team to pit on the back stretch of the raceway. Most speedways have just one set of pits, but Darlington, like some of the other short tracks on the circuit, has two. The front set of pits is parallel with the main grandstand and the flagman stand. The back set is parallel with a much smaller set of seats. The back stretch is a less desirable vantage point for the fans; they always want to see the start/finish line. That's were the action is. Moreover, television coverage tends to ignore the action on the back stretch set of pits. In fact, there were no television cameras aimed at the back stretch pits at Darlington.

In the past pitting on the back stretch was a detriment. When caution flag pit stops were permitted, teams pitting on the front stretch could duck into the pits when the flag fell, while those on the back stretch had to go around another half-lap before getting to their pits. By the time a car entered the back pits, a team in the front pits would be almost finished with their drill if it was a four tire stop, or completely finished if it chose only to change two tires and gas the car.

However, with the new pit rules, the strategy had changed. Now, instead of coming in under caution, most teams would wait until the green flag fell restarting the race and then pit.

"Pitting on the back stretch used to be an omen," Hupperich said before the race, "but, now it could work."

After a caution, all cars would have to take the green flag at the restart before pitting or risk going a lap down. This meant that those teams on the front stretch would have to go a complete lap before reaching the entrance of pit road. Labonte, and those other cars on the back stretch, could dive into the pits as they entered turn two after getting the green. Under those conditions, it could be an advantage to pit on the back stretch.

Race day at Darlington was the warmest of the young season. The sun beat down sending the temperatures into the high sixties or low seventies. Though the warm weather was welcomed by the spectators, it meant that the drivers would be a little uncomfortable as the heat increased in the cars.

For the driver introductions, Darlington officials put the drivers in convertibles and drove them around the raceway, adding a touch of class to the process. Once the cars did their parade lap, Terry walked over to the pit area where the team was sitting until the race started. There he talked with his parents, who had remained in the area after Bobby's second place finish Saturday. Terry's father runs Bobby's operation. Terry's wife Kim and son Justin stood nearby. Justin, at ten years of age, is the oldest of Labonte's two children and frequently attended the races with his mother. Their daughter, Kristin, rarely came along.

As race time neared, Terry walked to his car parked a few feet away from the pit wall. Kim reached out and handed Terry a small silver coin to put in his uniform pocket. It was from Justin —a good luck charm.

"Good luck Daddy, good luck," Justin yelled to his father as Terry started to climb into the cockpit. Terry cast a glance over his shoulder, smiled, and continued to climb through the padded rollbars there to protect him in case of a crash.

When Labonte started to enter the car, Donnie Crumley and Steve Loyd went around to the passenger's side. Loyd climbed into the car as if he were helping Labonte tighten his belts, though it was all an act. Crumley stood outside the car, hoping to block the view of any NASCAR inspectors. Loyd began loosening a set of bolts holding down a hunk of heavy metal made of tungsten mounted underneath the dashboard on the right side of the car. He reached under the dashboard and slid the metal over to a compartment above Labonte's legs. The added weight on the driver's side of the car would, theoretically, give Labonte a little better handling control in the turns.

NASCAR inspectors weigh the cars as part of the pre-race inspection process. Two measurements are taken — full car weight and right side weight. When the car was pushed through inspections, with the moveable weight on the right side of the car, it passed. If the car was weighed just before the race, it would not have passed. The team could get around the weight restrictions during the race because NASCAR officials only take a total body weight measurement after the race, provided Labonte won. The car would easily pass this measurement.

"It's tungsten so it's really heavy," Bryan Robertson said later when asked about the weight. What if NASCAR decides to check? "If they were checkin' everyone, the way we're runnin', they'd let us go right around."

The switch made, Loyd climbed out of the car. Crumley then removed a Sunoco banner that had been taped to the windshield to help keep the heat level down in the car as it sat on pit road. The two then headed across the infield to where the team would pit.

The team used the heavy metal addition for most races, the only part that differed was if the metal stayed in the car for the race or was taken out before. Sometimes, Crumley would reach in and take the metal out, wrap it in the banner covering the windshield and walk down pit road struggling to look natural. Other times it stayed in, bolted under the dash, as at Darlington.

The team went to great lengths to disguise the slab of metal. On the occasions when the weight was to be removed before the race a piece was used that had been cut to look like a roll of duct tape. In fact, a piece of tape was wrapped around the metal to make it look realistic.

The race starts at 1 p.m. Pitting on the back stretch the team isn't able to watch the start, but Labonte gets off okay. The first caution comes out early when Alan Kulwicki's Ford breaks loose and slams into the wall on the front stretch.

During the caution, Labonte radios back to Loyd in the pits that the car is loose. With only twenty-six laps on the tires it is too early to come in so Labonte will have to work with what he has until pitting makes sense. The caution lasts for five laps.

When the race restarts the cars run only three laps before a five-car accident stops the action again.

"Spin, spin in front of you," shouts spotter Danny Culler over the radio.

As he enters turns three and four Labonte sees Dale Jarrett's No. 21 Citco sponsored Thunderbird, Harry Gant's Skoal backed No. 33 Oldsmobile and Chad Little's Tyson sponsored Ford spinning high on the track, wheels locked and sheet metal rippling. Immediately, he slows and heads for the inside of the track.

"Watch your rear," shouts Culler again, as cars behind Labonte start spinning as a result of trying to avoid the accident in front of them.

Terry squeaks through the mess by driving down near the infield. He narrowly misses being hit by Gant's spinning car after it hits the outside wall and careens to the inside. He passes through unscathed.

"Terry if you weren't within two-tenths [of the leader] we were going to pit you now," says Loyd.

"I don't know, I lost a lot of track position in that little wreck there," Labonte replies as he makes his way around the raceway under caution.

"Terry, we might want to ride it out a little while."

"Okay, okay."

Before the race, Herb figured Terry could go forty-five to fifty laps on the better wearing radial tires. With the good position, Terry didn't pit for his first set of tires until lap 65.

By lap 98, Labonte is turning laps 1.5 seconds slower than race leader Michael Waltrip in the bright yellow Pennzoil Pontiac. Waltrip has out raced most of the cars on the speedway and is coming up behind Labonte. Two laps later he passes Labonte putting him a lap down. The long stretch of green flag racing has taken its toll; the leaders are lapping Labonte as the field becomes more and more stretched out.

As Waltrip goes by, each of the team members reacts differently, though they all feel the same way. Frustrated. Kelly Hunt, who is sitting on the pit wall, just shakes his head and looks down. Loyd walks to the back of the pits to smoke. The team knows the car doesn't have enough power, and without the power it will be almost impossible to make up the lap, let alone finish in the top ten. Other cars have made up a lap, some even two, but it will not happen here.

On lap 125, Loyd radios to Labonte asking how the tires feel. However, Labonte has trouble hearing the radio message because of a problem with his earplugs. He thinks Loyd is telling him to pit.

"He's coming in," says Culler.

The team is unprepared. As Labonte slows his car coming down pit road as they scramble to set up. Normally, they would have been in their positions a lap earlier. They change four tires, add gas and set Labonte on his way. By lap 160 he has worked his way up to fifteenth, although his lap times are erratic. One good lap is followed by a lap two-tenths of a second slower. The tires are also inconsistent, making the car handle much differently between sets of tires. At one point he brushes the wall coming out of turn two, slowing the car momentarily. "That sort of took away my momentum," he would say later.

Terry holds on to fifteenth through lap 180 and then falls back in the pack. He regains the spot on lap 220.

As the race wears on, team members' interest in the event begins to wane. It's a long day. Not being in contention for a top spot tends to lessen the excitement of the event. Three hours, forty-one minutes and fifty seconds later the race is over. Terry finishes the race in fifteenth, one lap down. Ricky Rudd, involved in an early accident, wins the race and the $62,185 that goes with the trophy. Labonte earns $9,735, and the finish moves him up three positions to twenty-sixth in the championship points race.

"That sonofabitch just about wore me out," he says as he climbs from his battle torn car. Scraped paint and minor dents mark the right side of the car and the front bumper shows signs of contact. "We just weren't good enough, we weren't the car to beat ... It was better at the end, but we weren't right. We didn't have the car the way we needed. We weren't good enough to start with."

nine

A Bump Here a Crash There

"A real team if the guys go to get drunk, they get drunk together."
Kelly Hunt

After Darlington the NASCAR circuit moved to the short track portion of the season, running on tracks in Bristol, Tennessee; North Wilkesboro, North Carolina; and Martinsville, Virginia. Each track is a half-mile long, each is rich in NASCAR history and lore, and each was designed for a vehicle nothing like the those that run there now.

Bristol, first up on the short track schedule, is perhaps the most exciting raceway on the circuit. Located north of Johnson City, Tennessee, the track sits snuggled between lush rolling hills and quiet streets. With banked turns steeper than those at Daytona, Bristol is the fastest half-mile track the NASCAR circuit visits. It's a fan's raceway. Not a bad seat in the house. Most fans there have been either on a waiting list for some time or held the seats year-to-year.

During the week between Darlington and Bristol, Terry and Steve Loyd flew to Ohio to test a new braking system that they hope to be able to test under race conditions later in the season. Designed by Delco Moraine, the brakes use anti-locking technology, something that has not been used on Winston Cup cars before.

Terry is using a car at Bristol that the team calls "Spider" for the way its light blue roll cage appears against the dark blue of its body when viewed from afar. The car is a couple of years old. Tired as NASCAR racers go.

"That's an old car," Labonte said. "I bet it's three or four years old." The color of the roll cage gave it away. The newer cars in Hagan's racing fleet had roll cages that were painted white or a light grey. The older cars, some that may have been around when Hagan's primary sponsor was Piedmont Airlines, carried the light blue cages. "I ain't never seen an old car that's run good. Who knows how many times that thing's been wrecked."

Later Herb Hupperich says the car is only two years old and that it was run three times the year before with finishes of seventh, fifth, and sixth.

No matter how old or new the car is Labonte is not comfortable with it. In early practice sessions the car is tight. Terry has to wrestle it into the turns, causing him to lose two-tenths of a second in the 36 degree bank. Two-tenths on this speedway is a lot.

The team continues to fiddle with the car before qualifying Friday afternoon. Springs are changed. The lower A-arms, which connect the wheel to the chassis, are removed and swapped for another pair, changing the angle at which the wheels rest on the roadway.

By the time qualifying comes around, the car is still tough for Labonte to drive. Not being able to go deep into the corners slows the car down. His qualifying lap of 16.780 seconds is only good enough for thirtieth starting position. Rusty Wallace, with a lap of 16.254, will be on the pole.

Labonte's qualifying run depressed the team. A lot of work had gone into preparing the car and again Labonte's qualifying effort was dismal. Labonte blamed the problems on the car, the way it handled. Some on the team blamed the results on him. They had seen his qualifying laps so far this season and were confident it was a problem with his mental preparation. Often in practice he would cut laps faster than his qualifying efforts and then when he did qualify it was like the car slowed down. Their only hope would be to move up to twenty-first by being the fastest during second round qualifying.

At 8 a.m., Saturday, it was raining, but that didn't keep fans from sitting in the bleachers, hoping it would stop long enough for the support race to be held or even some Winston Cup practice. The race they had come to see wasn't scheduled to start for another six hours, though that didn't seem to matter. The teams, meanwhile, worked under tarps on pit road with the same hopes as those in the stands.

The pit area at Bristol is tiny. It was designed well before the days when teams used huge transporters hauled by diesel tractors. Those vehicles are way too large for Bristol. Instead, teams rent eighteen- to twenty-foot U-haul or Hertz trucks and park in the infield. Most of the necessary equipment is shifted to the rental trucks and the transporters are parked outside. The system works fine, although, once cars are on the track, there is no way to leave the race way. Teams must be sure they have everything they need inside the track. Mechanics work on the race cars parked diagonally on pit road. All the teams work on one side of the speedway, fender-to-fender. On race day half the field will move to the other side, where they pit.

Makeshift tents protected the cars and mechanics from the rain. Those not working on the cars took cover in the rear of the rental trucks, which were left open. There are no garages in the infield at Bristol, just a concession stand, restrooms, a medical facility, small lounges for the drivers and a pressroom.

The rain fell constantly for the early part of the morning. Two early bird fans stayed in the stands, one dark green poncho protecting them from the rain. Back at the truck some of the guys on the team sat on coolers and boxes talking about racing. A half-filled coffee pot sat on the edge of the electric lift, a twenty-five-foot-long orange extension cord running from the truck to the pit wall kept the unit warm. A box of half-eaten donuts was off to the side.

"We don't have the chassis right, I know that," Herb said to assistant engine builder Gary Wagoner, "but if we could have qualified fifteenth, sixteenth, or seventeenth with our pit on the front side, we'd be better off."

Terry again did not use a qualifying motor because Hagan's team lacked a qualifying motor program. This was important because 98 percent of the teams used qualifying motors and then replaced them with a race motor designed to last 500 miles or more. The qualifying motors were lighter and faster, but would not last under race conditions. Once the other teams switched to their race motors, Labonte's times were comparable to theirs, but Labonte would be starting further back in the pack. But even with the speed differences eliminated, Labonte's car was still not handling as well as was needed to win a race.

Hupperich and Wagoner continued talking about the potential for building a qualifying engine that would skirt the NASCAR rules until Loyd walked up to the truck.

"There's a window about fifteen miles away," Loyd said. He had just returned from the NASCAR trailer where the radar showed it would clear up for a little while this afternoon. It did, but by the time the track had been dried it was too late to hold second round qualifying. Terry would have to start thirtieth, based on the first round effort. He was among good company at the back of the pack. Former Winston Cup champion Bill

Elliott, himself having a rocky start to the season, would start the race next to Labonte.

Terry was upset with the starting position. He had told Hupperich a day earlier that he wanted to do well because a good friend was very sick and he wanted to win as a farewell to the man. Starting thirtieth on a half-mile track decreased his odds of winning three-fold.

The poor starting spot did nothing to improve team morale. The team had needed at least a good qualifying round, if not a good race, to pull it together.

"This isn't a team," Kelly Hunt said later. "On a real team if the guys go to get drunk, they get drunk together. They shit together, they eat together. You've got your groups here."

Hunt has been in racing for eleven years. He is the team's humorist. He's called "roundboy" around the shop because of a few extra pounds he carries on his twenty-two-year-old body. He had wanted to get into racing so badly that with a wife and a newborn child, he left a job at a chemical plant paying $325 a week to sweep floors at Richard Childress' race shop for $125. His take home pay after taxes was about $80. He originally went for an interview at Hagan's but there were no openings. Hagan sent him over to Childress' shop where he talked his way into a job. It's a move he does not regret.

"It didn't start paying off until 1984," he says about making money in racing. He makes good money now, though, he knows guys with similar experience making more money on other teams. He tries to keep his salary reasonable, he says, because when times get tough the team will let the higher priced talent go first. Around Hagan's shop he tends to serve as a de facto crew chief, although it's a job he does not aspire to. Instead, he'd rather be a team manager. In addition to Hagan's, Hunt has worked for a couple other teams including Bobby Allison's team. He worked there for thirty-two days a year ago, before returning to Hagan's.

"With Bobby [Allison] if you said 'hey I saw another guy doing this,' he would consider it. Here, forget it. Steve's [Loyd] a little green. I don't really like him, but I respect him. Well, at times not even that."

As the performance continued to drop, fingers were being pointed. It's the car, it's the driver and so on. Whatever the cause, and it may have been a lot of both, it was hurting the team. Word of Terry's qualifying position was not what Hagan wanted to hear when Hupperich called Friday night. He too had to take some heat from the race committee earlier in the week, and despite promises that the situation would get better, it didn't appear it would happen here. It's easy to make excuses about poor race finishes, but qualifying is a different story. Hagan was sure there would be more questions to answer after this race. More important, he and Labonte were due in at Sunoco headquarters following the race for two days of promotional stops.

"The only thing I can do is give them [the team] a don't quit attitude," said Hupperich as the rain fell Saturday morning. "It's only the first quarter and though we're behind by fourteen points, there's still three more quarters to go. The scenario with Sterling had been we would start the season off strong and drop. Terry wanted to get things sorted out at the start of the season and at the end of the year be stronger. Then we could come back even stronger next year.

"What we need is the support of our sponsors," he continued. "In our business we're judged by how well we run Sunday or how well we qualify. We're not allowed to have problems. You find the problems and solve them. You learn from it then you succeed. The biggest thing is for people not to give up on us. All of your skeptics and doomsday people . . . they're the first ones to pat you on the back when you win, it's common sense."

The rain let up slightly before noon and the safety crews hit the track hoping to dry the surface in time for the Busch Grand National race that afternoon. The Winston Cup teams were hoping the rain would hold off long enough to get in some practice before nightfall. With the rain, and then the Busch race, the track surface would be much different from what they experienced during practice on Friday. They had already complained that the surface was tight because of a sealer that had been applied weeks before the race, now they were unsure how the cars would respond to the track.

Terry's brother Bobby won the Busch race, notching his first win of the season. Terry helped out by acting as Bobby's spotter for the race. When the race was over and the Winston Cup cars returned to the track for the first time since Friday, Labonte's car handled no better. It was still tight in the turns and it was still slower than some out there.

"The biggest thing is we're not ready when we get to the track," he said. "The competition is so close there's only three-tenths of a second between the front and back rows."

With many of the stops along the way, racing stories lead off the local newscasts. Bristol is no different. One newscast aired two race-related stories before airing news about a big gambling crackdown at a local VFW hall. Every town on the circuit opens up for the NASCAR teams and the thousands and sometimes hundreds of thousands of fans that follow. Hotels respond by doubling or in most cases tripling their rates and "welcome race fans" signs become the norm. No one misses out when the NASCAR circus moves into town.

Race day came with little fanfare. Though overcast, it appeared any rain would hold off until after the race. An early morning sun dried any remnants of the rain from the day before. Like clockwork fans started appearing in their seats at 8 a.m., for a 1 p.m. race. The pits had been alive for more than an hour and the teams had spread out to where they would pit during the race. Labonte's starting position left little to choose from when NASCAR officials came around for pit selections. Steve Loyd chose the second to last pit on the back side. Richard Petty would pit behind Labonte. Both pits were located at the end of turn two.

Terry arrived at the track around 8:30 a.m. After checking with Loyd and looking at the car for a moment, he left with Paul Mecca to attend a hospitality function held outside the speedway near turn one. In addition to driving the race car, it is incumbent on Labonte to make appearances at the sponsors request. He receives $75,000 a year to make at least twenty-five such appearances, which take little more than an hour per appearance. While simple in nature, Labonte doesn't like the appearances; yet, it is part of the job. He is also required to make up to ten non-race appearances for the sponsor at no charge.

When Mecca and Labonte arrived at the hospitality tent, a small group gathered around the driver. Labonte took a seat at a nearby table and started signing postcards, t-shirts or anything else the invited guests wanted signed.

After the line had started to thin out an attractive, slightly plump woman in her mid-thirties shuffled up to the table and sat down. She slid a Dale Earnhardt postcard toward Labonte.

"You have incredible eyes," the woman said staring at Labonte. "Just look at me, that's how I pick my drivers." He stared back, embarrassed and blushing. "Oh god," she moaned, "oh god."

Labonte handed her his own postcard and started to sign it. "That's Gilly with a G," she said as he started to make a J. "Oh it don't matter." She slid her body closer as she got up and left. Labonte looked at Mecca and laughed.

"Boy I hope I win so I don't have to answer all those questions next week," Labonte said when almost everyone is gone. He's not looking forward to the trip to Sun's headquarters in Pennsylvania. Another poor performance and there's bound to be a lot of questions about what's going on. A win might make them forget for a moment. An hour later it is time for Terry to return to the pits.

Race strategy will again be influenced by a change in the rules regarding pit stops. NASCAR announced midweek that caution period pit stops were again permitted. However, the cars would be numbered either odd or even based on their qualifying position. When the caution flag is displayed, odd-numbered cars can pit on the first lap, even-numbered cars on the second. When the cars go back onto the track for the restart, odd numbered cars will always line up on the inside row, even on the outside. During the last fifty laps of the race, the cars on the lead lap can move to the front of their respective rows.

Shortly before race time, a Winston show car circles the track with Miss Winston hanging from the window waving. Right behind is a Coca-Cola truck, a Valleydale Meats truck (the race sponsor), a convertible carrying the Bud Girls and another with the Unocal Racestoppers, Richard Petty's 1970 Superbird, a miniature car driven by a guy in a pig costume and a recruiter for the Air Force driving a miniature airplane.

At 1 p.m., the drivers start their engines, and the race begins. Labonte's early lap times are consistent, though race leader Rusty Wallace is gaining from behind as the field spreads out. Then, on lap 17, with Wallace a mere fraction of a second behind Terry, a car breaks loose and spins into the high bank in turn three. Terry is spared from going down a lap.

Terry takes advantage of the caution to pit for four tires and gas. It takes the team 26.87 seconds to complete the task, seconds longer than the fastest of NASCAR's crews.

Soon after the double file restart there is another caution. Labonte wants to come in for fresh tires, and some wedge. The car is not handling properly. Loyd thinks otherwise and instructs Terry to stay out on the track. He says they will try to fix any problems the next time he pits. It doesn't take long to see the new pit rules are having a negative impact on Labonte. Under green flag conditions Terry can work his way up through the pack, only to have the advantage nullified when he has to restart on the outside. At each restart he is forced to run a handful of laps on the outside groove of the track before he is able to drop to the faster inside groove. By then he has lost several spots.

On lap 32, as Terry comes out of turn three into four, Dale Earnhardt's and Sterling Marlin's cars collide in turn four, blocking a portion of the track. While their cars spin and hit the wall, Labonte steps on the brakes and swerves. Instantly his car breaks loose and spins 180 degrees down the front stretch, barely missing the wall. Quickly, he rights the car and continues as the caution comes out.

"Danny take a look at that right side," Loyd says to spotter Danny Culler. "If you even think that tire's rubbin' then we'll bring him in and out."

There's no damage this time, but during another spin on lap 48 the front of the car gets smashed in a few inches.

Five laps later, the caution falls again.

"Ya know, lining those cars up double file is just making it worse," Loyd says as Labonte circles the track under caution. "Just stay out of trouble and we might make it to the front."

Terry battles his way up to ninth place by lap 190 of the 500-lap event. To get there is a battle. Each restart puts him further back in the pack. Terry's frustration with the race shows in an incident with Alan Kulwicki. Kulwicki is running behind Terry and tapping on his back bumper trying to get around him. When Kulwicki starts to pass, Labonte turns the steering wheel slightly, forcing his car into Kulwicki's Ford. The race is under caution again.

"I got tired of him bumping me," Terry says as he completes another lap under caution. "I just hit his door a bit."

Labonte is able to stay in the top ten as the race proceeds despite several caution flags that stop his progress. On lap 405, Sterling Marlin heads into turn one and comes out of it in a 180-degree spin. He slams rear end first into the wall atop the raceway. The impact sends a jack stand used to hold the trunk up through the oil tank positioned behind the drivers seat. The car bursts into flames as the oil spreads throughout the driver's compartment. With flames shooting out from the windows, the car slides to the bottom of the track.

Immediately Bryan Robertson grabs a fire extinguisher kept in the pits and runs full speed to Marlin's car. "Get back here," Loyd yells into the radio, knowing that Labonte will have to pit under the caution. Robertson continues running toward the burning car, reaching it as Marlin climbs from the car and is sprayed down by a fireman from the safety crew. Marlin is airlifted from the raceway suffering from burns to his hands, face and back. The heat from the fire was so intense that it melted Sterling's visor to the top of his helmet.

While the safety crew cleans the track, the sky starts to turn grey and dark. Big clouds loom over turn two, almost certain to bring rain to the raceway shortly. Terry wants to pit during the caution but Loyd says no. Pitting now would mean the risk of losing valuable track position, and it appears there will be a rain delay, or worse, soon. Loyd's decision proves the correct one when it starts raining minutes later. The race is red-flagged at lap 458. At first team members stay in the pit areas under umbrellas, hoping for a short delay. But it soon becomes apparent that the rain will continue for awhile, so they move to the truck.

During the delay, Terry's son Justin sneaks past the security guards and over to the truck where Labonte is sitting. He asks about the fire. Terry only saw the fire for a moment, so the conversation moves to the driver who has been directly in front of Terry for most of the race.

"The one that really scares me is Jimmy Spencer," Justin says.

Labonte laughs. "He's scaring me from where I'm sitting."

Sterling Marlin's crash had an impact on several members of the team. Though no longer their driver, he is still well liked. "I didn't want my bud to get burnt," Robertson would say later about his dash with the fire extinguisher. Donnie Crumley also was concerned about Marlin's condition. The two men were friends back in Tennessee, and it was Marlin who helped get Donnie the job with the Hagan team.

Even with the concern for Marlin, the atmosphere around the truck is upbeat. There are just forty-two laps remaining in the race and, for the first time, the team is close to finishing in the top ten. With Labonte up near the front most of the day, the team's attitude is great. Everyone is attentive and interested in what is going on during the race. In the past, when Labonte would run in the back of the pack, the team only came to life during the pit stops. When not in contention, boredom set in.

Roughly one hour and forty-five minutes after the race was halted, it is restarted for the final dash to the checkered flag. On the restart, the new pit rules really come into play. Rusty Wallace, who had been running behind Terry on the track, is able to move to the front of the pack because he was the only odd-numbered car on the lead lap. He will start the race with an advantage over Davey Allison, who had led before the race was halted. Terry would remain in ninth position.

When the green flag is waved, Wallace jumps out to take the lead and is able to hold off a last lap charge from Ernie Irvan. Labonte finishes ninth, completing all 500 laps and earning $9,575. The finish puts Terry in twenty-second overall. His blue Oldsmobile is scarred on all surfaces from the battle, which involved nineteen caution flags for a total of 134 laps. The average speed for the race is only 67.673 mph, the eighth slowest of the modern era.

Herb Hupperich's comment after the race echoes the whole team's sentiments. "We really needed this. We've been fighting back all day."

ten

Marketing the Product

"It doesn't matter if you won a race two weeks
ago, people would say when are you going to win."
Terry Labonte

The team's top ten finish made Labonte and Hagan's trip to
Pennsylvania a bit easier to face. Both arrived Tuesday morning
to begin a two-day stay at the home of their sponsor Sun Refining and Marketing.

Tuesday afternoon, Mark Metcalfe, driver of the Sunoco
show car sets the car up in downtown Philadelphia. The brightly
painted stock car, a source of curiosity in the city, causes some
people in the lunchtime crowd to stop for a moment, ask a question or two, and then continue on with business.

By Tuesday evening, Hagan and Labonte are mingling
with top executives of the company at a small dinner party. The
evening is uneventful as the two racing partners make small talk
and answer questions about the race program. Hagan is at home

in these situations, able to converse with just about anyone. Labonte finds these types of gatherings a burden. For him small talk with strangers doesn't come easy.

On Wednesday, Hagan and Labonte make a full-scale charge on Sun's Marcus Hook refinery and another local office building. The day starts early with a stop near the area where Sun's gasolines are tested. Labonte, sitting behind a four-by-four card table, signs autographs for those employees able to get away from their jobs for a moment to look at the car on display. Having been in racing for thirteen years, Labonte is used to the autograph drill. Mecca hands him stacks of cards and he signs one after the other. This session is light compared to a time when he was with Richard Jackson's team and signed 1,000 autographs a day for three days.

Though used to it, this is the part of the job Labonte likes the least. He's uneasy when dealing with the fans and often his expressions make this obvious. Idle chitchat is bothersome to Labonte. He simply smiles instead of answering questions he finds uninteresting. Nonetheless, he also understands it's an important part of the deal.

"You got to get us a win 'cause they're wreaking havoc on me every Monday morning," says a plant worker wearing a blue company issued jumpsuit. Like the others in line before him, the man offers Labonte some encouragement, asks for an autograph or two and walks away to return to work.

Despite Labonte's presence, Sterling Marlin's fiery accident at Bristol is fresh on the minds of many of the workers. He was their driver just a year ago, and during the two years Sunoco sponsored the Hagan team he had made several visits to the refinery. Sun keeps employees up to date on the team's performance through post race newsletters. A majority of those in line ask about Sterling. Labonte answers them pleasantly, although he would like to get out from Sterling's shadow as soon as possible.

Sterling is the only driver these people knew. What sticks in their minds are the times he ran out front or finished in the top five. They seldom remember the times he finished way back in the pack. The employees thought, as the racing committee did, that the addition of Labonte would put them in front for good. In that sense, until Terry wins Marlin will be the driver they remember. Labonte's low-key personality does not help matters either. Though Terry is always polite, Sterling was much more open to the fans than Labonte. Fans asking Labonte for an autograph will get little more. He distances himself from them as he does the team.

"Shoulda got one for myself," says a plant worker walking away from the table with an autograph. "What if he gets famous someday." Most of those talking with Labonte are unaware that he's won the Winston Cup championship.

"Seems like a personable guy," says another who collected autographs for his granddaughter and daughter. "Marlin, I guess they had a conflict there."

After a half-hour or so, Terry picks up and moves to the next location at the refinery where an area has been roped off using yellow plastic caution tape.

Besides the autograph sessions, Mark Metcalfe drives the show car around the facility for the employees to see. The trip to Pennsylvania is just one of some 180 stops Metcalfe will make with the car before the year is over. The show car, actually a retired short track car, is part of Hagan's promotional responsibilities to Sun. He must have car and driver at Sun's disposal for whatever the event — car show, new gas station opening, company picnic.

The show car operation is run like a separate business. All of the major teams have a show car program. It is another form of marketing for the sponsor. Tour the hospitality tent area at a speedway and one is likely to find a dozen show cars laid out for race fans to fondle. Metcalfe, a Hagan team member for ten years, is in charge of the program, although his itinerary is set up by Sunoco. In 1990, he won the award for the most miles logged by a show car driver with 64,000.

"This is one of the loneliest jobs in racing," says Metcalfe as Sun employees ogle the car. "People think this is a glamorous job. I'd love to come home during the week. I'm on the road three or four months at a time." Because of his work schedule, he may only get to attend a handful of races during the season.

The thirty-two-year-old Army brat was born in Texas and ended up in North Carolina. He worked six years for Bill Aldridge, founder of a local oil company who had also been very close to Terry and his brother, Bobby, before coming to Hagan's. Aldridge once owned the land that Terry built his race shop on. He originally had the property earmarked for a truck stop, but when the bottom fell out of the truck stop business he divided the land and gave some to Terry to build his shop.

Metcalfe's travels with the show car have taken him all over the country from the Midwest to the Bronx, New York, perhaps the most unlikely place for a show car display. "I've gone to places where people don't know who Richard Petty is," he says in amazement.

"The hardest part is taking care of the equipment. People destroy things," he says as he watches over the car. "And everybody wants a hat."

After a few minutes Metcalfe fires the engine on the show car and drives to another section of the refinery. Like clockwork the card table is unfolded and Labonte pulls up a chair to sign more autographs.

"Hey, push that car into the river so we can get some work done here," shouts a foreman as his staff gathers around Labonte's table.

"The races haven't been much fun," says one fan. "I've got two cases of beer ridin' on you."

The entourage breaks for lunch. Labonte, Hagan, Mecca, and committee members Doug Plyler, Bud Campbell, Dennis Byrne and Al Contino gather in a small room just off the main cafeteria. During lunch someone plays a promotional tape from the season before, hyping driver Sterling Marlin and the Sunoco team. Labonte looks uncomfortable as a few on the committee brag about what is on the screen. When the tape is finished the group sets out for its next stop, an office building a short drive from the refinery.

After Terry has signed about two dozen autographs, the next man in line says to Terry, "We always thought it was Sterling. Must be that dang car."

As the man walks away Terry sighs and says, "It doesn't matter if you won a race two weeks ago, people would say when are you going to win."

This session and the trip are almost over. For Terry it can't come too soon.

eleven

Too Hot to Handle

"That's what that Sunoco sponsorship is about,
to put us up front. If not, we're going to be out
the door."
Donnie Crumley

Loyd and Labonte flew to Talladega for one last test before the
race there in May. The results were disappointing. The car did
not handle well and it is decided that they will use the other
speedway car in the fleet instead. "We've just fought this car too
long . . . This one was wrecked last year and it ain't never been
the same," Hupperich said shortly before the team headed
out to qualify for The First Union 400 at North Wilkesboro
Speedway.

Rain caused a postponement of first round qualifying until early Saturday morning. In prequalifying practice,
Labonte was slower than a lot of the field. In addition to still not
using a qualifying motor, Labonte believed that the rear gear,
which controls the ratio that the rear wheels turn, needed to be

changed. Other teams were using a different set-up and Labonte thought that at least in this one area they should be on par with the others.

Instead of using one of Hagan's tired fleet, Labonte would use one of his own for this race. He had a few leftover from when he attempted to go out on his own at the end of the 1989 season, and had decided before the season at which tracks his cars would be better than those in the Hagan stable. His cars were visibly better than Hagan's, cleaner and equipped with the latest devices, though they were rear-steer cars. Still, it didn't matter who's car they were running, it was still the same crew setting it up for the races. And that crew was not sure what to do.

"I think to qualify we need to run the correct [tire] pressure," Labonte told Hupperich, who keeps track of the tires during practice and qualifying. Hupperich filled the tires with three pounds less than suggested by Goodyear representatives at the track. The hope was that reducing the pressure would improve the handling of the car. After the first practice, Labonte felt the car would handle better with a little more pressure.

If the pressure in the tires was a little low, the pressure on the team was as high as ever. Hagan had successfully convinced the Sunoco race committee that everything that could be done to get the team on track was being done and that results would be forthcoming. In reality, however, the team was not much further along in understanding the new technology then they were at the beginning of the season. Adding to the team's problems was the talk around the garages of disharmony among the team members.

Indeed, the rumors had started to make their way into the press. The day before the Valleydale Meats 500 in Bristol, Ben Blake, motorsports writer for the *Richmond News Leader* wrote as part of a notes column: "The next split you hear of may involve (no surprise) driver Terry Labonte and car owner Billy Hagan. Labonte has been trying to set up his own team for a couple of years, and Hagan is not known as the most financially solid owner."

Furthermore, some of the media members at the track were asking questions. A few asked Mecca to get some quotes or to set up interviews with Labonte to discuss the matter. Instead of an interview, a pit note was released to all the media. Labonte did not like doing interviews, and after his qualifying performance he was in no mood to answer questions. He was sure the questions would eventually get around to the state of matters within the Hagan operation and that was an area he didn't want to discuss.

"I guess we've got a long way to go tomorrow," Labonte said in the pit note, largely crafted by Mecca. "Our tires didn't come in as quickly as we thought they would. The car pushed in the middle of the corner and was loose coming out. I think we'll be okay after we get going tomorrow."

"We were trying to solve the steering problem with springs and shocks, but first we've got to solve the steering problem," Hupperich said. "We've got to do nothing but work on the steering. We've been listening to a bunch of engineers, listening to guys on paper. Then Joe Blow with a fifty cent racer comes in and blows our doors off. We outscientificed ourselves, engineering too much." In his own way, Hupperich was right.

One thing the pit note did not touch on was Steve Loyd. There was plenty of blame to go around, but when a team is performing poorly some of the blame has to fall on the crew chief.

Loyd, forty-two, grew up about forty miles west of Corpus Christi, in Driscoll, Texas. In 1975, he started helping out a local race team that competed on the same tracks in Corpus and San Antonio that Labonte had raced at. Then, in 1985, there was an opening at Hagan's shop and Labonte called Loyd. He started out working on cars at the shop, preparing them for the races. It would be a year before he was allowed to attend the races. In September 1989, Loyd became Hagan's fourth crew chief in three years.

Loyd, in his second full season as a crew chief, was not well versed in some of the new technology in racing, and even less knowledgeable on leading a crew. These shortcomings could have been overlooked if Loyd was receptive to suggestions from his crew, but he wasn't. Often his comments to team members bordered on browbeating. "No one respected him 'cause the way he treated them. Steve treated everyone bad," Bryan Robertson said later. "Can't expect to be respected when you do that." As much as anyone, Loyd needed a good race to relieve some of the pressure.

North Wilkesboro sits in the western portion of North Carolina in an area once referred to as the moonshine capitol of the South. The speedway, slightly banked and six-tenths of a mile long, was built in 1949 and paved in 1957. One of NASCAR's first tracks, it sits not far from the shop of Junior Johnson. The track slopes downward from one end to the other, giving the impression that it was designed for fans. However, the track was built that way because the track owners did not have enough money to have the land completely leveled when it was being built. The track is about an hour and forty minute drive northwest from the Hagan race shop. Team members meet each morning in Thomasville and then carpool to the speedway.

After practice, the team prepared the car for qualifying. Water was added to the radiator to keep the motor cool. As Dewey worked the engine, Harold and Herb took the tires off the car and put them in the lounge of the transporter where the heat was on full power. Warm tires are faster than cold ones. A flat bladed fan was installed, rather than the normal curved one, to cause less drag and Livengood added fresh spark plugs to give Labonte the best chance possible when the qualifying session got underway. When it came time to push the car through inspection, they remounted the warmed tires. When Labonte drew the twentieth qualifying position, the warm tires were useless. By the time his turn came up to run, the tires would be cold again.

Labonte qualified in the thirtieth starting position. His lap of 19.715, or 114.121 miles per hour, was two miles an hour slower than pole sitter Brett Bodine in the Quaker State Buick. Because of the rainout on Friday, there was no second round efforts to fall back on.

"Damn it pisses me off we didn't qualify good," Terry said after the session. "We're doing something wrong. I ain't never qualified good in an Oldsmobile."

When the support race was completed Labonte and the rest of the field headed out for practice. Between qualifying and the last practice, the team got the car in better shape. Other teams switching to their race motors were unable to sustain their qualifying times. Terry had the fastest car on the track during the last practice, according to unofficial times tracked by Motor Racing Network commentators doing a live radio broadcast from the track.

"We've got to get somebody here to work on the chassis," Donnie Crumley, a weekend tirecarrier and a fabricator in the shop on weekdays. "That's what that Sunoco sponsorship is about, to put us up front. If not, we're going to be out the door." Crumley, like other team members and race observers, believed that with the amount of money Sunoco was spending on the team, it was in the team's best interest to get the manpower needed to put the team in victory lane.

Tension among team members was high Sunday morning. Something upset Hupperich. He started arguing with shop foreman Johnny Siler in front of the truck, but as the conversation escalated they moved between the transporters to block anyone from hearing their discussion. When Hagan arrived at the track shortly thereafter, he entered the discussion. Finally a meeting was called between Hagan, Loyd, Labonte, Hupperich, and Siler. When the meeting broke up, their faces indicated it hadn't been a pleasant one.

Because of his starting position, Labonte would have to pit in the very last spot on the track, deep in turn four. According to Hunt, a few years earlier that spot was nothing but grass. This would be the first time it would be used under race conditions. The location meant Labonte would have to use every bit of brakes he had to slow down and then make a sharp left turn into the pits and stop.

"Damn, we're almost back in town," Hagan says when he gets to the pit area.

There was, however, some welcome news about pitting unveiled by NASCAR earlier in the week. The sanctioning body announced that pit stops would return to the rules used a year ago with one minor exception. Only cars on the lead lap could pit during the first lap under a caution flag. No more odd- and even-numbered cars. NASCAR would continue to enforce speed restrictions on pit road. Excessive speed there would be penalized. With cars being lined up for restarts in the order they returned to the track from the pits, fast teamwork would be the key. NASCAR put the safety of pit road inhabitants in the hands of the drivers, where many of the drivers believed it should be in the first place.

The race features a lot of banging between the cars, which is the nature of short track racing. With not a lot of road to maneuver on, passing requires some contact. A spin in turn four is the early result of the bumping. Labonte barely slips by as the cars collect in front of him. Terry instructs the pit that his brakes are gone. Brakes fading are commonplace at short tracks, where the drivers mash the gas down the straights, only 670 feet at North Wilkesboro, and then step hard on the brakes in the turn. The problem is amplified when running in traffic because cool air is blocked from entering ducts in the front of the car that direct air onto the brake discs.

As the race wears on, Terry's car starts to show signs of the battle he is fighting. At one point Terry rams the car in front of him after it brakes for an accident. The front end of the car, just above the bumper is smashed, but there is no visible damage to the engine or radiator.

By lap 70, Terry has worked his way up to seventh place. He is on the leader board for the first time since Daytona. The team is excited. The short track has eliminated any advantages other teams have on handling and the race is more a matter of driving skill. If Labonte can avoid the continuous stream of wrecks littering the raceway, he might make out alright when the 400-lap race is over.

A pit stop on lap 165 for tires and gas illustrates some of the problems with the team. After returning to the race Terry radios in, "Felt like the right front was going down."

Steve talks to Billy Siler, who had taken over the tire position from Herb. Loyd radios back to Terry that the tires had three pounds less air in them than normal, despite Labonte's request a day earlier that they run regular air pressure. The tires from there on out would be inflated to the proper pressure.

Another caution flag comes out on lap 194. Terry radios to the pits that the engine temperature is climbing rapidly. He finally is forced to come in under green on lap 207. Loyd and engine builder Dewey Livengood jump over the pit wall and lift the hood. They are going to spray the radiator down with water and add water to the system. While sitting there the car quits. The earlier damage to the front of the car did have an effect. All of the coolant has leaked out, without notice, from a small hole in the radiator.

Having battled his way into the top ten, Labonte is now through. "These guys can't run a few laps without wrecking out there," Terry says back in the garage. The area is empty, its only visitors during the race are those who have finished early. Terry would finish thirty-first, third from the bottom, worth $5,000. The finish costs him two places in the overall points race, dropping to twenty-fourth. The race would finish with seventeen caution flags in all, consuming 65 of the 400 laps.

"We blew an engine. We had moved into the top ten before it happened, so that showed that the car was running good. We just can't buy any kind of racing luck right now. We're running good but we're just not in the right place at the right time, it seems."

As Terry leaves the garage to watch the rest of the race, someone tells him to have a good day.

"It's not been a good day . . . it's not been a good week," he says as he continues to the track.

Labonte's luck appeared to be getting better after qualifying for Martinsville a week later, although it didn't last. He qualified thirteenth and for the first time this season he didn't have to worry about second round qualifying efforts. He was guaranteed a starting position near the front of the pack.

Asked about the qualifying efforts by a reporter, Labonte said he wasn't happy. The reporter was a bit taken aback by the negative response given to him by the straight-faced driver. He asked why?

"I told all my fans to buy tickets on the back stretch," Labonte joked. It may have been the best line of the weekend.

Martinsville is short like North Wilkesboro, so any major speed advantages others might have would be dulled somewhat. Labonte excelled in these situations, having cut his teeth on these sized tracks in Texas.

Once again, Labonte is the victim of bad luck. The new brake system the team has been testing is getting its first race tryout. After the first caution, Loyd asks about the car.

"Car's not bad, but I'm about out of brakes; I can't stop in the corners. Seems like they got hot."

"If the brake problems get so ya can't stand it, reach down and turn that ABS [anti-lock braking system] off," Loyd tells him.

Terry pits on lap 86 for service. When he comes in water is sprayed on the radiator and brake ducts to try and cool both off. When he heads back onto the track the car is still running hot. The water temperature is now up to 260 degrees. "Come on in here and lets cool it off," Steve radios to Terry. "Might be low on water."

"Here they come," says spotter Danny Culler as the field makes its way around the track, passing Labonte still in the pits. "We're gonna get lapped."

"Can't help it, it's too hot," Steve says. On lap 128 they call it quits, the temperature problems unsolvable during the race. Had they continued they risked blowing the engine, which would have cost $25,000 or more to replace.

"The car was okay before the engine problem," Terry said afterward. "We weren't as good as we were in yesterday's practice. But without the problems we probably could have stayed on the lead lap all day."

After Martinsville, Terry had dropped again in overall points standings, to twenty-eighth.

twelve

Managing the Rumors

"It's like putting the brakes on."
Terry Labonte

In August 1987, as Billy Hagan started to get his personal life
in order, he turned his attention back to his race team, now in
complete disarray. Hagan had leased the team to J. Wayne
King and, in the nine months or so King was in charge, it had
fallen apart.

Team members who had been with Hagan for years were
searching for other jobs. King, on occasion, told them that he
would close the place down and sell off the cars. Before he could,
Hagan stepped in to take back his team.

"King had it for three-quarters of a year," Herb Hupperich said. "Just about enough time for it to go under."

Hagan picked Hupperich to be his team manager that
summer. It was a move some laughed at.

Racing is a small fraternity. When someone who's not a familiar face enters the circle, questions are asked. Hagan's hiring of Hupperich was no different. And, with the King fiasco in the not too distant past, Hagan's staff also questioned the move.

Hupperich grew up in Mississippi the oldest of three children born to a car mechanic and his wife. His father wanted the good things in life, a real go-getter. With a wife and son at home, the elder Hupperich drove to Louisiana to look for work. On his arrival there, he saw a boat preparing to take off for an oil rig at sea and walked up to the man checking names. His name, of course, wasn't on the list. He begged the man for a job, but was only able to get a promise that if something opened up he'd be called. Two weeks later, Herb's father was heading out to an oil rig.

"He wanted better things, though he never seemed to get them," Hupperich remembers.

His father was away most of the time on oil rigs. Herb, his younger brother and his sister were raised by his mother. "Mom couldn't tell me nothing," he says laughing.

His father worked his way up through the chain of command in the business and set his sights on being a chief engineer, a goal he accomplished at nineteen. Years later, Herb entered the business and became a rig superintendent at twenty-four.

"It's about God damn time," was his father's reply, when told of the promotion.

Hupperich became familiar with Billy Hagan from his days on the oil rigs. Many times Hagan's Stratagraph company was hired to monitor the wells after they had been drilled. Although the two never met, they did know of each other.

Back in Mississippi, Hupperich owned his own short track team. He drove competitively between 1978 and 1981, and later went on to be a car owner. With someone else driving, Hupperich's team won the track championship in Jackson, Mississippi. The team also won a race that allowed them to compete in a more prestigious race in Charlotte. However, Hupperich did not have the money, or an engine, to make the race.

To solve the money problems, Hupperich sold stars on the side of his car for $20 apiece. Next step was rounding up an engine for the race. He called Hagan. "I knew of Billy, but I hadn't met him," Hupperich says. "I called him and asked if he'd loan me an engine. He said yes."

He never made the race, but he did gain a friend in Hagan. Hagan admired Hupperich's "nothing ventured, nothing gained mentality." He also respected Hupperich for being able to supervise an oil rig. Occasionally their conversations turned to racing, when Hupperich mentioned he would some day like to get into Winston Cup racing.

Not too long after their conversations, Hagan called Hupperich and offered him the position of team manager of his Winston Cup team. Hagan had recently ended his lease deal with King and was taking over the operation. Hupperich was to be his liaison to the team.

"I said people are going to think you're crazy," Hupperich says explaining the conversation. "He said, 'yeah, they will.'" A week later Hupperich was on his way to North Carolina.

"In a lot of ways the type of work he was doing was similar," Hagan says now about the hire. "The logistics of moving twenty or thirty people on and off a rig are similar to running a racing team. They're both high dollar businesses that can't afford to be shut down. He liked racing and sometimes it's good to bring new blood in. I was trying to make Stratagraph survive and this was something he wanted to do."

Hupperich, thirty-nine, stands about six feet tall and weighs 240 pounds. He speaks with a deep southern drawl and occasionally quotes from the Bible to get his point across. His stocky build and ever present unlit cigar make for an intimidating impression. The cigar dates back to his days in the oil business. As the story goes, Herb would constantly open his mouth before thinking about what he was saying. One time he said something that was going to cost the company a lot of money. An old-timer on the rig walked over to him.

"Open your mouth," the man said.

Hupperich did and the man stuck a cigar in his mouth.

"Now, when you go to say something bite down instead."

The job of team manager is similar to being a camp counselor. Hupperich is responsible for coordinating travel and accommodations for the team, paying bills, dealing with the sponsor, and handling the day-to-day business aspects of the team. However, Hupperich's reach extends into the mechanical area of the business, which some resent. Hagan, essentially an absentee owner, has given Hupperich the power to make major race site decisions. Hagan does reserve the important final decisions for himself, but Hupperich is in charge of carrying them out.

"Herb runs the place," Terry says. "He sits there and everybody brings his problems to him. He's like a baby-sitter. He's sincere. He gives 100 percent, although, sometimes he does something and I look at him like 'why did you do that?'"

Hupperich came in and tried to run the team like an oil rig. However, on the rigs there are life and death situations, at Hagan's there are not. Hupperich's abrasive manner played better on the rigs. He always felt if he got too close to someone he might not be able to make the right decision down the road. The men on the rigs, though maybe not liking the approach, understood this was Herb's way of keeping his edge and keeping them alive. This was the mentality Hupperich brought to Hagan's team.

Hupperich's oil rig mentality was not working with the team. His manner meant that no one could get close to him. These guys are like a family and want to be treated that way. They put in long hours and want to be able to take a day off when possible. Team members complained that the most minor requests were declined for no clear reason. The problems could be seen in the team meetings held after the first few races. "It's just

little things, a lot of finger pointing. You're afraid to say anything or you'll lose you job," said one team member. "Herb, he
treats people bad," said another team member, afraid to have his
name used. "See, he can get garage passes but he never does that
for us. Billy's a lot like Herb, he don't care about us."

Two days into May the *Winston-Salem Journal* reported
that Hagan was one of three owners looking to make a possible
change. The story suggested that Hagan was interested in hiring
Barry Dodson, a veteran crew chief, to replace Hupperich.
Hupperich was already at Talladega for the next race the day the
story ran, so he didn't see it. But he quickly became aware of it.
Others who did see it talked about it in small groups when they
arrived on Saturday. Most were encouraged by the news, wanting
it to be true. They hoped someone else could come in and turn
the team around.

"I hope it happens," said one team member. "Something's got to happen. It's a combination of Steve [Loyd] not
knowing and Herb being hard to deal with."

News of his job being on the line made Hupperich reclusive at Talladega. He spent a lot of time in the lounge playing a
computer game. He didn't neglect his work, he just wasn't as
outgoing as normal.

"My daddy told me, 'boy, as long as they're talking about
you you're okay,'" Hupperich said. "Someone came up to me at
the track and said, 'you been talkin' any oil field jobs, Herb?' I
said, 'why?' He said, 'if you don't get that thing figured out
you're going to be lookin' around.'"

Stock car racing is well reported in the South and the
towns where speedways are located, so it was no surprise that the
Hupperich article had appeared in print. Those involved in
racing's "inner circle" talk a lot. As a result, rumblings about
anyone in the circle usually made it into print. Hupperich wasn't
the first to learn about a possible change through the newspaper.

"It hurts me," he said about the news. "I sit there and
think about it awhile. I'll feel sorry for myself, and then I say to

hell with it. I'm going to do this until the day comes, then I'll walk out the door."

Word of Hupperich's impending replacement overshadowed what was happening on the track. Labonte was driving one of Hagan's older cars at the superspeedway. The car dated back to when the team switched to Oldsmobile. Indeed, this car was the first they had ever hung a Cutlass body on in 1988. A rear-steer car when first built, it had since been converted to front-steer. The car had not been raced in two years, but everyone agreed that it would be better than the car used in the Daytona 500, which Labonte claimed was loose. They had fought to make the new car work better, but it still was not handling well in testing.

"We looked at the numbers," Hupperich said Saturday morning. "We said, God damn, this car shows better than all the work we did on the new one."

The older car was half a second quicker than the newer one right off the transporter. With a little work at the track it was even faster. Terry qualified with a 49.93, or at 191.819 mph, to take the twenty-fourth starting position. And when drafting with other cars, he cut laps in the range of 49.20 or better.

Talladega is the largest and fastest speedway on the NASCAR circuit. Bill Elliott holds the qualifying record at 212.809 mph, set in 1987. Since Elliott's record, NASCAR has required engine builders to install thin metal plates between the carburetor and manifolds to cut speeds. The restrictor plates work much on the same principles used in water flow restrictors to save water, only in racing they cut valuable horsepower.

At Talladega, the drivers run with the gas pedal mashed to the floor. Drafting, two cars running right behind each other almost touching bumpers, is essential to success at the track. Two cars together can run faster than one alone. In the days before restrictor plates, when drivers had more pedal response, drafting had an even larger impact. Often the second car in line could run slightly less than wide open while the leader had his pedal to the floor. When the second car was ready to move, he had some power left to make the pass.

During practice, the cars line up and wait until a pack of cars comes by. One behind another, different colors, the cars resemble the boxcars of a freight train working their way around the track, each group interrupting the semi-quiet moments as they pass. The drivers are looking for other drivers who can become drafting partners during the race. Maybe a Ford drafts better with an Oldsmobile. A Chevy runs with a Pontiac. Each is trying to find the right combination.

"This is where the drivers got to use their heads," Hupperich said while timing cars during practice. "There's no horsepower to pass, you've got to try and fool people."

Terry waits on pit road for a pack of cars to come around.

"There's a freight train settin' up," said Herb. "You got Rusty [Wallace], Dale [Earnhardt], the 5 car [Ricky Rudd] moving slow." The group is low on the speedway, warming their engines for practice. "They're coming out of four."

Once up to speed the cars stay in a straight line. Occasionally, like the Navy's Blue Angels air team, a car drops left or right and moves forward, then moves back into the line.

"When you get out of a draft you can go from second to fortieth in two laps," Herb said.

Out on the track, exactly that happened. Terry's car was too slow to stay with the top qualifiers and he lost the draft. He came back into the garage. A few moments later he guided his car back out onto pit road to wait for another pack of cars.

"There ain't nobody to run with," reported Steve Loyd. "Just sit there on pit road for a minute."

A moment later, Labonte is drafting with Rick Wilson, in the Snicker's Buick. He completes a lap in 49.90. Then he goes high in the tri-oval and drops back two car lengths, losing almost a second. He would later call this a "slow draft."

"It's like putting the brakes on," Terry said explaining drafting. "Before the restrictors you used to be able to let off the throttle some and stay where you were. Now you run wide open."

Rained caused the delay of the support races and practice Saturday afternoon. Wasting time while the rain fell, Terry and Herb played a fishing game Herb has on the computer used to keep track of lap times during the race. Herb won the game and the fictitious $58,000 prize.

"Damn, that's more than we've won racing," Herb said laughing.

"Yeah," responded Labonte ducking his head.

While they were joking, they were not too far off in their estimations. Through the first eight races, Labonte had accumulated only a little more than $82,000 in race winnings. For comparison, Hagan estimates his weekly race expenses at $80,000.

When the team arrived at the track on Sunday it was raining, though it appeared there would be some clearing shortly. Immediately, they went to work preparing the car for the race. About an hour before race time, the rain stopped and the safety crews started to dry the track. However, it wasn't long before the skies darkened again, and threatened rain. The safety crews continued to circle the track, and successfully cleared the surface for the race. Roughly fifteen minutes behind schedule, the cars were brought out onto the track to start the race.

Because of the size of Talladega, the team is going to try something different. Instead of Loyd staying in the pits for the race, he will be up in the spotters stand. Tex Powell, a racing veteran Hagan had hired as a consultant, would run the show from the pits. Other teams had used the technique with success. The theory behind the move is to put the crew chief in a place where he can see the entire raceway.

After a few laps NASCAR gives the one-to-go signal. As the cars reach turn three, spotter Danny Culler reports it is raining at his end of the raceway. Labonte adds that it is raining where he is too. When the cars reach turn four heading for the start/finish line, it starts pouring rain all around. The race is stopped and briefly the teams stay in the pit area hoping the storm will pass. Culler and Loyd remain atop the grandstands.

But, as the rain continues and the winds pick up, team members scramble for cover in the transporter or under the garages. Fans wade to their cars in the parking lot. The radio broadcasts are interrupted by reports of a tornado forty miles west, near Birmingham. The team members are stuck where they are. Their only choice is to stay in the transporter until the weather passes or the race is halted. Already a long line of cars has formed to exit the infield of Talladega. Parts of the vast stretch of land inside the asphalt track are flooding; some cars are up to the windows in muddy water. What was once the ideal parking spot has now become a very bad one. With the infield flooded, and lightning striking all around, NASCAR calls the race off and schedules it for 11 a.m. the next day.

When Monday came, the track was still wet from the rain the night before. Safety crews were needed to dry the surface, causing the race to start a bit late.

From the start of the race it is obvious Labonte does not have the power to run with the front of the pack. He spends the first sixty-nine laps running in the middle, while the leaders break away. Then, as the cars pass the flag stand on lap 70, Ernie Irvan tries to squeeze his Kodak Chevrolet into a gap between Mark Martin in the Folgers Ford and Kyle Petty in the Mello Yello Pontiac. There isn't enough room. Martin's car turns sideways and the rear end lifts up. Just then his car is tagged by the #90 Thunderbird of Wally Dallenbach, Jr. The crash sets up a chain reaction that claims twenty cars. Labonte's car spins down the front stretch, finally coming to rest against a retaining wall in the muddy infield. The front of the car is pushed forward, the left side dented. Other cars are spread through the Talladega infield in various stages of impact. A few are simply stuck in the mud, while others are severely damaged. When Kyle Petty's car comes to a stop, his left femur is fractured.

Labonte is uninjured in the wreck; he is extremely angry with Irvan for causing the accident. So are many of the other drivers caught in the storm of spinning cars. While Irvan says he wasn't responsible, all fingers point towards him. Labonte's later comments to the media about the crash are mean spirited, though for the most part they are just a way for him to vent his frustration about the race and the season to date.

"Irvan was looking out of one of those eyes that don't go in the right direction," Labonte told the *Richmond Times-Dispatch*. "Everybody that saw what happened, said [Irvan] was on the move again."

Before the crash, Irvan had been involved in several accidents in which he may have moved a little too early in the race. He had earned the nickname "Swervin' Irvan" because of his loose driving style, which had claimed the cars of several other drivers in the past.

Labonte is unable to return to the race. The car is destined for the boneyard. The final race results will list Labonte in thirty-seventh position.

Meanwhile, Harry Gant in the #33 Skoal Oldsmobile, spared in the crash, continues on toward the front of the pack. He takes the lead for the final time on lap 178 of the 188-lap race. However, with a few laps to go his car is running out of gas. Gant's teammate, Rick Mast, in the #1 Skoal Oldsmobile, pulls behind Gant on the next to the last lap and appears to push him. NASCAR rules allow one car to push another as long as it doesn't happen on the last lap of the race. Gant circles the track on lap 188 with his engine sputtering, and, as he comes out of turn four for the final time, his engine quits. Luckily he has enough power to coast past the finish line and claims the $81,950 in prize money.

After the race several drivers complain that it appeared Mast did push Gant on the last lap, although NASCAR maintains there isn't conclusive evidence to warrant changing the final results.

thirteen

Building for the Future

"Hell, at Talladega I'd been fired."
Herb Hupperich

By the time it is completed, a new Winston Cup race car costs upwards of $100,000, with about half of the price tag coming in the form of an unfinished chassis. With Hagan's monthly payment from Sunoco being about $175,000, new cars were not at the top of the team's expenditures list.

Still, early on in the season, Labonte was fairly vocal that part of the problem, mainly his on track performance, was caused by him being asked to drive old, tired race cars that he felt should have been sold off to make room for new ones. Instead of spending the money on new cars, Hagan had been simply having the old cars reconfigured for the front-steer technology, which Labonte found unacceptable.

A few races into the season, Hagan ceded to his driver's wishes and ordered a new front-steer chassis and the team went to work building a car for Labonte, a car best suited for tracks like Charlotte Motor Speedway and Richmond International. They set The Winston at Charlotte (May 19) as a target date for completion of the new 194-inch-long Oldsmobile, and they met it.

The Winston is a non-points race featuring the winners of races from the previous season or those who have won a race in the first half of the current campaign. Before The Winston is the Winston Open, in which non-race winners try to gain entry into The Winston, and a shot at the big money that comes with the title. Terry Labonte has raced in each of the five past events. Since he was winless so far in the 1991 season, to get into his sixth straight race, he would have to finish in the top three of the Winston Open.

Until North Wilkesboro, Labonte and Darrell Waltrip were the only drivers to have been in The Winston previously, but not be eligible for the 1991 running. Waltrip, however, won the First Union 400 and a starting spot in The Winston. While Waltrip did get in, the topic of past winners or Winston Cup champions not making the race received a lot of attention from the media. Several letters to the editor in major racing publications called for changes in the rules. The changes came, but not in time for Labonte to be guaranteed a starting spot.

Labonte qualified third for the Winston Open using the brand new car built especially for the Charlotte races. In a test session on Thursday, Labonte was clocked as one of the fastest cars on the track. Unofficially, Labonte's fast lap around the 1.5-mile-long speedway was at 172.029 mph.

While Terry's qualifying time for the race was fast, he finished only ninth in the Open. A poorly timed pit stop put him out of contention midway through the race. He would miss his first Winston since its inception in 1985.

Missing The Winston hurt, though there was a silver lining in the sense that the team had actually built a good car.

Labonte was confident with the vehicle and it showed on the track. He figured that with a few minor adjustments, the car would be ready for the Coca-Cola 600 in a week.

Qualifying for the Coca-Cola 600, the sport's longest event, took place Wednesday, May 22, and Thursday, May 23. The first twenty spots would be set on Wednesday. The race on Sunday would bring to a close a week's worth of festivities at the Charlotte Motor Speedway that started with the Winston Open and The Winston the weekend before. The week included parades, parties, fireworks, a race of NASCAR legends and, finally, the Coca-Cola 600.

Labonte was the thirty-second car attempting to qualify for the Coca-Cola 600 on Wednesday. Some fifty cars lined up trying to make the race. Only forty, plus any provisionals, would start on Sunday. Large numbers of cars qualifying for the races at Charlotte was not uncommon. The race paid a big purse, and the field was big. Moreover, most racing teams are based within a short drive from the speedway, so the expense of trying and failing was not that large. When Terry's qualifying run was over, he was the fifth fastest. However, several faster cars had yet to take their turn on the track. When the last motor was silenced, Terry was sitting in thirteenth.

Head engine builder Dewey Livengood disliked Labonte's starting position because of the number 13, though the team was relieved they would not have to go through the second round qualifying ritual. Instead, they could spend the practice time before the race working on their race set-up. The car was, perhaps, the best they had had all season, though Labonte said it was loose coming out of the corners and tight in the middle.

The support race for the 600 was a 300-mile Busch race, in which Terry would compete. He would start thirtieth, using one of his own Busch cars bearing the Sunoco colors. At race time the temperature was very high, and the humidity hung in the air like fog. The glue used to hold the lug nuts onto the wheels was melting. The race itself was uneventful. Terry finished tenth, his brother finished eighth. The $3,800 Terry won was just about enough to cover his tire bill for the race.

After a short rest, Terry went back onto the track in his Winston Cup car for the last practice session before the race. The last session is typically the most important because, with the support race finished, the drivers can get a feel for the track under the conditions they will race. NASCAR's last hour of practice at the end of a day is often referred to as happy hour. Cooler temperatures associated with late afternoon allow the cars to run a little faster than earlier on the same day.

After a few laps Terry came back in; the car was still loose coming off turn two.

"Hey, are we jerking off running with these tires?" Terry asked.

Already he has run forty-nine laps, or almost seventy-five miles on the tires, and under race conditions that's about all the tires can take. Bryan Robertson mounted a new set of tires on the car and Terry went back out. The car was too tight in the middle of turn two. It felt fine going in, but once there, it was tight. Practice ended before the car could be fine tuned.

Pre-race check lists are hung on the rear of the car on Sunday for the first time since the Daytona 500. Other teams routinely used the check lists, though Hagan's squad dropped the idea after the season opener. One by one, team members checked the items before pushing the car to the inspection area.

Sitting in the back of the transporter Hupperich prepared the radios the team would use during the race. As he did, one of the race committee members came up and sat across from him.

"So what's the scuttlebutt," the committee member said trying to make small talk. Herb said he knew nothing and continued working. After a few moments the man left.

"What kind of scuttlebutt do you think he was looking for?" Hupperich asked. "Hell, at Talladega I'd been fired. If they want to find a scapegoat they will, but until then you got to do the best you can. You can't worry cause then you make more mistakes."

Races at Charlotte are like circuses. The actual races are similar to the others, it's the events built around the races that turn silly. Track promoters turn the pre-race festivities into an entertainment extravaganza. Coming at the end of the Persian Gulf War, track promoters had wooden tanks built and exploded, with the remaining tanks falling victim to a monster truck. A flyover by armed forces jets and a wooden battleship built outside the raceway are the icing on the cake.

Following driver introductions the race starts normally. Then, on lap 9, while the race is under caution, Terry radios back to Loyd that the engine is misfiring. It happens only in the turns.

Immediately, the crew scrambles to get ready for an unplanned pit stop. Hearing the news, Dewey Livengood looks at Loyd and then looks away. What could be wrong? Livengood moves to the pit box and prepares another carburetor for installation. If they have to, they will make the change right there on pit road. On the track, Terry loses a handful of spots.

"Danny you can stop givin' him his lap times until we get this problem fixed," Loyd says.

It is happening again. Hearing of the trouble with Labonte's engine, looks of desperation washed over the faces in the pits. They are about to suffer another freak occurrence that will take them out of contention of another race. Not once in the days of practice before the race did Labonte complain of an engine misfire. The power plant worked flawlessly until now and it was unclear what was causing the problem. What was clear was Labonte's diminishing on track position.

However, after a couple of early cautions, Labonte reports back that the misfiring is only occurring under caution and only in the turns. When the car is running at top speed, the problem disappears. By lap 50, he is running in twenty-first, some eighteen seconds behind the lead cars. He is a lap down by

150. As in earlier races, the tires put on during pit stops have been inconsistent. One set will be loose, another tight. Moreover, Loyd has Crumley change the wedge in response to Labonte's complaints. But the change is negated when each new set of tires reacts differently.

On lap 166 the caution flag comes out for an accident on the track. "Pit this time," Loyd says, as Labonte circles the track under the first lap of caution.

Labonte wheels into the pits and the team moves into action. When the service is complete, Labonte races onto the track. As he leaves the pits, the NASCAR inspector assigned to watch Hagan's pit procedures walks over to Loyd. He shifts his headphones to speak and then walks away.

"Terry, I had my head up my ass. We pitted on the wrong lap, just go to the end of the longest line," Loyd says over the radio. "I shouldn'ta done it . . . I'm smarter than that."

Labonte has to drop to the rear of the pack for the restart because he came in on the first lap of a caution when he was a lap down. However, by lap 200 he has moved into fourteenth place, behind Bill Elliott in the Coors Light Ford Thunderbird. Labonte pulls the front bumper of his Oldsmobile Cutlass up to the back bumper of Elliott's car and waits to make his move. Going into turn two, Labonte swings his car wide looking for an opening around the outside. Elliott does the same, successfully blocking the move. Labonte remains on Elliott's tail. The two seasoned drivers continue their game for about five laps. Terry tries the inside groove and then around the outside. Each time, Elliott blocks Labonte from passing. The game is costing Labonte about three-tenths of a second each lap, a fact he radios back to Loyd.

As they barrel down the front stretch nose-to-tail at 170 mph, the front of Labonte's Oldsmobile taps the back of Elliott's car. Elliott breaks loose and goes spinning into the grass infield. Labonte goes by, the obstacle in his way removed.

"Steve, tell him I didn't do that on purpose," Labonte says.

Steve tells spotter Danny Culler to relay the message to Elliott's spotter and to Elliott's crew chief.

Labonte, assisted by a couple of good pit stops, methodically moves up through the field. There is nothing special about the way he is going about the race, it is just typical Terry Labonte driving. Smooth. Patient. Conservative.

By lap 360, Labonte is in tenth position. Then, on lap 384, as he enters turn one in a low groove, Hut Stricklin in the Raybestos Buick turns into him. The two cars spin near the bottom of the track and onto the infield. Labonte continues going forward, although the collision has damaged the steering. Terry drives the car into the pits, where Steve Loyd and Bryan Robertson, using a string drawn between two jack stands, attempt to right the steering.

Despite the extended pit stop, Terry is able to complete the race in tenth place, only one lap down. Once he takes the checkered flag, he drives the car into the garage and over to the transporter.

"With every set of tires, I had to run a different place on the track," Terry says as he emerges from the car. He is sweating heavily. His uniform is soaked from perspiration, and from Gatorade he dumped on himself during stops.

"This was the best ya'll looked all year," says Terry's father, Bob, sitting with his son at the transporter. "You drove your ass off."

"If we were just a little bit better we would have been pretty good," Labonte says. "The best thing is that we had a pretty good race car."

"You don't look bad," says Loyd, who had made his way back to the pits. "You would have looked like shit had you run a few more laps."

"The best part is we got us a good race car and we still got it," says Terry again.

The finish pushed Labonte up one spot to twenty-seventh going into the Budweiser 500 at Dover Downs International Speedway in Dover, Delaware. The Budweiser 500 is considered a much more demanding race than the Coca-Cola 600. Dover Downs is called the Monster Mile, for its high-banked turns and the strain it puts on the drivers.

Hagan could see a measurable improvement in Labonte's performance and attitude at Charlotte because of the new car. Labonte said over and over after the race that it was a good car and he was happy with it. Hearing that made Hagan think about building more. Shortly before the start of the Budweiser 500, Hagan told Labonte he'd make him a deal. He'd order a new car if Labonte would guarantee him two poles and two wins before the season was over. "You've got eighteen shots at it," Hagan said. Labonte laughed at the deal, though he said he would try. Hagan then told Hupperich to go ahead and order a new chassis. They hoped to get the new car built for the next race at Charlotte in October.

On Saturday Labonte raced in the Busch series event. Labonte's Busch operation is kept separate at the track, though some of Hagan's crew are paid to work in the pits for Labonte. "We hoped we could learn something on Saturday that we could use on Sunday."

Terry starts the Budweiser 500 in eighth but fights inconsistent tires all day. At the start the tires are ill-handling, causing Terry to drop back five spots in the first few laps. By the halfway point of the race he is seventeenth, two laps down. In the next seventy-five laps Terry manages to make it up to fifteenth. Up ahead, Harry Gant and Ken Schrader trade the lead.

"Steve you're going to have to tighten this up somehow. I don't know but it's pushing," Terry radios to the pits.

Initially, Loyd is going to put a piece of rubber in the right front springs. After talking with Billy Siler and Dewey, he decides to go with new tires and a round of wedge. Terry comes in on lap 353.

When he pulls in front tire changer Steve Wilson runs to the right side of the car and changes the wheels. Bryan

Robertson does the same for the rear. As they tighten the last lug nut, Kelly Hunt drops the jack and the three run to the right side. When Robertson goes to tighten the lugs on the rear tire, his air gun jams. He slams the gun on the asphalt hoping the lug will spring free. It doesn't. He scrambles for the backup gun behind him. By the time he turns around with the new gun, Wilson has moved from the front wheel to the rear and completed Robertson's tire.

"Good thinking Steve," says Loyd.

Robertson also thanks Wilson, but he is upset. Even though it is something that happens to every tirechanger at some point, it still cost Labonte a few seconds in the pits, and positions on the track.

"It takes five years before someone will react the way Wilson did," Kelly Hunt tells Robertson, now standing to the back of the pits angry with himself.

Shortly after the stop a tire punctures sending Terry into the wall in turn one. Terry continues around the track and to the pits.

"Terry, the wheels are all bent out of shape, just park it," Loyd says after assessing the damage. Dewey and Siler tell Steve to have Terry come into the pits. Maybe they can straighten the car out. Steve throws his gloves at the pit box and tells Terry to pit. They straighten the steering out enough for Labonte to finish the race, seventeen laps down.

Pitting for repairs instead of parking the car was a good move as Terry moved up to twenty-sixth overall with his twenty-fourth place finish. The newest car in Hagan's stable has now been christened. The right side is bashed in from contact with the wall, but the all-important chassis is undamaged.

fourteen

The Road to the Top Ten

"When you're not running the way you want,
then the morale gets down."
Steve Wilson

Terry Labonte has had a bittersweet relationship with road courses. Like any affair, the relationship has had its moments. It has truly been a give and take relationship, with Labonte, perhaps, coming out on top more often than not. However, whenever the relationship turned nasty, Labonte got hurt bad.

Over the years Labonte has proven to be a tough competitor on road courses. When Riverside in California was open he grabbed five poles there. He has also done well at Sears Point International Raceway in Sonoma, California, the road course that replaced Riverside on the schedule. But in November 1982, the Riverside course got the better of Labonte. He was shooting for the lead when a front tire blew, sending him head-on into a cement retaining wall in turn nine. The wreck not only totalled his car, but fractured his leg, some ribs and smashed his face bad enough to require plastic surgery. He also wrecked there in 1986.

Labonte now says the 1982 accident was the worst moment in his career. "They had to cut the car to get me out," he recalls, almost laughing now. Though at the time he says if his wife had asked him to quit racing he would have. It took him two races at Riverside before he got over the fear of wrecking in turn nine again. The fear behind him, he rebounded back into the front of the Winston Cup road racers.

Sears Point is the first road course on the Winston Cup schedule and falls smack in the middle of an exhausting six-week stretch of racing that takes the team across the country and back. It isn't the number of races that is so tough, but the travel. From Charlotte they travel to Dover. From Dover they go west to Sonoma, and then to Long Pond, Pennsylvania. From there they head to Michigan and finish the stretch in Daytona.

Getting ready for Sonoma required the team to work on two cars at once. Prior to the race at Dover, the team worked not only on the one for use at the mile-long speedway, but also Terry's road racing car for use at Sears Point, on June 9.

There just isn't enough time between races to complete the work. Following Dover, truck driver Harold Hughes has to return to Thomasville to unload the Dover car and load the road course machine. He then has just one day at home before leaving for the West Coast.

The traveling wears on the whole team, with Hughes probably getting the worst of it. He does most of the runs alone, though he'll bring help for Sonoma. Included in his preparations is an extra box of racing hats to help him get through the various weigh stations that could slow the trip down even more.

"They always want hats," Hughes said. "And you'd better give 'em some if you know what's good for you."

Labonte wants to drive his own car at Sonoma, a twisting twelve turn road course set in the wine producing country north of San Francisco. He had the car built to his own specifications

Terry Labonte takes the Sunoco Ultra Racing Team's car #94 through a practice lap.

Team owner
Billy Hagan
(left) and
Sunoco Racing
Committee
Chairman Bud
Campbell are
all smiles after
Labonte won
the pole at
Watkins Glen.
*Photo courtesy
Marilyn
Campbell*

The difference between a successful and unsuccessful pit stop amounts to just seconds, so every team member has to know his job and perform it quickly and cleanly.

Mechanics Jesse Coke (left) and Bryan Robertson (right) maneuver the backup engine for installation into the Sunoco car #94.

The King. Richard Petty, the man who made stock car racing what it is today, plans to make 1992 his final season.

Dewey Livengood makes adjustments to a backup engine before installing it. The engines are Dewey's babies and he takes great care in making certain they are right.

Herb Hupperich owned his own short track team, but his hiring as team manager for the Hagan racing team was greeted with some skepticism by racing "insiders."

Pete Wright and Terry Labonte discuss the car's performance after a practice run in Atlanta. Wright joined the team after Steve Loyd departed for Roush Racing, and his experience had an immediate effect on the performance of the team.

Ted Musgrave (55) rammed Labonte at Talladega in July. Here he races next to Chad Little and ahead of Bobby Hillin (53) and Darrell Waltrip (17).

Billy Siler mounts the headers on a backup engine.

Speed in the pits is a necessity. Here Kelly Hunt races around the front of Labonte's Oldsmobile with jack in hand at the Hardee's 500 in Atlanta.

Kyle Petty (42) prepares to pit as Harry Gant (33) goes by. Petty was injured at the Winston 500 in May. Gant won five races in 1991 and finished fourth on the points list.

Steve Loyd started the 1991 season as crew chief for the Hagan racing team. When expectations for the team were not met, Billy Hagan was forced to relieve Loyd of his duties as crew chief.

Geoff Bodine in the Budweiser car leads Harry Gant (33), Mark Martin (6) and the rest of the field down pit road at the Pyroil 500, won by Davey Allison.

The final set-up of a race car is the result of changes made during practices. Here Jesse Coke makes some adjustments to the rear suspension as Dewey Livengood looks on.

Terry Labonte sits inside the Sunoco Ultra Oldsmobile after a practice session.

Terry gets up on the bumper of Darrell Waltrip in an effort to pass Ricky Rudd in the Tide Chevrolet Lumina at North Wilkesboro.

It is important that the car look good on the outside as well as run smoothly on the inside. Here truck driver Harold Hughes takes time to clean the windshield.

Dewey Livengood started the 1991 season as the chief engine builder for Hagan racing, and ended it as crew chief. The improved performance of the team under Livengood bodes well for the future of the Hagan team.

Racing under the lights has its pitfalls. During pit stops, teams have a

hard time seeing on the left side of the car. At Richmond, Johnny Siler uses a flashlight to guide Bryan Robertson reaching into the front wheel well to pull out a spring rubber, while Donnie Crumley stands ready with a tire and Kelly Hunt hangs on to the jack.

The team pushes the Sunoco race car forward into position for first round qualifying at Phoenix. Terry's time of 28.83 was fast enough for twenty-eighth position, but he dropped lower in the starting grid after a poor second round attempt.

Terry Labonte drives down pit road before the start of the Pyroil 500 in Phoenix. He started from the thirty-fifth position, with Jeff Purvis in the Folsom Racing Chevrolet next to him.

Terry climbs into his car before the Tyson Holly Farms at North Wilkesboro. Despite qualifying nineteenth, he was confident going into the race. The team and the cars were improving and he was growing closer to the team.

Crew chief Dewey Livengood removes the carburetor so that NASCAR officials can inspect it.

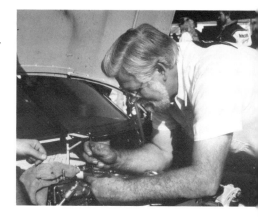

Team members (from left to right) Johnny Siler, Bryan Robertson, Donnie Crumley, Billy Siler and Kelly Hunt glue lug nuts on to tires during action at Bristol. Because of some problems with the track, flat tires were a problem for many of the teams.

Sterling Marlin in his 1991 ride—the Maxwell House Ford Thunderbird. Marlin spent four years with the Hagan team before jumping to Junior Johnson's in 1991.

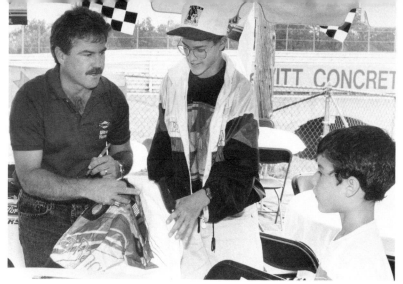

Race car drivers are never far from a pen. A large portion of a driver's time at a track outside of the car is spent at hospitality functions such as this one at Watkins Glen where Terry signs autographs and answers questions for fans.

Ernie Irvan, surprise winner of the 1991 Daytona 500, drives in a pack that includes Mark Martin (6), eventual 1991 points champion Dale Earnhardt (3) and Alan Kulwicki (7).

Tire carrier Donnie Crumley takes a moment during the hectic weekend to relax. A Tennessee native, Crumley understood that the team had to improve its on-track performance in order to preserve Sunoco's support.

Team owner Billy Hagan watches the action from his seat atop the pit box, while Herb Hupperich, and his "ever present" cigar, mans the computer.

A NASCAR inspector oversees the repair work done to the damaged front valence of the Sunoco car at the Atlanta Motor Speedway. Labonte finished fifteenth in the season-ending Hardee's 500.

Terry Labonte and Sun Refining and Marketing
Company President David E. Knoll enjoy a chat
during down time at the track.

Terry Labonte leads the way during practice at Watkins Glen, with Ricky
Rudd (5) and Lake Speed following behind him.

and is comfortable with its ride. Since Hagan didn't have a road course car that was worth working on, just some converted short track cars, the decision was an easy one.

Road course cars differ from their oval brethren in weight distribution and braking power. On an oval, the driver only steps on the brakes slightly, if at all, in the turns, while a road course requires much more braking.

Unlike oval courses, only the overall weight of the car counts on road courses. Instead of shifting weight to the left side, teams move internal parts around to get a better balance. Road courses include left and right turns, offsetting one side weight advantages. In Labonte's car the oil cooler, normally behind the driver's seat, was where the passenger seat would be. The transmissions are also different than those used for the wide out racing of speedways. Road course configurations demand constant shifting, some of it done with out using the clutch. Indeed, racers often joke about which will last longer, the race or their transmissions.

The team was excited about going to Sonoma. Labonte's record on road courses in the past was well known and he was confident about this trip to Sonoma. Part of that confidence came from running his own car and part from all the effort he had put into learning to drive on road courses.

Road courses demand top driving skills more than flat-out speed. In fact, a good road race driver is best at out braking his competition. "You race the track more so than the other competitors," Labonte said. "It's more of the driver versus the track."

Labonte's record on road courses was respectable, but because of his record in 1990, and his performance thus far in 1991, Labonte was being overlooked by the media. Through the first dozen races of the season, including the non-points Winston Open, Labonte had a starting position average of twenty-one and a finishing position average of a dismal twenty-two. His return to Hagan had not produced the magic predicted at the start of the season, and touted in press releases and news stories.

The team was still in terrible straights. Team members were avoiding Herb, only speaking with him when needed. They followed Loyd's orders because he was the crew chief, but they talked badly of him in his absence. Morale was low around the shop. What once was a fairly close team had fallen into little cliques, each talking about the others. Instead of being a team they had evolved into hourly workers who worked on race cars and complained about their bosses. "Herb is shitting Billy's money with his salary, " said one of the more experienced team members. "It would be fine if he wouldn't stick his nose into things he doesn't know, like settin' up a car. I could run this team on a million or a million and a half. There's no way this team shouldn't be making a million dollars."

The stress level around the team was still high. Bud Campbell's seven race limit had been extended further, though many members of the racing committee couldn't understand the poor performance. What they understood was that Sun Refining and Marketing was funnelling $2.1 million into a team that was doing worse than teams with far less funding. News of Hagan's team being on a cash-only basis with some of his suppliers led a few committee members to wonder how much of the $2.1 million was actually reaching the team. In times of trouble people often assume the worst; racing is no different.

Making matters more uncomfortable was the decent performance of last year's driver, Sterling Marlin, who, with Junior Johnson, was sitting in eleventh place overall. Terry was in twenty-sixth. Prior to the season, some on the team had said there hadn't been a win in years because of Marlin; they said he couldn't drive. His action on the track in the early part of 1991 made them think twice.

"You've gotta sit and take it," said Herb. "Not a sonofabitchen one of them knows how to fix it. That's asinine. When you're running bad the heat's going to be applied."

"The reason why you race? You race to be competitive," said Steve Wilson, a fabricator at Hagan's shop and a front tire changer on race day. When you're not competitive, when it gets to the point where you can't change that, it gets to me, it gets to Johnny [Siler], it gets to Greg [McElreath]. The person who can shrug it off and say, 'that's just another race,' is not competitive.

"When you're not running the way you want, then the morale gets down. If it doesn't, you've got a problem. It don't matter if we're running for first or twentieth, I run out there and change that front tire as fast as I can. I want to be the best that I can."

When it comes to talking about what's being done by the management to help build morale through the tough times, Wilson refuses to talk.

Wilson has strong racing bloodlines that go back to the early days of the sport, including ties to Richard Petty, the sport's most recognized figure. After his stint in the Navy, Wilson went to work at Petty Enterprises fixing race cars.

"My family, it's all they've ever done," Wilson said, between making trips to a nearby garbage can to release squirts of juice from the glob of chewing tobacco in his mouth.

A job in racing is something Johnny Siler wanted, too. "Hell, I always did," he said. Siler, the shop foreman, stands about five-foot-seven, with big droopy eyes. Like Wilson , he always has a jaw full of tobacco. A quiet man, Siler has been in the sport for a long time. Before joining Hagan, he operated his own business fixing damaged race cars. He would travel from shop to shop repairing the damage done the weekend before. He joined Hagan's shop shortly before Hupperich took over from J. Wayne King.

"You go through tough times. It's kinda like a boxer, he knows he's going to get his bell rung. But, he's got to get back up. If he does, he might land a blow that wins the fight. These tough times are not going to last," Herb Hupperich said. "These guys weren't used to this, problem after problem. They're all winners in their own right. If they get down, they're not doing their job, you got a damn mess on your hands."

Hagan's racing and financial problems were not the only ones being discussed within the racing industry. Stuck in the middle of the recession, the nation's automakers were reporting the largest losses in their history. About twenty-eight teams, including Hagan's, are directly supported by General Motors and Ford. Moreover, news reports started lumping Sunoco in with other sponsors reconsidering their futures' in the sport. Though, speculative in nature, the reports worried everyone. Like the auto manufacturers, Sun was suffering financial woes, reporting losses for the first part of the year and evaluating possible staff cuts.

Now, for the first time this season, team members actually felt they had solid chance to visit victory lane. They had a chance to put everything behind them, if even only for a week, when they arrived at Sears Point. Victory lane was a place they had not visited for three seasons.

The team got to Sonoma on Wednesday and had a day of rest before the track opened on Thursday. There were a few hours of practice on Thursday and qualifying Friday. A confident Labonte scored his best qualifying effort of the season, just .027 seconds off the pole won by Ricky Rudd. Labonte was on the front row next to Rudd, considered one of NASCAR's better road course drivers.

"I feel like we've got a good race set-up," Terry said after qualifying was complete. "We're awful close right now so we're not going to change much, I know that. We're just going to get it as good as we can so we can run a good consistent pace."

During Saturday's practice sessions the car was a little loose. The right rear was a bit too heavy. Steve Loyd and Kelly Hunt each adjusted the rear springs and Terry was back onto the track. "I believe I can beat the 3 [Earnhardt] and the 17 [Darrell Waltrip], " Terry said after a few practice laps.

Hupperich watched the practice from his usual position on top of the transporter, though the view at Sears Point is minimal. Indeed, there really isn't a good spot to watch the race from anywhere at the track, except possibly from the Goodyear blimp. The 2.52-mile-long race track snakes up and around the sun seared hills of Sonoma. From the pits, only a sharp hairpin turn is visible. Some teams will use more than one spotter for the race.

The 1991 race is the third visit to Sonoma for NASCAR. The sleek wide bodies of the General Motors and Ford products look shoehorned into the track, which is better suited for smaller Indy-type cars. Around the track are the garages of the Sears Point regulars, who continue to work on their cars as if the NASCAR boys aren't there. A much different crowd populates the race track. The beer swilling crowd has its contingency, but those fans from the West Coast seem to be more of the wine and cheese set.

Hagan couldn't make the trip to Sonoma this year; he had a race of his own to run. At least one driver in the race wouldn't miss the Cajun team owner. Tommy Kendall, an experienced road racer often hired by Winston Cup teams without road course savvy drivers to run those tracks, remembers Hagan well from an incident a year before at Watkins Glen, the other road course on the circuit. After the Glen race, Hagan chased Kendall around his car, swinging his cane, because he thought Kendall had caused an accident involving Sterling Marlin. Kendall hadn't and Hagan eventually apologized for the mistake. Nonetheless, shortly before the start of the Banquet Frozen Foods 300 at Sears Point, Kendall joked that he had to keep looking over his shoulder for Hagan.

Terry was much more intense before this race than previous ones in 1991. Instead of joking with team members, he spent his time thinking. In past weeks he had watched the support race from the top of the truck. This time, he quietly climbed on top of the cabinets in the transporter, unrolled a tarpaulin and fell asleep.

"At Dover, he was down here cuttin' up with everybody," said Herb, explaining Labonte's mood. "This time he has a shot at winning."

Hupperich had done some extra planning for the race. In the days leading up to the trip to Sonoma, he watched a videotape of the Sears Point race the year before over and over, each time keeping track of the shifting patterns of Morgan Shepherd, who carried an in-car camera for ESPN. He documented these shifting patterns on a map of the speedway for Terry.

"I told Terry that last year the first four or five guys spent the start banging each other. I told him if they start banging, stay out of it, but stay close to the leaders."

Labonte is a strong willed driver and will only rely on advice given by other drivers. While he appreciated Hupperich's information, he was not likely to use it. He would run the race the way he wanted and only that way.

The start at Sears Point is a difficult one. The cars must first go through a hairpin turn and down a short straight to get to the flag. Then it's a quick left turn and up a hill. Labonte does not get a good start. He is caught on the outside of the turn going up the hill and falls back to fourth before getting in line. Ricky Rudd jumps into the lead.

Terry pits on lap 7 after the caution comes out for an accident on the course. Getting to the pits requires drivers to go wide into the hairpin turn and then around the outside of the track to their pit areas. Hagan's team has the third pit from the end.

Team members complete their work quickly and Labonte exits the pits. However, when he is ready to leave, a tire from Mark Martin's car blocks his exit. Terry throws the car in reverse and turns out of his pit, hitting another tire Martin's team left in the roadway. The impact bends the steering and will affect the handling of the car for the remaining sixty-seven laps.

Labonte stays in the top ten for all of the race, although he never is able to make a serious charge for the lead during the two hour and thirty-three minute race. While Rudd jumped out to an early lead, Rusty Wallace, another of NASCAR's finest road course racers, leads the race most often. But on lap 160 he loses the lead to Tommy Kendall, never to regain it.

Davey Allison captures the lead on lap 72 when Kendall and Mark Martin collide, taking both out of contention. Allison navigates the course with Rudd right on his tail. As the two cars enter the hairpin turn, in full view of the pit area, Rudd gives Allison's car a small nudge, spinning Allison's Thunderbird. Rudd takes the lead and wins the race, but NASCAR black flags Rudd as he passes the front stretch. He is being disqualified for intentionally spinning Allison. As Rudd runs the track for what he thinks is a victory lap, Allison steers his car into victory lane and starts celebrating.

Both teams argue with NASCAR's leadership, maintaining their driver should be awarded the win. After much discussion, NASCAR's competition VP Less Richter levels a five-second penalty on Rudd, dropping him to second place.

As Labonte climbs out of his car he says to Loyd, "We ought to take these springs and throw them away. It was loose. I was spinning the rear tires all day. I saw that tire there in the pit and I thought I missed it. It knocked the toe-in out and it wouldn't turn well."

"You missed it alright, but you didn't see the other one," Loyd says laughing.

"The race set-up wasn't as good as it could have been," says Terry as the team loads the car on the transporter for the trip home. "We had a good qualifying set-up, what we didn't have was a race set-up."

The sixth place finish is worth $14,400 and moves Labonte up to twenty-second in points. After the car is secured on the transporter, each of the team members grabs a beer and heads for the airport. Another race is under their belts, seventeen remain.

fifteen

Seven Cylinders

"It was good; damn it was handling good."
Terry Labonte

The afterglow from Labonte's sixth place finish at Sonoma lasted less than a week. Following Sonoma the NASCAR circuit moved to Pocono International Raceway in Long Pond, Pennsylvania, where Labonte qualified fourteenth. In the process, he and seventeen other drivers broke the track record.

Once again Labonte was complaining that the car was loose. During Saturday morning's practice session, the car was loose going into turn one and loose in the flat spots. He thought, perhaps, the right front spring was not stiff enough.

"I think maybe it needs two front springs," Terry said in the garage after the first few practice laps.

"That's what I'm thinking," replied Steve Loyd. "Maybe a 1600 and a 1400." For the remainder of practice Saturday morning Loyd and the crew switched springs in and out and adjusted the wedge. In all, they may have changed the entire set-up on the car a couple of times before Labonte said the car handled well enough to race.

Doing well at Pocono was important for the Hagan team. Sun Refining and Marketing's headquarters is less than two hours away in Philadelphia. Pocono was about as close to a home track as Sunoco could get. More important, Sunoco sponsored a series of races at the 2.5-mile-long tri-oval, so the company name was displayed prominently above the speedway scoreboard. Several top Sunoco executives as well as most of the race committee would attend the race on Sunday.

"I've qualified first or second at every track except Talladega . . . third there," Labonte said on his way back to the garage after making an appearance at the Sun hospitality tent. What's the difference between a good round and a bad one? Without hesitation, he says, "the car."

The race starts on time and after a few laps Terry is on the radio with Loyd.

"They're killing us with the gears," he says, with a touch of anger in his voice. "We got the wrong gear in the car."

The rear end gear that is in the car prevents Labonte from going into the turns as fast as he wants to. Other drivers are able to go deep and still keep their engines revving high. Labonte has to back off earlier, making it difficult to gain any ground.

When Labonte finishes his message, Livengood looks at Loyd with a snarl on his face. Livengood's quiet manner keeps him from voicing the displeasure that can be seen in his expression.

The caution flag is out on lap 19 and Labonte darts into the pits. Bryan and Steve mount four tires while Harold Hughes and Dan Gatewood fill the gas tank with high-octane racing fuel. Donnie Crumley takes out two rounds of wedge.

"Those guys kill me coming out of the corners," Terry says as he drives around the track under caution.

"Well, we'll learn for the next time. Just stay out of trouble and we'll be alright," replies Loyd. "Just be patient with us."

Terry pits again on lap 50. Hunt, Wilson and Robertson run to the right side of the car. Donnie Crumley follows with a racing tire under each arm. As he reaches the front of the car, Lake Speed, pitting in front of Labonte, turns sharply into his pit, clipping Crumley in the process. One of the tires flies toward the pit from the impact, but Crumley is able to hang onto the other. They complete the stop and climb back over the wall with Crumley grabbing his back. His teammates ask him about his condition and the accident. He is shaken by the hit, though he claims he's alright.

"I've got hit before, by Kyle [Petty]," he says. "But it wasn't that hard. Terry came in short so he wouldn't get caught. Lake Speed came in short and blocked him in."

Crumley has been on the team just over a year. He joined last season after Sterling Marlin suggested he call Steve Loyd. At the shop he works building car bodies, though, he feels more comfortable as a mechanic. He took the job to get his foot in the door, settling for less money than he'd like and hoping the position will grow into something bigger. Well mannered, Crumley is bearish in appearance and speaks softly with an accent native to Tennessee. A likeable guy, he's the type who will spend minutes looking for something that often is literally at his feet.

Notwithstanding the gearing problem, Terry remains between tenth and fifteen for most of the day until it starts raining. The drivers are red-flagged on lap 138. After an hour and forty minute delay, Labonte continues running toward the front of the pack. Though not in contention for the win, he is a bit more competitive than previous races. However, with 70 laps remaining in the 200-lap event, a rocker arm fails, cutting off power from one of the engine's eight cylinders. Labonte is reduced to running the remaining laps on the inside lane of the speedway to stay out of trouble. He finishes twenty-first.

"The car was too tight to start," he says after the race. "It got better. We had the wrong gear. It was running okay. It was staying on the race track. Every time we [pitted] we lost four to six spots.

The team returned to Thomasville after Pocono to re-group. A few days later they left for Michigan International Speedway and the Miller Genuine Draft 400. First round quali-fying on Friday put Labonte in twenty-first position, fastest of those not guaranteed a starting spot. If the conditions remained the same Saturday, Terry would stand on his time.

"It's this much Terry," said Kelly Hunt, holding his hands apart about six inches describing the qualifying efforts. Spreading his hands wide apart, he added, "It's this much other things."

When they got to the track on Saturday the tempera-tures had dropped some thirty degrees, bringing with it faster speeds from the cars yet to make the starting grid, including Labonte's. He qualified Friday with a lap of 42.150 seconds. His early laps Saturday were around 42.09, though he was still inconsistent.

"How'd the car feel to ya, Terry?" Loyd asked. "What did ya have a bad second lap?"

"No, but if we're going to requalify we're going to have to put some new tires on this thing."

Terry understood the consequences of the cooler temper-atures and what needed to be done on the track. He knew he wasn't the fastest car out there, but by standing on his time he risked falling further back in the pack. Some of the cars that were much slower a day earlier on a warm track were now much quicker.

"We're sittin' ducks," Labonte said to Loyd as they planned the strategy for qualifying. "We gotta go."

"How do we make it better?" asked Loyd.

Labonte shrugged his shoulders.

They selected tire set No. 5 with a stagger of an inch and a quarter on the front and an inch and seven-eighths on the rear. The compounds used to make bias-ply tires result in slight fluctuations in the circumference of these tires. Despite being made the same way, two tires of the same style may be different in terms of circumference. Racers use these changes to their advantage and have found over the years that having slightly larger right side tires on the car improves the handling. Throughout the weekend, the tires are measured for any changes in the circumference which would effect the car. The bigger the difference, the more dramatic the change in handling.

Earlier in the week Steve Wilson had resigned from the team to go work for Stavola Brothers Racing, the owners of the Snickers Buick driven by Rick Wilson (no relation). Steve's brother Ken was hired to take over the team, also struggling this season. Pocono would be Steve's last official appearance for Hagan; he was to start at Stavola's on Monday. The move was understandable, and also not unexpected. Wilson, like a lot of the others, was unhappy with the way the team was being run.

"It's one of those family things," Hupperich said about Wilson's departure. "But, it's different when one brother is in power and the other is a subordinate. We've always said if you're not 100 percent with us, here's the door."

Wilson looked forward to working at Stavola Brothers. The sixty-five-mile commute from his Greensboro home to Charlotte was not a problem. His brother lived nearby, and along with some other teammates they were to carpool with a company supplied vehicle. He was also getting a big raise with the move.

"When he called to ask me about it, he asked if I would have a problem working for him," Wilson said. "I said, I have no problems working for someone who knows what they're doing."

Most of his Hagan teammates reacted positively to the move, though Loyd and Hupperich avoided Wilson at the track. And Labonte had little to say to him.

"The driver's a prick," Wilson said about Labonte. "If a man wants to go and better himself you should congratulate him and say good-bye, not these guys."

Wilson's resignation was not the only bad news the week of the Miller Genuine Draft 400. Rumors were surfacing that Oldsmobile was going to pull some of its factory support from NASCAR and that Hagan's team was one that Oldsmobile was considering dropping. A factory program is worth some $200,000 to $500,000 in sheet metal, technical help, wind tunnel testing and the use of new street cars, and loss of such benefits would dramatically impact the team. No firm decisions were made, though General Motors was experiencing huge losses and was seeking areas to cut.

On top of the possible loss of Oldsmobile money from his program, Sun notified Hagan it was going to enforce a contract clause and audit his books. He had ten days to prepare for the auditors. The clause is not usually enforced, but with the rumors of Hagan's finances being unstable, the committee agreed to go through with an audit.

Some team members were excited. They figured Sun would find something that would force a change with either Loyd or Hupperich. In their minds, both would be an ideal result. They knew Hagan was on a cash-only basis with some suppliers. They also complained that their paychecks were sometimes postdated, putting a hardship on their families. The bottom line, however, was that there was a good chance nothing would happen.

When second round qualifying was over, Labonte's lap of 42.002 seconds was good enough for twenty-sixth. Going back out was a smart move for the Hagan team. Had they stood on Labonte's time from a day before, Labonte would be in thirty-first position.

A few hours before the race, Hupperich sat alone in the rear of the transporter, reading one of the racing newspapers frequently left on the bench seat. His pre-race responsibilities had been completed, so there was nothing to do but wait.

"What's wrong?" asked Labonte as he took a seat across from Hupperich.

"Do ya ever get tired of talking to people?" Hupperich replied.

Labonte said yes. As if to drive home the point, someone with a program walked over asking for an autograph. Terry put on his public relations face, signed the book, and the person walked away.

From the start of the race it appears Terry might finish well. Quickly, he weaves through the pack and moves into the top ten. The car is strong, and as the race wears on it gets better. At the 100 lap mark, Terry is in ninth place. Nevertheless, after a late pit stop, Terry notices the engine does not have the muscle it had earlier. With 60 laps left in the 200-lap race, Terry loses power. A rocker arm bends, and for the second consecutive week he finishes the race on seven cylinders. The mishap angers him. Engine builder Dewey Livengood, who pours hours into getting the engines together, is disappointed. His creation has failed.

Terry motors around the track down near the apron, staying out of the way of faster cars. His engine, missing some power, is audibly ill. He rapidly loses track position.

Noticing her husband has dropped off the pace, Kim Labonte walks through the pits and up to Loyd, standing on the side of the pit box.

"Did he lose a cylinder?" she asks.

He answers yes.

She mumbles a profanity and walks away.

Kim's interest in the sport is limited to watching her husband race. When he's out of the race, her interest wanes. She married into the racing life. She and Terry met when she worked for his sponsor back in Texas. A short time after he moved to North Carolina, they married and she followed. The couple's children each saw a speedway before they were ten weeks old.

Like the rest of the racing wives, Kim fears for her husband's life week in and week out. She's stood by and watched him win the championship, and she was there when he required an ambulance to leave the raceway. After Terry's bad wreck in 1982, he said he would have quit racing if Kim had asked. She didn't then, and she hasn't since. It's something Terry is grateful for. He says he wouldn't know what to do otherwise.

Following the race Terry wheels the car back to the garages. He is mad. The car had performed well, and then the motor expired. Making matters worse is that this is the second week in a row this has happened.

"It was good; damn it was handling good," he says. "I thought early in the race we were pretty good."

Though he is upset after the race, Terry does not carry on like a maniac. He handles the pressure well, choosing to leave his anger at the track instead of taking it home to his wife and kids.

"He handles it better than most," Kim says. "I'd be ranting and raving and throwing things."

sixteen

A Needed Change

"If this were all easy, there'd be eighty cars out there."
Billy Hagan

Steve Loyd and Terry Labonte have a long friendship that dates back to their days racing on the short tracks in Texas. While Labonte was leaving his mark on the track, Loyd spent his time working for free on the crew of another team.

In 1975, while working for a tractor company, Loyd would go to the local race track in Corpus Christi. Two of the top drivers at the track were Terry Labonte and Slick Yoemans.

One night after the races, Loyd walked down to the pits and asked Yoemans if he could help out. He was willing to work for free, which was good because Yoemans' team operated on a shoestring. If they won a race, Slick's father bought dinner. That was the extent of Loyd's pay.

Loyd helped Yoemans for ten years until Yoemans left Texas for North Carolina to join Labonte in a salvage business. Yoemans still runs the business, with Labonte as a partner.

Soon after Yoemans left Texas, there was an opening at Billy Hagan's Thomasville race shop. It was 1985 and crew chief Dale Inman was leaving to return to Petty Enterprises, working for his cousin Richard Petty. Immediately, Labonte thought of Loyd to work under Inman's replacement.

During a four-year apprenticeship under some of the most knowledgeable players in the business, such as Pete Wright, Steve Hmiel and Jake Elder, Loyd learned the business from the bottom up. Quietly he stood on the sidelines watching these men set up race cars, waiting for his turn at the top.

Though Labonte left Hagan's team after the 1986 season, he and Loyd remained friends. When the crew chief position at Hagan's opened up in the fall of 1989, Loyd turned to Labonte for advice. Labonte told him to take the position, and told him what to ask for concerning incentives. Hagan promoted Loyd to crew chief with five races remaining in the 1989 season.

At the end of 1990, Labonte's return to Hagan was being billed as a family reunion. Loyd said there was not another driver he'd rather work with than Terry. And Labonte returned the compliment by saying they had known each other so long they wouldn't have to go through a learning period.

However, after the first fourteen races of the season, it was obvious that the relationship was not working. The fifteenth race of the season, the Pepsi 400 at Daytona International Speedway, was the race that broke the proverbial camel's back.

Loyd carries his forty-two years on a slim six-foot frame. He looks younger than his age, though he jokes that being crew chief has cost him a few hairs and greyed a few others. His low-key personality, while helping him get through the tough times, also made it difficult for him to be a leader.

Loyd is a likeable guy. A single father, he cares deeply for his nineteen-year-old daughter. In his spare time Loyd gardens and listens to country music.

Loyd had struggled all season with the move to front-steer cars. Despite a midseason addition of Jesse Coke, a mechanic with experience on front-steers, not a lot of progress was made in mastering the technology.

Missing the free test date before the race and bringing the wrong car to Daytona were two more nails in Loyd's coffin. And, when Labonte parked the car after eight laps of the Pepsi 400, he sealed his friend's fate.

The next day, and for just about every day during the following two weeks, phone calls went back and forth between Hagan, Bud Campbell and Terry. The team was in real trouble. Morale was low and the structure was fragmenting. At the halfway point there was little to show for the season. The team was distressed, blaming each other, and the driver, for the problems.

"Yeah, there was a lot of shit that went down here," Hupperich said. "Decisions [about which car to bring to Daytona] were made with full knowledge of the driver and Steve. Somehow, it's conveniently forgotten that they had anything to do with it. It turned out like I demanded it. I'm just thankful that I've got a job."

By all comparisons the team was below the level of the season before. According to The Sponsor's Report, a media tracking firm, the Sunoco team amassed one hour and sixteen minutes of television time by the halfway point in 1990. That time, according to the report, would have cost $880,090 if the company had gone out and bought the same amount of advertising on the networks that aired the races. For the same period in 1991, Hagan's team only accounted for twenty-one minutes and forty-five seconds of air time at a value of $439,320.

Hagan's relationship with Sunoco, while bound contractually for another year, was in jeopardy for the long run. Hagan had to do something and it had to be substantial. He also had to do it quickly.

"I think it was a lack of adequate attention to the overall management of the product because there was absentee ownership," Bud Campbell said. "We felt he put too much faith in the fact that this thing was going to work itself out without putting himself into it."

"With everything that's been going on, they've pretty much had Billy on a rotisserie," Hupperich said after the Pepsi 400. "Sun was just waiting for something to happen."

Hagan called Loyd and relived him of his crew chief duties. He could remain with the team, but not as its leader. Instead, he was to return to race car preparation where he had started. He was being replaced by Dewey Livengood, an eleven-year employee and the head engine builder.

"I told him I had pushed him along too fast. I put him in the deep water before he could swim that good," Hagan said. "He was sinking and the whole ship was sinking with him. He recognized the situation and he knew we were going down instead of up. It takes a pretty good man to stay in a situation where he was on this level [holds his hand high] and is now down here. Anytime a person gives their utmost effort to the cause, they don't have to back down because it didn't work."

In making the change, Hagan also admitted there was a problem with the team. Having spent most of his time in Louisiana attending to his other businesses, he had not seen what was happening in the Thomasville shop. He realized that his predictions at the start of the season were off.

"I expected a lot more than happened," he said. "I didn't thoroughly evaluate all of the problems that there were. I had a sense of false security. The problem was that I had a series of problems that didn't add up, they multiplied."

Halfway into the season, Hagan understood that Loyd's and Labonte's inexperience with front-steer cars was taking much longer to overcome than originally expected. He also realized that while Labonte and Loyd were friends, they had never worked together in that type of situation before.

"It wouldn't have been as bad had Steve been a crew chief longer and had more confidence," Hagan said. "The further we went along the more obvious it got, until it reached a boiling point. If this were all easy, there'd be eighty cars out there."

Few people in the shop believed in Loyd. He hadn't originally been hired for the position of crew chief; he was a mechanic. Deep down he seemed to have his own doubts that made him apprehensive.

"The worse part about it is he wasn't a good leader, in getting people to work together," said Labonte.

Livengood, the elder statesman of Hagan's team, was an unlikely candidate for the top spot, yet a good one. He'd been with Hagan since 1980. Before that he worked for veteran driver Dave Marcis for another seven years. However, his entire career at Hagan's had been in the engine shop, trying to extract horsepower from hunks of steel. Nonetheless, he was stable. As people came and went through the other side of the shop, Livengood was a constant in the engine room.

His leadership capabilities were immediately questioned by some around the Sunoco race committee. His background did consist of a short, though successful, period as a crew chief for a Trans-Am team. Yet, the times had changed dramatically in the ten years he'd spent in the engine room. If Loyd had limited experience with front-steer cars by the midpoint in the season, Livengood's was minuscule. But, what Livengood did have, what mattered most, was the respect of his fellow teammates.

When Hagan called Dewey and asked if he would become crew chief, he was interested, though concerned. The crew chief's head was always the one to roll if something went wrong. Having invested a lot of years at Hagan's he wanted to make sure there was a future. He was also concerned about his wife, Doris, who served as the team scorekeeper.

"Well, I don't know," Livengood said. "What will happen to me if it doesn't work?"

Hagan assured Livengood that as long as he wanted to build engines, he could do it for Hagan Racing.

"Okay, I'll give it my best try," Livengood said. Livengood then called Labonte for his approval.

Labonte, like Hagan, knew there had to be a change. However, Labonte expected Hagan to go outside the team and find someone with a lot of talent working on front-steer cars. The decision to go with Livengood surprised him, though, he went along with it.

"When Billy called and told me it was Dewey, I told him the only person I have more respect for is my dad," Labonte said.

Livengood's first race as crew chief was two weeks away, at Pocono.

seventeen

Teamwork

"When you lose a lap here, you've got a long
day for ya"
Dewey Livengood

Dewey Livengood is a solid 240 pounds of racing veteran. Despite his size, he shuns the spotlight and is so quiet it is painful. Sporting a full head of grey hair and matching beard, he is the team's grandfather figure. Now he is the crew chief.

For the past few months, when the team was crumbling around him, he kept his mouth shut, all the while tending to his motors. Having been in the business so long, he could see where some of the problems were, but could do little about them. And each time Labonte complained about a motor, or when one quit unexpectedly during a race, Dewey took it personally.

In the two weeks since Daytona, the team had taken on a completely different complexion. The team was the same, but the atmosphere was now much more casual. Livengood's immediate effect on the team was calming, yet professional.

Instead of Terry Labonte and Steve Loyd making all the decisions and the team members blindly carrying out their orders, Livengood let those on the team do what they do best. He still made the final calls, yet, for the first time this season, the crew chief was making decisions with input from those around him.

Livengood, forty-nine, is known and well liked by most of his motor building counterparts, though his shyness costs him the attention of the media. Labonte praised his work before the season, saying he was one of the most underrated engine builders in the business. Hagan agreed.

Livengood is also extremely superstitious. He would rather Terry not qualify in the thirteenth position. And the color green, considered bad luck in racing, makes him cringe.

"We used to run the number 44," Harold Hughes said. "But when we got Sun they changed it to 94. Dewey says that a 9 and a 4 equals 13 and he's been bitching about it ever since. He hates it when we qualify thirteenth. He would rather give up five spots than start there."

Herb Hupperich also supported the move and the way Dewey was handling the team. "We got some boys who can do the job," said Hupperich. "This will give Dewey a chance to understand what we've been doing . . . the man's smart."

Hupperich also believed that Livengood had the strength to manage Labonte. While Livengood had asked Labonte if it was alright that he became crew chief, he also had Labonte's respect. Together they could work to make the team better.

Notwithstanding Livengood's promotion, the Sunoco race committee still had some questions about the team. While chairman Bud Campbell took a wait-and-see approach, others wanted even more dramatic changes. Moving Livengood in didn't help, they argued. That was just stirring around an already weak broth. What the team needed, some believed, was for

Hagan to go out and pay money for a big name crew chief and chassis wizard to help solve the front-steer problems.

No one lacked respect for Livengood, but he didn't have a deep background in front-steer cars. And Hagan and Hupperich had been blaming the team's troubles on the switch to front-steer cars. When Hagan didn't bring in a chassis genius, a few of the committee members didn't believe Hagan had their best interests in mind.

With all of Sun's questions and concerns, there wasn't much they could do. Yes, Sun did have a contract with Hagan through the 1992 season. Yet, it contained no performance clauses, no minimum levels of efficiency to be achieved by the team on the track. All it said, in basic terms, was that he had to carry Sunoco's colors and, at the beginning of the season, tell the race committee exactly how he proposed to win the championship. Hagan was fulfilling his end of the agreement. Sun had to rely on the team's pride and desire to win. The results were less than desirable, but all Sun could do as Hagan's primary sponsor was ask for changes. The only real grounds Sun had to pull its precious sponsorship dollars was if Hagan severely breached the contract. Failing to make three consecutive races was cause for breaking the deal, but with Labonte at the wheel Hagan was virtually guaranteed a starting position.

A week before the team headed to Pocono, they tested again at Talladega. The results were not reassuring. Not only did the car handle poorly, but Labonte feared the motor was not strong enough to make the race. The Diehard 500 at the 2.66-mile-long superspeedway was only a week away.

"I don't know if we'll make the race," Labonte said as the team prepared the car for the Miller 500 at Pocono International Raceway. "We need a motor. We don't have any money. I might try to get someone to loan me one."

Labonte thought he might be able to get a motor from Richard Petty. Petty's crew chief, Dale Inman, was the crew chief for Labonte when he won the championship in 1984. The two had remained good friends since, and Labonte had helped Petty's operation with their road racing efforts. A new motor from one of the better engine builders would cost more than $20,000 just to rent.

"I think I can get one from Richard, he might let me use one. But, ya gotta be careful with stuff like this 'cause you'll piss a lot of people off. They gotta find out what's wrong. If we put it in and it runs the same, well?"

The team had yet to replace Steve Wilson. Instead, pit stop duties had shifted to cover the gap. "Some guys when they leave, they don't leave a very big hole," Hagan said about finding a replacement for Wilson. Hupperich had interviewed a few people, although not may were interested in the terms. One candidate working for another team made the trip from his home in Charlotte to the shop and found it was too long, according to Hupperich.

Away from the transporter Labonte discussed Hupperich's and Hagan's excuses, "They can't get anyone to work for them."

Tex Powell, who had helped out for a few races, was also gone from the team. His knowledge came with a price, and there was talk that Hagan's financial state kept him from meeting it. According to Labonte, he saw early "that he couldn't do anything here."

Hagan's operation was not opulent by any standards. The team had what it needed to work, but not a lot of extras. There wasn't a shop full of new cars, and, according to some on the team, Hagan was behind on some bills. Hagan was slower than others had been in paying Labonte his race winnings. Other teams he raced for paid the winnings either weekly or monthly, but it was done on time. Labonte's deal with Hagan only stated that he be paid his money on a timely basis.

"Here it's whenever you go to Herb and say I need some money," Labonte said. "Hell, I don't know what he does with his money, he sure doesn't pay his bills."

The Miller Genuine Draft 500 would be Livengood's first race at the helm of Hagan's faltering race team. His debut making the calls would come before some 2,000 employees of Sun Refining and Marketing. Once a year the company brought to the races any employee who wanted to go. The day was an elaborate affair with special t-shirts made up and a buffet lunch. In addition, the employees got tickets to the races and other promotional items. Topping it off, Bob Campbell, the president and chief operating officer of Sun was the grand marshall of the race. Sun's bill for the entire day falls in the neighborhood of $250,000.

Labonte qualified twenty-second for the race and stood on his time during the second round. When the nine cars that went back out to requalify finished, Labonte was bumped to twenty-third. The position didn't bother Labonte much; in 1989, he had won this race from the same starting position. Moreover, by this point in the season, it was clear that his qualifying efforts were not always indicative of his race performance.

Sun bused the employees to Pocono International Raceway from its southern Pennsylvania headquarters. Once there, the buses made a lap around the track and dropped the employees off near the pits. After a brief tour, it was back to the tent where Labonte and Mecca performed a pre-race stand-up routine. Typically, and Pocono was no different, Mecca asks Labonte a handful of questions about racing such as how does this track compare to others and what's stagger? The two have a repertoire to pull from and the talk goes over well. Though quiet on the track, Labonte has a way of winning over audiences. The routine appears to be original everytime the two perform it.

While Labonte and Mecca were on stage, two friends were off to the side waiting in the beer line. "Wouldn't it be something if he won today," one said to the other. "Yeah, I've been waiting three years for that."

Once the performance was over, Labonte moved to a table near the edge of the tent. A crowd followed forming a long line for autographs that snaked throughout the area. One by one, the employees came up and asked for Labonte's signature, be it on a postcard or the shirt they received for coming to the races. Children asked Labonte to autograph their remote control cars, designed to look exactly like the Oldsmobile he will drive in the race.

After stopping at the hospitality tent, Terry returned to the truck to change into his race uniform. There's no on site physical preparation for a race. Drivers are not normally seen loosening up before a race the way football players warm up. Drivers do work out at home. But, between now and the time he fires the engine on pit road, Labonte's preparations will be limited to the ideas in his head. Labonte shuns the notion that he does anything to get ready for a race. When asked how he prepares for a race? He pauses, flashes a devilish grin and responds, "Watch a Clint Eastwood movie."

The pre-race procedure under Livengood deviated little from the way Loyd handled it, except for the drivers' meeting. Before each race, Loyd and Labonte attended the drivers' meeting together, mandatory for participation in the event. If either missed the meeting, the team would be fined. However, at Pocono, Livengood sent Billy Siler in his place. The car was a little behind in preparation, and checking the valves in the engine usually came last. Livengood, not one to delegate his duties, spent a good deal of time checking the work of others to make sure everything was right. As a result, the car was one of the last through inspection.

Three laps into the race the caution flag is out. Labonte and Livengood do not say anything to each other over the radio as Loyd and Labonte likely would have. When the caution comes out again on lap 11, Labonte says the car is pretty good, his standard off the track phrase when anybody asks how the car is. He pits under caution on lap 22 for tires and gas. When he goes back onto the track after the stop, he has lost seven spots.

The car is running good. Then, as Labonte heads out of turn four, driver Dick Trickle and his car spin down the front stretch, taking Labonte with them. The rear of #94 swerves left than right as Labonte fights to take control of the car, but he can't. By the time he has gained control of the vehicle, Terry finds himself facing into traffic. Thankfully he also finds himself near the entrance to pit road, and he drives his damaged vehicle into the pits. There the team changes the tires and puts gas in the car. The rear left quarterpanel is severely damaged. Using hammers and metal bars, they beat the twisted sheet metal away from the wheel.

Labonte returns to the track a lap down. NASCAR penalized him one lap because he entered the pits before they were officially opened. Despite their work to keep the car in the race, the team knows it will be tough to make up a lap at Pocono.

"When you lose a lap here, you've got a long day for ya," Livengood says.

Labonte motors his way through the pack, passing many of the same cars he had passed before his earlier pit stop and the accident. He makes it to the top portion of the field by lap 70. Soon after getting there, Hut Stricklin's Raybestos Buick spins coming out of turn four, collecting Richard Petty's STP Pontiac, Bobby Hillin in the Mello Yello Pontiac, Ricky Rudd in the Tide Chevrolet, Alan Kulwicki in the Hooters Ford and Darrell Waltrip in the Western Auto Chevrolet. Cars spin wildly in front of Labonte's Oldsmobile. Quickly he ducks to the inside near the wall separating the track from the pits, and continues through a cloud of billowing white tire smoke to the front. Suddenly, it looks like Labonte will get his lap back after all. In an instant drivers who thought they had a good chance to win are eliminated from the race. The team is up and cheering on top of the pit wall.

"Good driving Terry," Dewey says. "Was there a full moon last night?"

"I can't believe that 43's still running," Terry replies. "The last time I saw him he looked like he was twenty feet in the air."

"He was," says Culler.

Thanks to his driving skills, Labonte, for a moment, is the last car on the lead lap. He has passed the leaders caught in the accident. However, he is in front of the leaders, and their much more powerful cars, at the restart. What he needs is a quick caution; it doesn't come. He continues running between eleventh and sixteenth for most of the race, and is in fifteenth when it starts to rain. After about a two-hour delay, NASCAR officials restart the race only to have it rain again. The 200-lap event is halted at 179 with Rusty Wallace leading, just short of running out of fuel. Labonte finishes fifteenth. The finish is good enough to keep him in twenty-sixth place in the points race.

eighteen

Rooked

"That's about as close as we can come to wreckin'."
Terry Labonte

Outside of the main gate of the Talladega Superspeedway sits the International Motorsports Hall of Fame and Museum. The round buildings of the museum store the remains of some of the sport's most devastating accidents. Next to the wrecks are a handful of the fastest American machines on record.

Terry Labonte knew when the team got to Talladega for the July running of the Diehard 500, there would be no speed records set by the Hagan-owned team. In fact, making the race at all concerned him. His beliefs weren't just bad vibes, they were based on the results of testing sessions behind the wheel of the car he would have to drive at the world's fastest speedway. The car was a clunker in every sense of the word.

Technically the car brought to Talladega, a five-hour drive from Charlotte, was the team's back-up superspeedway car. The one Labonte preferred was wrecked beyond repair in a multi-car crash at this same speedway in May and had not been replaced. Labonte was uncomfortable with the car they brought to Talladega, but there were no other options. Perhaps another one could be built next year, but for the time being this was it. Too bad they couldn't get rid of the restrictor plates—that would give them an advantage.

As at Daytona, the restrictor plates introduced in 1987 by NASCAR would serve to keep the speed of the cars at Talladega down to an acceptable level. Since first being used, the size of the plates had been adjusted by NASCAR four times to the current 7/8 of an inch opening. The plates are placed between the carburetor and the exhaust manifold to control how much air mixes with the fuel and a result is less horsepower. Restrictor plate engines produce dramatically less horses than the roughly 670 to 680 hp produced by the unrestricted engines. Though NASCAR insists the use of the plates increases safety by decreasing speeds, drivers complain the plates take away their ability to pass, causing the cars to run together and making accidents more frequent.

Before the Diehard 500, NASCAR announced another equipment change. Rear spoilers would have to be at a minimum angle of 35 degrees. NASCAR also said before the weekend's events got underway that the inspections of the spoilers would be tougher and that the cars would be inspected immediately following the race as well as before the cars went out onto the track. Any car found with a spoiler bent at an angle less than 35 degrees would be penalized.

Located about forty miles east of Birmingham, Alabama, Talladega Superspeedway occupies a large piece of real estate just off Interstate 20. Construction started on the superspeedway in 1968 with a price tag of $4 million. The first race was held there in 1969. With both front and back stretches extending over 4,000 feet and turns banked at 33 degrees, the track has had its share of closed-course speed records. In fact, former Sunoco-sponsored driver Mark Donohue pushed his Porsche over 221 mph at Talladega in 1975. Over the years the speedway has been the site of many first career wins for drivers, and has gained a reputation for upset winners.

Terry knew what he was talking about when it came to Talladega. He won the July event in 1989, and has consistently placed in the top five there. He knew what was needed to run with the front of the pack, and he felt the team didn't have it. Even before the team loaded the car in Thomasville for the trip to Talladega, Terry expected that it was going to be tough to qualify well.

After the first qualifying session on Thursday, Labonte was sitting in thirty-first place. Sterling Marlin captured the pole with a blistering 192.085 mph lap around the 2.66-miles-long speedway. Labonte decided Friday morning to go out and requalify. When it was over, he had slipped to thirty-fifth starting position in a forty-one-car field. His qualifying time was more than six mph slower than Marlin's.

Early Saturday morning, Labonte climbed into the cockpit and secured his safety harness to start his first practice session of the day. He reached for the power switch, then for the ignition, and the motor responded.

Labonte sat at the end of pit road, engine idling, waiting for another car to come around the track that he could draft with. A moment later the fluorescent orange and white No. 10 Chevy Lumina of Derrike Cope came out of turn four heading for the front stretch. Labonte eased out onto the track apron and tailed Cope around the track. The two, with a little more than a few feet between them, traveled around the track for a couple laps. Cope, with only two career wins in his six years on the circuit, had a car as slow as Labonte's and would start the race the next day in thirty-seventh. Together, Cope and Labonte created a slow draft.

"The car's running slow," Labonte said when he returned to the garage. "We're just about even with the 10. Hell, I couldn't even hit him."

Practicing before the support race, Labonte experienced similar problems trying to keep up with rookie driver Ted Musgrave. Trailing behind Musgrave aggravated Labonte. Musgrave's team only had a handful of cars, and early in the season had to sit out practice sessions fearing their engine would blow. Labonte had trouble swallowing the fact that Musgrave was running a motor worth a quarter of the one he had in the #94, yet it was Labonte who could not keep up. Musgrave had qualified ahead of Labonte, and was better during the practice.

Labonte returned to the garage and had Kelly Hunt and Bryan Robertson change the rear springs. Herb Hupperich was atop the transporter tracking times. Waiting for the adjustments to be made Terry asked, "Herb, any cars running out there?"

"Yeah," Herb replied.

"Any I can run with?" questioned Labonte with a touch of sarcasm and frustration.

The team had exhausted every possible option to make the car go faster, without success. It wasn't handling poorly, it just wasn't fast enough to tame Talladega. For the first time all season teammates Hunt and Robertson were able to take a lunch break without worrying about getting back to the car. They had done all they could. There was nothing to do but wait for the next practice a few hours away.

While Hunt and Robertson headed for the transporter, Barry Dodson, crew chief of the Team III Pontiac, walked over to Labonte standing in the garage. His driver, Dick Trickle, had qualified twenty-fourth.

"There are three groups out there," Dodson said. "There's a front group, then a second group, including us, and a bunch even slower than us."

"I believe we're in that third group," Labonte responded.

With a half-hour remaining in the last practice session before the race, Labonte strapped himself in and set out for the track. Livengood worried there may be a problem with the engine in the car; he suspected a bad cylinder. After a few laps, Labonte returned to the garage. Instead of pulling into the garage, he parked near the transporter. Bryan jacked up the right side of the car and took off the front wheel. Dewey lifted the radiator cap allowing the excess water to drain from the engine.

Hupperich, standing near the car, took a cigar from his pocket and lit it. He hadn't smoked a cigar all season, only chewed them, and his actions caught the attention of his teammates.

"Now I know why I don't smoke," he said choking on his cigar smoke. "I'm not smoking," he added. "I'm just smellin', there's a difference."

Wearing protective arm covering, Dewey reached in the wheel well and removed the spark plug from the suspect cylinder. Using a magnifying glass, he inspected the plug for signs of a problem. The plug appeared fine. The engine was to stay in the car.

As expected for Alabama in July, the weather was hot, very hot, and sticky on race day. Some drivers would use cool-suits for the race. Cool-suits pump chilled water through a plastic membrane worn under the uniform. Labonte would not be one of those drivers. For one, he didn't own a cool-suit; and two, his experiences with them had not been favorable.

"The first time I used one was during the 1984 or 1985 season when they first came out," he said, "and it broke. I took it off and threw it out the window during a pit stop."

Instead he would rely on an air cooler for his helmet to stay cool during the race. Using the air cooler meant that Terry would have to switch from the open-faced helmet he had been using for the first half of the season. The air cooler requires the use of a full-faced helmet, considered safer, and works by circulating air through a hose that runs through an ice-filled chest and into the helmet.

Because of the stepped up inspection process, it took much longer than usual for the cars to move through the procedure. While the advance team worked to get the car ready, there was some concern over the whereabouts of the race day crew members. They were scheduled to have landed an hour earlier, but with race time nearing they were nowhere to be found. Their chartered plane was circling the area, waiting for the skies to clear.

Since the race day crew was running behind, Hunt turned to former teammate Steve Wilson for help. Before leaving the team to work the Stavola Brothers Snickers Buick, Wilson was partly responsible for setting up the Hagan pit area and knew where everything was in the pit box. Hunt asked Wilson if he would help set up the Hagan pits until the race day crew could get there. He said yes without hesitation. The race day crew did finally arrive after an hour and a half delay.

By the time Dewey finished the final motor checks and the team pushed the car to inspections, they were the last in line. NASCAR, suspecting that teams were violating the spoiler and body height rules, was paying much more attention to fine details this time out. The suspicions were correct. In getting Labonte's car ready, the crew had stuck bars of soap covered with duct tape under the front springs, and then set the front air dam height. When the car was inspected, it passed. A few laps into the race, however, the soap would disintegrate from the pressure of the springs and lower the front of the car an inch or more, making the car faster.

Because they got to inspections late, they were also the last car on the track, arriving in their starting position moments before Labonte was to start the engine.

Running under the first caution, Labonte radios that when he pits he wants a couple rounds of wedge. The car is loose and he hopes the wedge will solve the problem. Terry pits out of sequence with the leaders on lap 49 for tires and gas. Before pitting he is running about ten seconds behind the leaders, though his lap times are just a few tenths of a second off. However, because of the early pit stop, Terry is down a lap by lap 67.

Thirty laps later, Harry Gant, in the Skoal Oldsmobile, spins in turn three. Labonte has to do everything he can not to get involved.

"That's about as close as we can come to wreckin'," he says during the caution.

"You barely squeaked through. It was so close I thought for sure you scraped the wall," spotter Danny Culler replies.

Coming out of turn two a few laps later, Buddy Baker taps the back of Ernie Irvan's Chevy Lumina, causing Irvan to spin and take a few cars with him. Labonte ducks to the bottom of the track, on the infield. He has almost come to a full stop when Ted Musgrave plows into the rear of his car.

"Danny, did he make it?" yells Dewey, not being able to see the back side of the track from the pits.

"No," says a disheartened Culler.

Terry drives to the pits. When he arrives the team surveys the damage. The front fenders are mangled and the rear quarterpanel near the fuel spout is caved in. More important, the crash ripped out air vents in the rear wheel well. The team beats and rips parts of the front fenders and then sends Labonte back onto the track. The work will have to be done bit by bit so Labonte doesn't lose too much ground. Still under caution, Terry needs to catch up to the pack and then head for the pits again. Four stops later the car is driveable, though the rear trunk lid is being held up with elastic cords.

While still under caution Culler asks about the accident. "Who hit you?"

"It was the 55. I had it cleared, I was in the grass. He hit me right in the ass and spun me around," Labonte answers.

The heat of the day and the extended workout with the consecutive pits has the team ready for a break. As the race continues under caution, most of the team takes timeout and gets some ice cream from a vendor in the pits.

The race finally goes green, but not for long. The caution is out again. Labonte radios to the pits that he is getting extremely hot and his feet are burning. The damaged area in the rear wheel well is allowing hot fumes, dirt and tire rubber to enter the driver's compartment, making driving almost unbearable for Labonte. He pits and Livengood dumps two cups of water through the window onto his feet. He comes in on the next lap, long enough for Harold to empty a half-bag of ice and about two gallons of water on his sizzling feet. Unfortunately ice cream is out of the question.

Despite the unscheduled pit stops, Labonte is able to stay in the race and captures the twenty-fourth position. When it is over, he drives into the pits.

"Ya didn't have much but ya stayed with it and I appreciate that," Livengood says after the last lap.

Terry heads toward the garage and parks behind the car of Ted Musgrave. When he gets out he starts looking for the rookie, but Musgrave has already returned to his transporter. Labonte walks to his without incident.

NASCAR's increased inspections required that the cars remain in a roped off area until checked again for infractions. When NASCAR inspectors reached the Sunoco Oldsmobile, they lifted the hood to make sure the restrictor plate remained. With the hood up, the scent of Irish Spring soap was evident, remnants from the blocks in the springs at the start of the race. If the inspectors smelled the soap, they did nothing about it. Labonte's performance was not significantly better because of the infraction so why bother.

"I had it missed. The 55 just drilled me right in the ass," Labonte says. "I was off the track and all of a sudden bam. The car wasn't great . . . we just wanted to try and salvage what we could and get the hell out of here."

nineteen

The Reality of It All

"We feel now that these elements are starting to mesh."
Billy Hagan

Death is as much a part of racing as tires and gasoline. Drivers accept the fact and move on. Just about everyone of them has been involved in a terrible accident that has made them re-evaluate their careers. Most return to the cockpit, forcing the thought of death to the deep recesses of their minds. But with each new fatality, or near miss, the danger seeps back into their consciousness. Whether a built in defense mechanism or the nature of the high speed sport, there is no long, drawn out period of public mourning when a brother dies. Races aren't cancelled, no pre-race memorials are held, just a funeral and the season continues.

Death behind the wheel was the furthest thing from Terry Labonte's mind when he prepared for Watkins Glen.

Labonte and the Hagan racing team were confident heading to Watkins Glen the second week of August. Indeed, they considered the 2.48-miles-long road course, snuggled in the mountains of upstate New York, to be their best chance at visiting victory lane.

Labonte's confidence seemed well founded. Seven weeks before he had dominated the Fay's 150 Busch Grand National series event held on the twisting, seven-turn road course. He won the pole and lead all but nine laps of the sixty-two-lap race. The win brought with it $16,525. More important, a Winston Cup test session earlier in the season indicated Labonte was running at speeds near the track record.

Their performance at Sears Point back in June helped build the team's confidence. They would use the same car, Labonte's own. Terry considered the car better suited for Watkins Glen because the track has more right turns than Sonoma.

Labonte had had some success at Watkins Glen previously. His best performance came in 1987 when he won the pole and posted a second place finish. Since then, however, he had not finished in the top five there.

Labonte takes road courses seriously. Early in his career he learned some of the secrets of road racing at the Bob Bondurant School of High Performance Driving. Some thirty other Winston Cup drivers have learned how to approach a road course from Bondurant.

Watkins Glen opened to competitors Thursday, August 8, three days before the running of the Budweiser at The Glen. Unofficially, Labonte was the second fastest car, behind Mark Martin, during the first practice session held Thursday. However, Labonte hadn't been pushing all out during the practice session. Instead, he was trying to get a feel for the radial tires being used on the road course for the first time. Yet, despite the feeling out process, he knew he had turned a few good laps during the session.

Qualifying was to start at 1 p.m., Friday. As the teams prepared their cars to qualify, rain began to fall. The inclement weather continued for hours, pushing qualifying deeper and deeper into the afternoon, nearly to the brink of cancellation. The thought of qualifying being cancelled was a nightmare for Labonte. He considered the pole essential to winning the race, and he felt he could capture it. If qualifying was not held, NASCAR would revert to the point standings to set the qualifying order. That system would put him in twenty-third starting position.

Four and a half hours after qualifying was scheduled to have begun, the rain stopped and the track dried. Terry was the twenty-fifth car in line to qualify. The team was confident, unlike any time during this season. Once the twenty-fourth qualifier pulled out of pit road, Labonte climbed into his car and went through his pre-race procedure as team members pushed the car to the end of pit road. There, under overcast skies, he started the car and waited for the signal from NASCAR to go.

Unlike other races, the car this time contained a qualifying motor. Livengood had built it for the race at Labonte's request. The requirements: one fast lap, that's all Labonte needed. The rest of the car was set up pretty much the way it would be for the actual race.

Drivers approach road courses much differently than the ovals. Instead of being concerned with pure speed necessary for success on the ovals, road course drivers have to look at the total picture, each turn is as important as the next. As hard as it is to get a car set up perfect for a track, it may be harder for a road course. Drivers may find the car handles real well in the turns, but a little off in the straights. The team felt they had Labonte's car set up correctly for Watkins Glen.

Labonte sat waiting, engine idling. Just then the sun broke from the clouds, lighting the speedway. "Maybe this means something," race committee chairman Bud Campbell said to his wife Marilyn as Labonte headed out of pit road under the sun.

Labonte completed his qualifying run in a track-record 1:11.851, at a speed of 121.652 mph. NASCAR's clocks had Labonte going 175 mph down the back stretch, exceeding the record there for Winston Cup cars, and going 3 miles per hour faster than anyone else. As he raced down the front straight to end his near perfect lap a puff of blue smoke came from the rear of his car, signalling trouble with the engine. But the engine had held for the run.

Soon after Labonte turned the engine off, the sun moved back behind the clouds. Qualifying was not yet over, and Labonte worried his time would be bumped. He knew that several other fast teams had yet to have their turn at the track. Until it was over, Labonte would remain serious.

When the last of the Winston Cup cars completed qualifying, Labonte grinned ear-to-ear. The seriousness was gone, he was on the pole with a record setting time, ending a streak of ninety-six races without a pole.

"It was a good lap," Labonte said afterwards. "I knew I could run a good one because I ran a pretty fast lap on Thursday and I wasn't really trying. I didn't mess up qualifying, which is unusual for me."

Joking with reporters, Labonte said the pole was important because his standings as a road racer had slipped. While the humor could be heard in his voice, the comment also contained a touch of sincerity. Despite his record at Riverside, albeit three years back, the press had largely ignored him. But not without good reason. Since the Winston Cup cars had returned to Watkins Glen in 1986, Ricky Rudd and Rusty Wallace had won all but one race. The exception was the 1986 running, which went to the late Tim Richmond. As a result, the media focused on both Rudd and Wallace at Sonoma and The Glen, limiting Labonte to mentions with the also rans.

The pole win instilled a desperately needed boost of confidence in Labonte and the rest of the Billy Hagan-owned team. For once, they started to work together. Some of the barriers between the driver and the team were coming down. And they could walk through the garages with some spring in their step. Week after week they suffered through freak accidents and failed parts. However, this week Hagan's entry mattered to the rest of the field. Labonte was the man to beat.

Winning the pole also increased the media's interest in Labonte. Previously, reporters' visits to the Hagan transporter were infrequent. Now, with Labonte sitting on the back step, the transporter became a regular stop.

"We started out the year with a new driver, a new crew chief and a new type of car, front steer," went Hagan's often heard litany. But after Labonte's lap he had a new ending that he could say with conviction. "We feel now that these elements are starting to mesh."

Hagan was hopeful that the pole would bring other benefits. Already he could see his team reacted well to being competitive. "Knowing you can win is 80 percent of it. Terry's walking around with his chest out and that's most important," Hagan said.

However, he also hoped that the pole, the season's first for Oldsmobile, would help him secure another deal with the manufacturer. Oldsmobile representatives had officially notified Hagan that next season the company was cutting back its race team support and his team was being trimmed from the program. The pole qualified Labonte for the Busch Clash next season. Oldsmobile, Hagan believed, wouldn't want to be the only manufacturer absent from the Clash and might be willing to strike a deal.

"I know one Mississippi boy who's happy about it," said Hupperich when asked about the pole Saturday morning.

Labonte practiced Saturday morning and watched the support race with Hagan later in the afternoon. During the support race, two NASCAR inspectors came to Hagan's transporter to test the engine Labonte used to qualify. In the rear of the transporter, Livengood stripped the engine down to the block for the inspectors to run their tests. The motor passed, although, done in the back of the trailer the process left room for controversy. Who's to know if there was something wrong? Afternoon practice was short to make sure there was enough time for a series of races to follow. Hagan raced in the final event of the day, an IMSA Firestone Firehawk series race, finishing eleventh.

For the first time this season, Labonte was comfortable with his car. During practice the team toyed with routine items, such as testing to see if the car worked better with new tires, "stickers," or scuffs. There was no slinging springs at The Glen, they had the car dialed in. In all, it was a successful session.

The team was taking no chances here. To avoid the race day crew from being delayed by the weather, they arrived on Saturday night instead of Sunday morning as had been the norm. They couldn't afford such a slip up with so much riding on this race.

The team returned to the track Sunday morning and immediately began to prepare for the race. The garage areas at Watkins Glen are awkward, designed for a much smaller race car than Winston Cup offered. To fit two cars in a stall the cars had to be parked at an angle, with the rear of both cars almost touching. While the team worked on the car, Hagan and members of the Sunoco race committee lingered around the garage, much happier than at anytime thus far in the season.

Off to the side, Paul Mecca stood near a small fence between the stalls watching Livengood adjust the engine valves as he did before every race. Jesse Coke was in the back of the car checking the rear end gear. Sunoco race committee member Harold Vaughn also looked on as the team worked and after a few minutes walked over to Mecca.

"Why are they doing that? Could this be where they're screwing up?" Vaughn said within earshot of the team. Vaughn couldn't understand why the team would take most of the car apart before a race even though the car was fast enough to win the pole. "Why not just cover the car up after qualifying and leave it alone?" he asked.

Mecca quickly pulled Vaughn away and explained that what the team was doing was standard operating procedure. "All the teams did it week in and week out," said Mecca, pointing to the nearby stalls. Vaughn didn't seem to believe Mecca's explanation and later asked the same question of Hagan and Labonte. He received similar responses. Labonte said the process was a way to make your own luck, that if the guys went looking for something they might be more apt to find it now rather than to have the part fail during the race.

It was questions like Vaughn's that irked Labonte, and the other team members. The committee set-up was ineffective to the point that he hoped his next sponsor did not have a race committee like Sun's. "There are like four or five guys who know what's going on, and the rest are neophytes. For my next sponsor I'm gonna ask, 'you got a race committee?' If they say no, I'll say, 'I believe we can do business.'"

A couple of hours before the race, Terry and Mecca made an appearance at a small hospitality tent set up overlooking the raceway. After signing autographs, Labonte fielded questions from the Sunoco employees and guests. His toughest competitor? Mark Martin. Rusty Wallace and Ricky Rudd would also be competition he said.

"It's tough to pass here," he said responding to another. "You've got to be quite a bit faster and then out brake them."

A little more than a half-hour later Labonte ended his stay and walked through the infield to the garage. As he did, a man with a young boy asked for a picture. He stopped long enough for the father to snap a quick photo of the kid under his arm. Continuing on, he stumbled across a penny imbedded in the dirt, heads up. "Maybe that'll be a lucky penny," he said reaching for the coin.

Dewey selected pit No. 38, a spot at the end of pit road near an opening. He chose the pit for two reasons. Being at the end of pit row would keep Labonte out of the crowd down near the front of the stretch. Pitting near an opening assured that the team would not get blocked in.

The team is unusually tense. Along with the pole comes a shot at the Unocal Challenge, a money fund that rewards a driver who wins a race from the pole. The kitty was up to $90,000. They were sure that they would be watched carefully during the race. The last thing Unocal wanted to do was pay $90,000 to a team sponsored by a rival oil company. Unocal would find news stories of the Sunoco team winning the Unocal Challenge embarrassing, they said, and Unocal would pressure NASCAR to find fault with Hagan's team.

"I know one thing, we sure as hell got to be on our toes," said Billy Siler shortly before the start of the race. The other team members felt the same way. Everyone was afraid NASCAR officials would resort to minor infractions that were normally overlooked as a way to end Labonte's day, and avoid upsetting Unocal.

More important, this was the team's biggest day of the season. For some, including Labonte, it was their first legitimate chance at winning in a couple of years. Each step of preparation was done with a little more care. Even the race day banter took on a little more serious edge. Though the team members were still managing to enjoy themselves, Livengood's reminders to be extra careful were keeping them on their toes.

With a few moments to spare before having to go out to the track, team members congregated around the tail of the transporter. Some ate, others just talked.

Billy Hagan walked over to the group, and, with his cane propped against his knee, took out a roll of money he had in his pocket. He handed each team member a $100 bill, a bonus for winning the pole, and thanked them. They were surprised with the offering, yet appreciative. Tucking the cash away, the team headed for the pits.

During two warm-up laps around the course, Labonte jerks the car right and left to heat the tires. Nearing the end of the second lap, Doyle Ford waves the green flag starting the race. Labonte barrels down the front stretch and dives into turn one. Quickly, his lead spreads to six car lengths over Mark Martin, and threatens to get even larger. As the two cars race down the front stretch on lap 5, driver J.D. McDuffie drives his Pontiac down the back stretch and into turn five, a sharp right that comes at the end of a long straight. When McDuffie enters the turn, his left front wheel breaks off sending the fifty-two-year-old driver over a grassy area, through a tire wall and into a guardrail, coming to rest on top of the No. 52 Alka Seltzer Pontiac driven by Jimmy Means. Means' car had spun in reaction to McDuffie. Means, able to get out of his car, looks into McDuffie's car and starts to frantically wave for help. An autopsy report would later say death arrived in an instant.

NASCAR stops the race while McDuffie's body is removed from the wreck and the track is prepared. During the break, Labonte and team members sit on the wall near their pits waiting for word about McDuffie. The mood is somber, and while the delay leads them to believe the worst has happened, no one mentions it. From their vantage point near the entrance of the garages they can see there are no ambulances moving. They hear no sirens signalling the injured being rushed to medical attention. Instead, NASCAR officials are shuttled to the crash site, with bits and pieces of news making it back to the teams. Someone reports that safety crews have covered the car with a blue tarp, usually a sign of death.

McDuffie was liked by all on the circuit. A burly guy with a cigar, he represented what the sport used to be. Without major sponsorship dollars, McDuffie hauled his car on a twenty-year-old ramp truck to races, occasionally borrowing tires to qualify and taking home any scraps the bigger teams had left over.

Mecca is the first of Hagan's group to hear of the death. He returns to the pits with the news, telling Donnie Crumley first. Crumley, without thinking, turns and tells Labonte. Labonte, visibly upset, moves away. He doesn't want to hear more.

"Donnie, why don't you use your head," Jim Coltrane says. "The man doesn't want to hear that." They begin to argue but just as quickly drop the subject.

An hour and forty-eight minutes after McDuffie's car had come to rest in turn five, NASCAR restarts the race without mention of the terrifying incident. As the drivers pull out of pit road, out of the reach of a radio or television, NASCAR officials report the death of McDuffie, shielding the drivers from McDuffie's fate.

Labonte doesn't allow the death of McDuffie to effect his driving. He charges out and takes a commanding lead. Effortlessly he guides the blue Oldsmobile through the straights and turns of Watkins Glen. Each lap is better than the last as he takes control. It is his race, and for once he has the car to take control. Martin, sitting a distant second, is running for position only. He radios back to his pits that he isn't going to risk wrecking his machine. He knows that without a mishap, Labonte is unbeatable.

Then, on lap 22, Labonte's bad luck catches up with him. His left rear tire blows out, spinning the car around and taking with it valuable track position. Labonte heads for the pits.

The crew goes to work, changing two tires and gassing the car. It takes a long time for them to complete the work. While they are working another accident occurs, drawing the caution. "Caution's out, hurry up, hurry up," Livengood yells as the pace car enters the front stretch.

"Damn it," Labonte says in anger. If the pace car passes him while he was in the pits, he will go a lap down. Hunt drops the jack and Labonte speeds through the pits, beating the pace car to the flag stand to stay on the lead lap. NASCAR penalizes him for speeding in the pits, and forces Labonte to move to the rear of the pack.

At the restart, Terry races through the pack and within twenty laps he is sitting in sixth place. He squeezes every drop of energy from the car, driving with an abandonment not shown all season. Labonte is aggressively attacking the track trying to get back the position he lost. He floors the gas pedal in the straights and slams the brakes going into the turns. He cuts the turns as sharp as possible, passing slower cars with each lap. The pressure begins to take its toll as the brakes start to give out on lap 36.

"I'm outta f___ in' brakes," he yells. The brakes are boiling hot from the strain of trying to stop a 3,500-pound car. Labonte pushes the car into the corners, faster than normal, and jams on the brakes. A caution period helps cool the brakes, and at the halfway point in the 90-lap event Terry is running ninth.

When Labonte heads out of turn five, he notices the engine seems to misfire. On the next lap, a valve spring breaks, taking the motor with it. After forty-eight strong laps, Labonte's race and the team's dream of seeing victory lane are over.

"The car was running real good," he says standing steps away from his oil leaking race car. "I thought something was wrong when I came off the turn before. I made it back around the track and it just quit. It's just too bad."

With a wisp of smoke, Labonte's day ends in disappointment. While the remaining cars continue to race, Hagan's dejected crew packs away the pit equipment and leaves the raceway with only the memories of being associated with the pole sitter.

About fifteen miles from the raceway, McDuffie's hodgepodge team parks his old blue truck in the parking lot of a local diner. On top sits the remains of McDuffie's last ride, hidden by a loose fitting tarp. After 653 starts without a win, McDuffie's engine has been silenced.

twenty

Engine One, Two, Three

"Oh my God, boys we got serious trouble."
Dewey Livengood

Three races under the leadership of Livengood and the team was showing improvement, if not in pure on-track statistics, in the way they worked together. The team was beginning to come together after spending most of the season splintered into groups. The relationships between the team and its leaders were also improving.

Herb Hupperich's relationship with those who worked under him had changed slightly for the better. Most of the team members still had trouble with his involvement with the mechanical side of the business, though they were able to be cordial around Hupperich. Hupperich was realizing that his life or death oil rig approach to management may have been acceptable on the high seas, but in racing it wasn't.

Around the garages at Michigan International Speedway, the new-found team togetherness was clearly evident. The
guys were joking and working side-by-side with less tension than
at any point during the season. That, despite, Labonte's twenty-
ninth place first round qualifying performance for the Champion Spark Plug 400.

The season had turned. Labonte had accomplished one
of the goals set for the team after their slump, capturing a pole
position. The first position also brought with it good news for
next season—entry into the Busch Clash.

"Now we have to finish races without any accidents or
malfunctions," said Hupperich early Saturday morning.

In practice before qualifying, and after, Labonte was satisfied with the strength of the engine, though the car was pushing badly. When he went into the turns, the car wanted to keep
going straight. As a result, even with the engine performing correctly, he wasn't able to go as fast as he wanted.

"Terry said if we could get rid of the push it would be a
bad mother," Hupperich said as Kelly Hunt, Bryan Robertson
and Jesse Coke worked to find the problem causing the push.
Like Watkins Glen, the garages at MIS are better suited for
smaller cars. Checking for alignment problems in the tight quarters is difficult, so the car had been pushed to an open garage
with a flat cement floor. Using string and a pair of jack stands
the team checked the alignment and found some areas that
needed adjustment.

In addition to the push, the team wasn't using a qualifying motor for this race. Starting the season without one, the
team had gradually phased a qualifying motor into the process.
Unfortunately, Labonte's flat out qualifying lap at Watkins Glen
that won him the pole had killed the motor. It couldn't be rebuilt
in time for Michigan a week later. Even with the qualifying
motor, some questioned whether Labonte's qualifying times
would be better. He had put together some good practice times in
the past only to come up with a substandard qualifying effort.

Though he would then complain about the car, some team members wondered if he just wasn't freezing up during qualifying. Labonte often said he hated the process. He would have liked NASCAR to track practice laps instead. He couldn't understand why sometimes he would do well in practice only to bust when the chips were down.

By mid-morning the team isolated the problem causing the push and Labonte was on the track practicing. Overcast skies had caused the temperature to drop since the day before, making the cars a bit faster than during the first round. Second round qualifying would start at 11 a.m. An hour into practice, Labonte turned a 42.26 second lap around the two-mile track, a little more than 170 mph. The lap was his fastest since they had unloaded the car a few days before.

Initially, Labonte was going to stand on his time. However, by 10:30 a.m., he and Livengood were wavering. Labonte wasn't the only one to have picked up speed from the day before. With a half-hour of practice remaining, they mounted new tires and Livengood prepared the engine for a qualifying run. The water was drained from the radiator and cool water added to bring the engine temperature down. Livengood installed the flat-bladed fan and Hunt placed duct tape over the brake vents to reduce drag. During the race, the brake vents would be open to cool the brake rotors when under strain. Here, however, the brake vents as well as the radiator duct would suck in air that would slow the car a tick. Labonte would only be on the track for a lap or two, so they didn't risk having the car overheating.

Labonte went out onto the track to simulate qualifying. One lap to get the car up to speed, the other one for position. When the simulated event was over, their stopwatches had recorded a lap of 42.08 seconds or somewhere above 171 mph. Labonte felt good about the lap, though he was not confident he could do it again. And he couldn't. His second round attempt took 42.134 seconds, slower than practice, but good enough to move up to twenty-fifth starting position.

After qualifying was over, the crew returned with the car to the garage. They were relaxed as they went about preparing the car for practice later in the afternoon. Qualifying had been successful with Labonte moving up instead of down as had been the case in other second round attempts. They made the right choice in going back out as Labonte would have slipped to thirty-eighth had he not. To a team measuring success in small steps so far, it was a good day.

Rain moved in for the start of the support race. Meanwhile, team members gathered around the front of the car in the garage. For about an hour, Livengood, Hunt, Robertson, Coke and Hupperich stood around the engine compartment talking racing and working on the engine. Hunt and Livengood traded race track tales as the others listened. They had both witnessed a lot in their years at the track, and it seemed like a duel. The victory would go to the one with the best story. While they talked, Livengood slowly loosened the four bolts holding the Oberg oil filter together. Lifting the top of the filter off, Livengood noticed metal particles mixed in with the lubricant. He picked up some of the fluid between his fingers. He did not like what he felt. The duel was over.

"Oh my God, boys we got serious trouble," he said swirling his fingers through the mixture. Metal in oil is a sign that a bearing has started to disintegrate. Further wear could cause the engine to blow. It was unlikely the engine would make it through the race, let alone the next practice. "We won't have to worry about changing the transmission, we got to change the whole motor," he said.

Immediately, they started the process of removing the engine. While Hupperich, Hunt, Robertson, Coke, Billy Siler and Harold Hughes worked to remove the bad motor, Livengood sat in the truck preparing one of the two backup motors kept on the truck.

The motors are Livengood's babies. He had tweaked, torqued and tested each one dozens of times before they were put on the truck as backups. He and the guys in the engine room devoted hours upon hours of their time to grooming these two engines and now he had to choose which of the two to use. Yet, earlier in the week he had already made the decision that these would be his second and third string. His first choice, now choking on metal bits, was in the car. They had done this dozens of times before, and the process went smoothly. One difference, not lost on Hagan, was Hupperich's role. Normally Herb did little actual work on the cars, but he was being extra helpful at Michigan.

"He's trying to keep his job," joked Hagan upon seeing Hupperich in the thick of things. In the past, he had stood by as team members did the mechanical work. At Michigan, he was all over the place.

"Terry's going to be upside down when he sees this, isn't he," Robertson said to Hupperich. Labonte had walked away after practice to talk to his brother and his father parked on the other side of the garages.

"Well, better now than tomorrow morning or during the race," Hupperich said.

The engine change was complete by the time the support race was finished. Terry climbed into the car and fired the engine. Before putting the motor through some tests, he glided around the track for nearly ten laps to break in the motor. Not long after, practice was over. The backup engine performed well, but not as well as the engine Terry qualified with.

"Car's pretty good, " Labonte said returning to the garage. "But, it sure didn't run like that other engine. It looks like it's running about 100 rpms slower at the start/finish line."

"Well, I know that, but there ain't nothing we can do about that now is there," Hupperich said over the radio.

The car was rolled back into the garage where preparations began for the next day. Livengood lifted the hood to make room for a fan to cool the engine. When he looked down at the hot engine, water was spurting from the radiator hose. He slammed his radio headset and grabbed a hose wrench. The large nut holding the hose in place turned effortlessly, it hadn't been tightened before practice. Immediately, as if they had practiced before, all the team members looked to the top of the trailer where Hupperich was clocking cars still on the track. Hupperich looked down, unaware he was in trouble.

Luckily Labonte was only on the track for a short time. Yet, there was still a chance that some damage could have been done to the motor. Team members pushed the car out of the garage to drain what water remained. As they did, Hupperich came down from the truck, oblivious to what had happened. Livengood was furious and let Hupperich know it. Hagan, who had watched the episode unfold, suggested Hupperich stay back from the car while Livengood surveyed the situation.

"The engine got hot," Siler said. "Not as hot as Dewey, though."

They decided to stay with the motor in the car. Labonte hadn't been out long and it wasn't as if all the water had leaked out. After covering the car, the team returned to their hotel for the evening. While the rest of the team grabbed fast food dinners and went to bed, Livengood worried about the motor in the car. It hadn't been that hot, but why take the risk? He wanted to change the motor as soon as the team got to the track Sunday morning. Only this time, he would do most of the work himself.

Changing the motor would take a large chunk of time out of the team's pre-race schedule, but Livengood knew it had to be done. Livengood, essentially, was making his own luck, something Labonte had eluded to earlier in the season when trying to explain the pre-race procedure to a Sunoco race committee member. If he changed the motor, he removed the risk that if some damage had been done the day before it would show up early in the race. If they didn't change motors and the engine blew, Livengood would be to blame. He was, however, sacrificing speed by installing what was his third choice of a power plant for Labonte's ride.

While the team changed the motor, Hupperich set up the pits, another job he did not do on a regular basis. This weekend he had his hands everywhere, including "some places where they shouldn't have," he joked later. The motor mishap embarrassed and angered him. He, as much as anyone, wanted to win. He wanted the team to do well. With each poor performance he knew Hagan was in for more trouble from the folks at Sunoco. That trouble would eventually trickle down to him. "If you do a lot of work, it makes the winning that much better," Hupperich said.

By the time the race started some of the hostilities had settled down, though Livengood still would not speak to Hupperich. It was because of Hupperich that Labonte would have to start the race in an untested engine, and it was because of Hupperich that Livengood and the rest of the team had to spend the morning installing the new motor. Livengood was not happy to say the least.

A week had gone by since J.D. McDuffie died in the wreck at Watkins Glen. Although the event was fresh in the minds of many of the drivers, it's not spoken about. The only outward signs of the tragedy are the placards at the refreshment stands saying the proceeds would go to McDuffie's family, and the small black stickers on each of the cars containing McDuffie's car number. McDuffie has not been forgotten, he is just being remembered quietly as is the custom in racing.

"Like someone was saying, J.D. will be riding with the winner, Sunday," Hupperich said standing away from Labonte.

The race itself is uneventful for the Hagan team. Labonte starts twenty-fifth and runs consistently in the same place for most of the race. At one point he is racing as high as fourteenth, but the car is loose the whole race making it impossible to get any higher. With each pit stop, the crew tries to tighten the car up with little success.

Dale Jarrett wins the race in exciting fashion, beating Davey Allison in a photo finish. It is Jarrett's first career win. Labonte has his own photo finish trying to pass Ted Musgrave;

he fails. He finishes in seventeenth, two laps down. Labonte's younger brother, Bobby, finishes thirty-eighth, completing only 38 of the scheduled 200 laps.

"This was our third motor," Labonte says after the race. "It was the backup for our backup. I wish I could have had that first motor in the car. It was stout and I felt real confident with it. We'll just have to give it another shot next week at Bristol and work for better."

twenty-one

Saturday Night Racing

"It's just not as much fun."
Bud Campbell

George "Bud" Campbell really enjoyed professional stock car racing before the 1991 season started. A season ago, he and his wife traveled around the country to fourteen of the twenty-nine races on the Winston Cup schedule. It was through that dedication to the sport that the couple became friendly, perhaps even close, with team owner Billy Hagan and team manager Herb Hupperich. Hagan and Hupperich provided a majority of their passes to the raceway.

However, by late August, eight months into his reign as chairman of the Sunoco racing committee, the sport had taken on a whole new perspective. He still enjoyed racing, but the demands involved had dimmed its luster. No longer was it as enjoyable as it had been the year before when he and his wife could attend the races as fans. Now, when they were at the track, he had to be concerned with how things were being done on the team and how could they be better?

The racing committee up to this point could best be characterized as frustrated. After nineteen races, the team languished in twenty-third position overall. Talk of winning the points championship had long been laid to rest, and finishing in the top ten was virtually out of the question. The best they could hope for was ending the season in the top twenty, which would deliver some monetary bonuses from Winston at season's end. As the team sank deeper in the Winston Cup standings, the tension level on the committee went up. They wanted results, now.

There was, however, a glimmer of improvement in the team's performance since Dewey Livengood replaced Steve Loyd as crew chief. Yet, the team still struggled when qualifying and was plagued with freak problems, be it engine failure or bad tires.

For Campbell, the most minor conversations eventually turned to racing business. And keeping the racing committee moving forward was becoming problematic. Each committee member had his own idea on how Hagan should be dealt with and what was wrong with the team. In addition to the racing committee, weighing heavy on Campbell's mind were ongoing meetings and discussions dealing with the future of Sun Refining and Marketing. Campbell, and several other executives, had been asked for recommendations to be considered when the company underwent extensive streamlining in September. His deadline was days away when the team headed to Bristol International Raceway for the Budweiser 500, the season's first Saturday night race.

"It's just not as much fun," Campbell said standing in the infield at Bristol, hours before the race would start.

Throughout the season, Campbell had given Hagan the benefit of the doubt. When things didn't go well at the beginning of the year, Campbell gave the team seven races before he would start to comment on the performance. When the race committee received word that Hagan was behind on some of his bills, Campbell took Hagan's explanation for the problems. In many cases, Campbell was alone in his thinking. It's not his style to browbeat people. Coming down hard on the team would only make things harder, he reasoned. He preferred to encourage them instead. Others on the committee wanted a tougher stance from the chairman.

Labonte's qualifying effort for the race didn't help matters any. In practice Friday afternoon, Labonte was running laps between 16.85 and 16.90 seconds. In qualifying, Terry forced Hagan's Oldsmobile around the high banks of Bristol in 16.834 seconds for twenty-eighth position. Only thirty-three cars were to start the race.

The top cars in the field were running two to three-tenths of a second faster, a lot considering the half-mile length of Bristol. His car also had a bad vibration, which was traced back to a bad driveshaft. Ironically, Bill Elliott won the pole using an old rear-steer car.

With the last practice session on Friday over, Livengood and Labonte sat on the tailgate of the rental truck which substituted for the transporter in the infield of Bristol. Hupperich and the rest of the team filled in around the two. Second round qualifying was scheduled for 1 p.m., on Saturday, when the track temperatures would be at their peak. To make any significant move in the starting grid, Labonte needed to be a half-second faster. On a hot track that was unlikely, although standing on their time could push them further back.

"We ain't gonna pick up no half-second," Terry said, a touch of anger in his words.

Before anyone could respond, four-time champion Dale Earnhardt squeezed between two members. "I'll tell you guys what," he said. "You guys should go and have a couple a beers before you make a decision. You shouldn't make these kinds of decisions on an empty stomach." He then walked off.

"So I should tell Billy that the car's loose going into the turn," Hupperich asked. He would have to report Labonte's qualifying results to Hagan, who was off racing somewhere else.

"No, tell him I screwed up. Tell him I've had enough," he said wiping a hand across his forehead. "Tell him to find somebody else."

Labonte, like the race committee, was frustrated and tired of the constant struggle. Again he would start from the back of the pack. Livengood and the remaining team members felt the same way. Week in and week out they were trying their best to give Labonte a good car. Sometimes they did, though most of the time they didn't.

All day Saturday the team worked on the car for the race that night. By the last practice session, the vibration was gone and the car was handling a bit better. Moreover, with the other teams reverting to their race motors, some of the speed disadvantage of earlier had been removed.

The lights shining off the short, steep asphalt of Bristol brings racing back to its Saturday night roots. Most stock car drivers, including Labonte, got their start at small raceways around the country racing on Saturday nights. In NASCAR this is about as close to those early days of racing that these drivers get, outside of visiting local short tracks on their weekends off, which they do. Drivers and teams like the Saturday night event because it gives them Sunday off, and also leaves Sunday as a rain date. There's a heightened excitement level watching the cars go around, their brake discs glowing from the heat and sparks flying from tail pipes banging the pavement.

With the sun setting behind the rear grandstand, the race starts. Despite a few spinning cars early, there are no cautions until lap 63.

"What's the deal with the car?" Dewey asks.

"It's okay."

Livengood turns to Billy Siler and shakes his head. After 63 laps, all Labonte can say is the car is okay. Livengood expects a bit more detail from his driver. A moment later it comes.

"The brakes are out. I ain't got no damn brakes," Labonte says. "I can't believe I ain't got no brakes. I've never been to Bristol and not had any brakes."

The team is trying a new braking system designed by Delco Moraine that incorporates anti-lock technology, which in situations of hard braking would help prevent skidding. Terry ran with the system in place at Martinsville and the brakes heated there, too. Throughout their stay in Bristol a Delco Moraine technician constantly worked on the brakes, taking heat readings and suggesting adjustments. When he heard Labonte's complaint, he shook his head and buried his face in his hands.

Following a round of pit stops, the green flag drops again. Labonte is sitting in second, a few lapped cars separating him from race leader Michael Waltrip in the Pennzoil Pontiac. As the cars fall into place under the green, Waltrip's right front tire explodes, sending him into the wall in turn four. Labonte dives under Waltrip to take the lead and go down in the record books as being the 12,000th lead change in the modern era of NASCAR. The first lead change in the modern era, considered the period after 1972 when the schedule was pared to around thirty events annually, came when Richard Petty passed A.J. Foyt on the third lap at Riverside.

Despite a few days of disappointing practice, Labonte held the lead for thirty-four laps, opening a seven-car-length lead at one point. But, on lap 117, one of his tires starts to go flat. Forced to pit under green, Labonte loses a lap that he is unable to regain.

Throughout the race, Labonte and a bunch of other teams struggle with tire problems. A new sealer applied to the track surface sometime in the months leading up to the race causes pebbles to break free and puncture tires. By the end of the race, the team had changed tires eight times because of flats. Yet, when it was all over, Labonte was in ninth place, seven laps off the leader. Alan Kulwicki, himself troubled by flat tires, wins the race.

"I'll tell ya, when I got a clear track [the car] works pretty good," Terry says.

Labonte is pleased with the finish and is in an upbeat mood when getting out of the car. Occasionally, he has been very angry and unapproachable after a race. This time he sits on pit road talking to anyone who stops by and signs autographs with his blistered hands. The race notched his third top ten points race finish of the year.

"I'm not so sure about those anti-lock brakes," Labonte says smiling. "I had my foot to the floor and ran right into the car in front of me."

"We had a lot of flat tires. The car was pretty good. We felt that in the last practice we were pretty good, though we were not right. We had a flat and we thought we were okay and then we had another flat."

A few steps away the car sits, bearing the wounds of a short track race. The front is bashed in from Labonte hitting the rear of another car, the left front tire shows a three-inch-long gash—ready to blow. Another lap and Labonte could have been into the wall. The left front fender is missing, cut away from an earlier accident.

A week later the team picks up its fourth top ten finish, and their best finish of the season with a fifth place in the Southern 500 at Darlington International Speedway. Labonte felt positive going into the race because Livengood had put together a strong engine combination for the track. While qualifying left Labonte in twenty-third at the start, his consistent driving style slowly took him toward the front. Down two laps at one point, Labonte raced back to fifth, and in the process regained one of his laps. Harry Gant took the Darlington crown.

Combined with his ninth place finish at Bristol, Labonte moved up to twenty-first in the Winston Cup points race, his highest position since the second race of the season.

twenty-two

Accepting the Challenge

"There are some people, they'd complain even
if you hung them with a new rope."
Billy Hagan

As the Sun Refining and Marketing Co., prepared to undergo
extensive changes, company president David Knoll was still
keeping his eye on the racing program. In a meeting with Knoll,
Bud Campbell and Geoff Plazer raised the question of offering
Hagan an incentive plan. Knoll agreed the company should back
the offering. It was clear the team's performance was improving
and Knoll believed a bonus might make the difference. He left it
up to Campbell and Plazer to structure it.

After some discussion, Campbell and Plazer offered a
challenge to Billy Hagan. Imagine the season was just starting
with the last race in Bristol, they said. If the team finished the
next ten races in the top ten, based on points accumulated by all
competitors, Hagan would receive a $100,000 bonus. In addition,

Sunoco would pay out $1,000 to every member of the team, including the team secretary. The crew chief and the driver would each be in line for slightly higher amounts.

A caveat in the deal was that if the team accepted the challenge, Hagan could only run thirty-five decals on the car next season, decals that could be worth as much as tens of thousands in post season bonuses. The decal count would be a drop from the season high of fifty-one, and down from the current forty-five to forty-eight. If the team finished eleventh through fourteenth, the deal was worth nothing. Nevertheless, if they finished fifteenth or worse, Hagan would give up an "equitable" amount out of his payout for next season.

Hagan agreed to the proposal, and upped the ante. After talking with Labonte, the two agreed to match Sunoco's contribution making it possible for each team member to get $2,000 when it was all over. Both sides agreed there would be no publicity for the program.

The Sunoco Challenge, as it was called for the rest of the season, was the first time the team had something to shoot for since the start of the season. Once the championship had been out of reach, they had no clear cut target to aim at. They thought week-to-week, not for the long term. Sunoco hadn't set any goals in their original deal with Hagan, outside of a clause requiring Hagan to submit his plans for winning a championship.

"Nobody expected this year to happen," Campbell said. "When we did the deal, everybody expected a giant leap forward. I don't know if [performance clauses] are in every contract, but they will be in the next go-round here."

By the time the team got to Richmond International Raceway for the first Winston Cup race held there under the lights, Sunoco and Hagan were in agreement about the bonus plan. They decided that the team would be told just before the race on Saturday night.

Terry qualified for the race in twentieth position, a mere one thousandth of a second separating him and the twenty-first place qualifier. That sliver of time meant Labonte had a starting position for the race and did not have to worry about second round qualifying. Instead, they could spend their time concentrating on the race set-up.

In practice the car and Labonte were inconsistent. Labonte had complained about this car the last time he drove it. He said there was a problem with the way the body sat on the chassis. Yet, nothing had been done to rectify the problem between races.

"I told them it needed to be fixed, it was never fixed," he said later. "It can be fixed. It's a problem with the body."

With the improvement in the team's performance, Labonte now believed they could be competitive. All they needed were a few new cars and possibly a personnel change here and there. It irritated Labonte when the adjustments he asked for weren't made, especially with the new cars slow in coming. During the season, the team spent a good deal of time repairing some of Hagan's older cars for resale while a brand new chassis sat in the shop waiting to be completed. It was unclear if they would get the new car done by season's end.

Though Labonte couldn't get a new car, the team had new uniforms. This was the second week in which the team would wear work shirts with the Sunoco logo on the back. The shirts were actually their work uniforms with the Sunoco logo sewn on the back. It was something the race committee discussed over and over since the start of the season that had finally been instituted. For once the problem wasn't the team's, the committee was just slow in approving the patch design. Sunoco wanted Hagan's team dressed on par with those on the other major race teams. Some had their sponsor's name embroidered on their jeans, while Hagan's team used regular work uniforms. The uniforms were sufficient, although they paled in comparison to what some better funded teams had.

The uniform change, though a good idea, was prompted somewhat by the team's poor performance. With the team's performance lacking for much of the season, the race committee's attention shifted from on track activities to some of the ancillary items. For its money, Sunoco wanted to project a first class image and that wasn't happening on the track. So committee members spent their time focusing more on incidentals. Once the uniform change was made, some switched their complaints from what the team members wore to how they wore it. Indeed, one committee member got upset because team member Jesse Coke helped push the car through inspections with the tail of his shirt hanging out.

"There are some people, they'd complain even if you hung them with a new rope," said Hagan sitting in the transporter early Saturday morning. "It's nit-picking. If we were in the top ten, we wouldn't be hearing this."

Moments later as Hagan talked to a visitor, Coke walked into the transporter, his shirt tail, again, exposed. Hagan grabbed his arm as he walked by.

"I know you're working but, when you get a minute, tuck in your shirt and they'll get off my back," Hagan said in a soft manner. Coke agreed and continued with his task.

By the last practice Saturday afternoon, the car was shaping up for the race. It was by no means perfect, Labonte complained it was loose.

It is still loose on lap 9 of the race when the first caution flag comes out. Running under caution, Terry radios in. "It's a little loose. Might need to put some wedge in it."

Livengood looks around the pits and pushes his radio microphone away from his mouth in anger. He shakes his hands. "Where's it loose?"

"It's a little bit loose going into one and a little loose coming out."

On lap 57, again under caution, Terry pits for tires. While in the pits, Donnie Crumley adds a round of bite to the rear. Soon after the restart, Labonte begins to move up than suddenly drops back a few spots. Thinking he has a tire going down, he slowed in case he had to pit. Instead, after a couple laps he is confident the tires are fine and again gets the car back up to speed.

By lap 150, Terry is running in eighteenth position. The car isn't handling well and the tires are making it worse. Each set reacts differently to the three-quarter-mile surface. First it is loose, then it is tight. Nothing they do betters the consistency. Not in love with the car before, Labonte truly dislikes it now.

At the 200-lap mark, Terry is nineteenth and a lap off the leader, Davey Allison. Labonte pits under caution during lap 219 and, when Bryan Robertson has a difficult time pulling a piece of rubber out of the right front spring, the pace car completes a lap knocking Labonte still another lap back.

Even with the lost track position during the stop, Labonte is able to work his way up to twentieth position by lap 250. At 350 he is in nineteenth, though now three laps off the pace. The race ends with Labonte four laps down but still in nineteenth place.

When Labonte arrives in the pits he is distressed. The car handled poorly all night and the anger is evident from his expression.

"The car's a piece of shit. Everytime I tell them to fix it they don't," he says when he gets out of the car. "They must think I'm lying." Instead of sitting in the rear of the transporter for a few minutes, Labonte heads right for the lounge. Paul Mecca waits outside for a moment before going in. Part of Mecca's job with the team is gathering post race quotes to report back to the race committee. After a few minutes, Mecca goes in.

"Terry can I get some quotes?" Mecca asks.

"I already told you," Labonte replies. "The car's a piece of shit. We lost a lap in the pits because our spotter didn't tell us where the pace car was."

Mecca waits for Labonte to blow off a little steam then turns his tape recorder on for the official quotes. He knows

Labonte is angry and, though they both understand it is Mecca's job, he doesn't want to push the matter.

"We missed the set-up," Labonte says as he changes out of his racing uniform. "The car wasn't very good. We kept after it all night. The engine was pretty good, we just hung in there and salvaged that finish. I don't think that hurt us very much in the points."

He was right, the finish actually helped him move up two spots in the standings to nineteenth. The team also remained within the top ten for the Sunoco Challenge.

Two weeks after Richmond, the series moved to Dover Downs International Speedway for its second visit of the season. Like Pocono, Dover attracted a large contingent of Sunoco staffers because of its proximity to the company's regional hub. As such, Hagan wanted a strong performance from his team. More important, he was expected back at Campbell's home in Pennsylvania for a meeting following the race. A bad performance would mean the questions would be tougher.

Labonte's qualifying attempt was weak. Having run laps faster in practice, his qualifying lap was good enough for only twenty-first position. There would be no going back out, which left Labonte in twenty-third position after second round qualifying was complete.

"On a scale of one to ten, with ten being happiest, he was a negative ten," said Hupperich about his conversation with Hagan the night before. Hagan had yet to arrive at the speedway, so it fell on Hupperich to inform the owner about the team's performance. Indeed, throughout the season the bad news was always funnelled through Hupperich. He had to hear it, deliver it, and suffer the results.

Early Saturday morning Bryan Robertson is asked if the car is fast.

"We qualified twenty-first, I don't know if I'd say that was a fast car," he said. That might have been the most diplomatic answer the questioner would receive from a team member.

As was the case at many race tracks this season, Labonte could extract a lot more from his car during practice than he could during the actual qualifying attempt. During practice Saturday morning, Labonte's car was strong through the one-mile high banks of Dover. He still was not as fast as some of the top teams, but he had cut the distance. Between laps Bryan and Kelly Hunt changed the springs and shocks to combat Labonte's complaints of the car being loose. With each adjustment they searched for the magic formula that would put Labonte in touch with the race track.

After practice Terry and a few of the team members gathered at the rear of the transporter. The atmosphere was calm and casual. Labonte, often reclusive when the car was not running right, remained with the team. The conversation came to a halt as two women with long blonde hair sauntered over to the transporter. Both wanted autographs and it appeared they had been collecting them all morning from other drivers. They both had signatures all over their shirts and one had had the drivers sign her pants.

"Can you?" asked the one without writing on her pants. She handed Labonte a black pen and turned so her back was to Labonte. Facing the circle of teammates she had walked through, she waited for Labonte's autograph. In front of an audience of his peers, there was no way Labonte can let the moment go.

"Sure can."

"Is there any room back there?" Her shirt is full but her jeans haven't a mark.

"Well sure there is," he replied.

Starting on the left side of her rear end and working his way across to the right, Labonte autographed her pants. She is shocked he signed her pants; she intended to leave them clean. When he was done her friend took the same position. This time he started with the right side and worked his way around to the front. Terry Labonte #94. As the two turned to leave the transporter, Mecca, standing near Hagan, asked if they wanted the team owner's autograph too.

"God, I'm gonna pass out being around all these guys," one said.

"I'll catch you," Siler said as the group laughed.

When the two are gone Campbell leaned in to Labonte sitting on one of the two benches in the rear of the transporter. "Boy is she going to be mad when she finds out that was just your finger," the chairman said. Again the group laughed.

The entire episode, although only a few minutes in length, indicated a step forward in the maturing of the team. At the beginning of the season, Labonte did not spend a lot of time with the team, and even less time joking with them. His estrangement from them increased as their performance weakened. As a result, it was easy for some on the team to point a finger at the driver, and blame all the problems on him. Now, with Livengood at the top and the performance marginally better on the track, they were a more of a team. There still weren't a lot of group activities for the men away from the track, no team dinners, but they were getting along better. And the communication between Labonte and the mechanics allowed them to get a better idea of what he wanted from his car.

When race time arrived Sunday, the temperatures were high and the humidity thick. Showers were in the forecast.

The team rearranged pit stop duties prior to the race, dropping Billy Siler as the rear tire changer for Chris Hussey, a team member from Bobby Labonte's Busch operation. Cars at Dover raced on bias-ply tires, which changed in size frequently during the race. Siler was needed more to keep track of the tires than he was changing them. With the bias tires, the stagger could change by the hour, dramatically altering the way they would affect the car's handling.

"They thought it was going to hurt my feelings or something," Siler said of the change. "Hell, all the tires I've changed, this is a break."

From the start of the race, Labonte reports that the car is loose, real loose. During pit stops, they try adjusting the wedge and bumping the rear spoiler up a bit, to put more pressure on the rear wheels. Nothing seems to have much of an effect.

"The car started out good and kept getting looser and looser," Labonte explains during a caution. "I thought I might find a better line, but there wasn't one."

Troubles during the pit stops are not helping the team any. Because of the hot temperatures, the glue holding the lug nuts on the wheels is melting. Each time they try to mount new tires, the lugs fall off, costing Labonte a few seconds in the pits. After one stop the NASCAR inspector walks over to Hunt, who handles the jack and whose job it is to make sure everything is okay before the car leaves the pits.

"Did you get all those lug nuts on the right rear?" the inspector asks, shoving his headset to the side so he can hear.

Hunt looked him in the eye and said yes. "Shit, I know 'cause every one of them fell off."

The inspector didn't believe him, but moved on. "I hope so," he says turning away.

By lap 150, Terry has moved up to ninth, and by 170 he is in seventh. Hagan swipes the air with his thumb each time Terry passes the front stretch. Hagan does this whenever Labonte is in contention and passing cars. When Labonte is out of contention Hagan could be found sitting back, arms crossed and feet up. Although Terry is moving up on in the field, he is getting no closer to race leader Harry Gant, who is dominating the field. On lap 240, Gant passes Labonte putting him a lap down. He is three laps down at 256.

Terry pits on lap 282 for tires and gas. The stop takes 23.84 seconds and he is gone. By now only two cars remain on the lead lap, and Gant was one of them. Twenty laps later, Labonte radios back to the pits there is a problem with the engine, a cylinder has gone. Then the car dies.

Labonte coasts into the garages, where he leaves the car bleeding oil, a trail of the lubricant spread to the entrance. "I made sure they'd have to get a new one," Labonte says as he gets out of the car.

"Something happened to the engine," he says to reporters who followed his injured car into the garages. "When it happens to us it's usually a valve or rocker arm."

Labonte dresses and walks away, angry and disappointed. He and his wife walk up a small hill in the infield to watch the race. After a while she leaves, he's better off alone.

Livengood and the team walk back to the garages where Labonte parked the car. Livengood reaches into the cockpit and flips the switch on the tachometer, which would tell him how high the rpms had been in the motor. When he presses the button, it doesn't respond.

"Donnie did you reset the tach?" Livengood asks Donnie Crumley, who is standing nearby.

Crumley nor anyone else touched it before Livengood. Labonte had. When he drove his lame car around the track for the last lap, Labonte revved the engine until it reached the redline section of the tachometer and it exploded. That was his goal, hoping it would force Hagan to buy a new motor. He also knew that if he was successful no one would ask. Hagan, unaware Labonte had redlined the car, spends the rest of the day telling people Bill Elliott can run 400 laps on seven cylinders while Labonte could only complete two.

Back on the race track, Harry Gant laps the entire field and wins his third consecutive Winston Cup event. Labonte's twenty-sixth place finish puts him in twentieth in the points race.

twenty-three

Setting Things Straight

"Terry must go brain dead when he's qualifying."
Bryan Robertson

Following Dover, Billy Hagan spent a day in Pennsylvania in meetings with Campbell and some of the members of the race committee. While the meetings did not result in Hagan agreeing to any major changes in the way he ran his program, he did reaffirm his commitment to spend more time at the Thomasville race shop. Hagan made the commitment after the Pepsi 400 at Daytona, when it became apparent he was unaware of what was going on with the team.

In previous years, Hagan visited the race shop maybe fifty days a year, according to team members. Most didn't mind that he was away. However, by being away from the shop, Hagan had lost touch with how the operation was being run. When questioned about back-due bills, Hagan had to defer to Hupperich, who oversaw the day-to-day affairs. Moreover, earlier in the season when the team was struggling, he wasn't there to see the gap building between his driver and his team.

Some on the committee wanted more of a commitment from Hagan. They wanted a solid agreement that something needed to be changed, something that would give them some rules to enforce if the goals were not met.

Throughout the season Labonte's cars had suffered from broken or bent valve springs, which forced the driver either out of the race or to finish way off the pace. The committee wanted to know what was being done to solve the engine problems. Earlier in the season, Hagan rented an engine from another team to test against Livengood's product. The test results were similar, though, admittedly, Hagan did not use an engine from the top engine builders.

Hagan returned to Thomasville after his meeting and gathered the team for their first meeting in months. Before the meeting, Hagan opened the suggestion box, which sat unopened for most of the season, and reviewed the questions. In the box he found a series of questions that well represented what the team was feeling this far into the season. He found questions many wanted answers to, but were afraid to ask. Some based on fact, others on fiction. Many left the impression that more than a few feared for their jobs.

Hagan addressed the questions head on. The financial problems, he said, were being taken care of. To prove his point, he laid out the business' income and expenses, showing the team spent more than it made. He also mentioned an anonymous letter sent to Sun claiming the team owed tens of thousands of dollars from back tire bills. This was false he said, the tire bill never reached those levels and what he owed had been paid. All of the financial problems were being settled Hagan assured them. No one could put a lien on the team and shut the place down as suggested on one of the scraps of paper in the box.

Many of the anonymous notes, if not a majority, questioned Herb Hupperich's role in operating the team. Why didn't Hupperich focus on managing instead of worrying about the cars? This, too, would be changed, Hagan said. For now on, Hupperich's duties were restructured and his reach into matters with the cars limited to managing. All issues about the cars would be controlled by Livengood.

"It was interesting," Kelly Hunt said about the meeting. Most of the team members felt positive about the meeting and its results. Finally, some of their grievances were being heard, without fear of losing their jobs. When it was over, the suggestion box was left to fill up again.

While the team had been working better together, there was still a lot of finger pointing when something went wrong. After Dover, with the problem with the lug nuts falling off during pit stops, one team member suggested that Billy Siler wasn't putting them on right. He said that Siler was doing it on purpose because they stopped having him change wheels. Another speculated that Labonte wasn't trying hard on the track because he didn't want to pay out his portion of the Sunoco Challenge money. Both complaints were ludicrous, but they serve to show how the team was getting along.

The team felt positive when it arrived at Martinsville later in the week. Using a qualifying motor, Labonte produced laps in practice on par with the faster teams, but, they were still having a problem setting the car up to match Labonte's driving style. The car was loose, so loose in fact that during practice on Friday Labonte spun, narrowly missing the wall.

Labonte went out to qualify. When all the cars had gone, his time was good enough for twenty-fifth place. He was three miles per hour slower than the pole sitter, Mark Martin in the Folgers Ford Thunderbird.

"Terry must go brain dead when he's qualifying," Bryan said early Saturday as the team prepared to take the qualifying motor out, "because the car ran good in practice."

When Kelly Hunt is asked about qualifying he doesn't say a word. He just points to the lounge of the transporter and moves his hands as if he's driving. His message is clear.

Because of Terry's performance on Friday, they decided to remove the qualifying engine and install the race motor before the second round began. Livengood and Labonte still planned on going back out to requalify, but the switch back to the race motor would give the team extra time to work out the handling problem. A little more than an hour after they started, the new motor is ready to be tested. Livengood reaches through the window and throws the ignition switch, bringing the motor to life. The area around him fills with the aroma of smoldering engine paint mixing with racing fuel.

Labonte set out for the first of his many practice laps Saturday morning. After each series he pulls the car up to the pit wall and scans the time sheet handled by Hunt. The numbers were decent, yet needed improvement. Terry had the team change the rear end gear before going back out. He was posting some of the best times at the track since they unloaded the car Friday morning, but still the handling wasn't exactly right. Labonte circled the track while Livengood and Hunt kept track of his speeds, comparing the times on their watches after each lap.

Second round qualifying was rapidly approaching and Livengood installed the qualifying fan and the team mounted new tires on the car. They wanted to see what Labonte could do with the machine under qualifying situations. In one lap he blistered the roadway, notching a time of 20.47 seconds or a little more than 92 mph. He then continued for another lap against Livengood's wishes. Livengood didn't want another lap on the engine or the tires before qualifying.

Labonte pulled the car up to the pit wall and the team quickly stripped the tires off. With NASCAR's public relations representative Chip Williams sitting in the rear of the transporter, Hupperich and Hughes load the tires off the car into the lounge where the heat has been turned on full force.

Hupperich stored the tires there until it was time to requalify. Terry's qualifying lap was quicker than his trip around the track a day earlier, though so were those of his competition. His second round time pushed him further back to twenty-sixth. But had he not ran again, the team might have been forced to use a provisional.

On a small track like Martinsville starting position was important not as much for the spot on the track but for the spot the team would get in the pits. Martinsville's half-mile accommodates two pit areas, one on the front and the other on the back stretch. The back stretch was the last place the team wanted to be. Even under the best circumstances, pitting there would be trouble. When all the cars entered the pits, the teams on the front stretch can complete their work before the teams on the back stretch start. Even the fastest pit work could not make up for that advantage.

In practice Saturday afternoon, Labonte was getting more comfortable with the car. Hunt, Coke and Robertson spent the time changing springs, tires and the sway bar, trying to tighten the car up a bit. The changes worked, although Labonte still wanted the car a little tighter. Terry is happy with the numbers recorded during practice and so is the team. However, with the car loose, he worried it would become harder to control during the race.

"I've seen this picture too many times before," Labonte said to Hupperich as the two sat in the transporter watching the support race. "It will be good for a couple of laps and get worse."

"Why don't we put it back to where it was yesterday when you said it was too tight?"

"The track is different now," Labonte responded, gritting his teeth in mock anger.

The next day the team was late getting the car to the inspection stage. When they got there the exhaust pipe was too low to the ground and had to be repaired before they could push the car to the track. NASCAR rules require the exhaust pipe to sit at least three inches from the ground. The pipe was no more than a half an inch too low, but it still had to be fixed. Hughes jacked the car up, while Robertson stuck pieces of wood under the exhaust. With a twist of the jack handle the car dropped onto the wood, bending the pipe upward. It took a few tries, but finally the alteration was complete. The team was free to push the vehicle into its starting position.

Minutes before the start, Labonte walks around the car and climbs in. Meanwhile, Robertson slips into the car from the other side and loosens the bolts that hold a piece of heavy metal under the dash on the passenger side and slides it over to the driver's side. When he's done fastening the metal, Labonte hands a small ratchet to Harold, standing outside the car trying to block any NASCAR inspectors from seeing the proceedings in the car. The pre-race, post-inspection weight adjustment over with, Labonte is ready to begin.

Moments later the drivers fire their engines and the race is on. Immediately, Labonte gains positions on the field, although the car is still loose. Coming out of turn two, his car fishtails badly, almost causing him to hit the wall. Others did hit the wall.

An accident on lap 44 puts the race under caution. Labonte ducks into the pits for tires and gas. As he enters pit road and makes his way down to Hagan's position, he accidently stops a pit early, but recovers quickly. With the team working on both sides of the car, Livengood sprays water into the brake ducts to cool the brake rotors, hot from constant use. Two dozen laps later, Labonte has moved up to seventeenth.

With each pit stop the car gets better and Labonte more confident. Up ahead on the track, Harry Gant in the Skoal Bandit Oldsmobile dominates the field. There isn't any talk of Labonte passing Gant, though there is a feeling that he can finish high on the scoreboard. Gant seems destined to win his fourth straight Winston Cup race with his commanding lead on the field.

Labonte cautiously stalks the field, passing one car at a time, waiting for the right moment to take another position. By moving up tight on the bumper of his prey and then ducking underneath, Labonte is making headway, while not in danger of ruining his own position or hardware.

"The car feels good," he reports during a caution. "Did you see I passed somebody?"

"Well, we made the scoreboard, we're in fifth," Livengood replies.

Good pit work became a premium. Although the team's pit work had been on average two to three seconds slower than the top teams during the season, at Martinsville the adrenaline is pumping. The stops are flawless and efficient. Despite their speed, they could not overcome the disadvantage placed on them by pitting on the back stretch. Labonte would go back onto the track having lost track position. After each pit stop he spends the first few laps under green passing the cars he had passed earlier in the race.

"I like this set of tires," says Labonte a few laps after a pit stop. "It was tight for about four or five laps then it got better. I must have passed a lot of cars."

"You got that right," Hagan says from atop the pit box. Hagan rarely spoke on the radio, but with Labonte in contention he is more attentive. Once again he is swiping the air with his thumb for every car Terry passes.

Labonte weaves through traffic and finally regains his track position. Then, on lap 210, a caution flag falls and he has to start all over.

"Boy this back stretch pittin' just sucks, don't it?" Labonte says while the team works on his car in the pits.

"10-4," says Dewey.

Labonte pitted in sixth and was in fourteenth at the restart. Nonetheless, he was not content to run in the middle of the pack today.

At the halfway point of the 500-lap race, Labonte passes Rick Mast to take over tenth position. Again he is methodically moving up, setting his sights on the car in front of him and taking over its position. Next up is Ken Schrader in the Kodiak Lumina. Labonte races up behind Schrader. As the two cars go deep into turn three, Labonte nudges the rear of Schrader's car and goes by. Moments later a caution nullifies his efforts.

"I really hate to get behind all of these cars again," he complains. "I was hoping we'd go green all the way. "

Teamwork is at its peak. The stops continue to get better. With the work complete and the gas tank full, Hunt drops the jack, a signal to Labonte to go. Turning onto pit road, Jimmy Spencer clips the front of Labonte's car. Thankfully the impact does no damage to the car.

"Well, I'm closer to the front than I was. That was a good stop."

It was Labonte's first compliment about the pit work all season. In previous races, he complained that pit stops were costing him track position. Often, he was right. Through the first twenty races of the season, the pit work was inconsistent. Great stops, stops on par with the best teams, were often overshadowed by pit work that took seconds longer than any other. In some early races, Labonte lost six to ten spots on the track because of delays in the pits. For now, however, it was coming together.

"Man I hope it goes green all the way. These lapped cars are a bunch of shit here," he says during a caution on lap 278. "This car feels really good for the long run and then somebody spins out."

"I figure you've passed at least fifty cars by now," Hagan says.

"I'd bet I passed more than that."

"You got that right," Hagan says laughing.

For the first time in a long time the mood in the pits is upbeat. The crew's in-race conversations don't revolve around the handling of the car. There is a lighter tone. For the moment they are enjoying the race, enjoying Labonte's success, and enjoying being a team.

At the restart Terry is seventh. Ahead on the track, Geoff Bodine in the Budweiser Ford and Rusty Wallace in the Miller Genuine Draft Pontiac pressure Harry Gant. Gant has had the dominant car for most of the race, although the cautions are keeping the leaders bunched together. Wallace slams Gant a few times down the stretch, then on lap 377, as they exit turn four, Wallace sticks the nose of his Pontiac under Gant's car and the two break loose. Both drivers maneuver their cars to the pits while Labonte moves up in the field and another caution comes out.

Gant's apparent removal from contention excites the team. He appeared untouchable during this and the last three races, which he won. If Gant is out of the race, Labonte may have a chance to win.

While Gant's team takes the caution period to repair his car, Labonte stays on the track and slides into third position behind the No. 6 Folgers Ford of Mark Martin and leader Ernie Irvan in the No. 4 Kodak Lumina. On fresh tires, Labonte can make a run at the top. Gant, meanwhile, is at the end of the pack, his damaged car still on the lead lap.

Under green, Labonte gets up close to Martin going into turn three. Like a cat toying with a mouse, Labonte touches the back of Martin's car, only to have him slip out of reach. While Labonte and Martin play, Irvan is pulling away. The running order stays the same as the laps tick off, all except for Gant, who is charging for the front. Labonte drops to fourth as Gant zooms by on lap 474. Gant is able to push his mangled machine to the front, while Irvan drops off the pace.

Labonte's car has been handling well. Under long stretches of green flag racing the car came to him, and grew stronger. Under green flag conditions, Labonte can run with the pack. Unfortunately, with Labonte still in the top five, the caution comes out, bringing the race to a halt.

"Terry if they [the leaders] come, we're just going to get right sides," Livengood says. "What do ya think?"

Hagan, sitting on top of the pit box, wants Labonte to stay on the track and maintain his position. He's pointing to the track, but doesn't say anything. When pit road opens the leaders flood in. Labonte comes too, taking on two tires in 13.88 seconds.

Terry holds fifth place at the restart, but twenty laps remain and Mark Martin is on his rear bumper trying to take the position. Around they go, nose to tail. Each turn opens an opportunity for Martin, which Labonte quickly closes. Labonte's worn right side tires, not replaced during the last pit, are becoming a problem. His Oldsmobile isn't holding the track well enough to go deep in the turns.

"Make him go around you," Danny Culler says over the radio. Labonte closes down the inside, forcing Martin to the outside. Coming out of turn two, Martin slips the nose of his car under Labonte's. Labonte fishtails violently but recovers, although not before yielding the position.

Gant holds onto the lead and notches his fourth consecutive Winston Cup win. Labonte finishes sixth, marking his fifth points-race top ten finish and only the second time this season he finished on the lead lap. The sixth place finish is worth $12,900.

Labonte drives his car through a crowd of people standing in the garages and over to the transporter. Visibly he is upset with the finish and with Martin's pressure late in the race. Grabbing a cup of water from Paul Mecca, he walks to the transporter without a word.

"That last stop, that was the last thing we needed," he says. "Our only hope was not to go out tenth or so. The left sides wore out. The world's smallest muscleman got me."

"Pitting on the backstretch killed us," says Livengood after the race.

twenty-four

Pumped Up

"We just kinda adjusted ourselves out in left field."
Terry Labonte

Just off of business route 85 over the High Point border and into Thomasville sits the home base for Hagan Racing Teams, Inc. From the road, the shop is indistinguishable from the other small businesses that dot this narrow, winding stretch of Ball Park Road. Only the large blue transporter filling most of the front parking lot and a small lighted Sunoco logo identifies the place to visitors.

Once a one-bay garage, the shop was expanded several times to reach its current 20,000-plus square foot footprint. It's divided into three buildings. The engine shop occupies one, race car preparation another, and the third is the fabrication department, where the bodies are built and painted.

Outside the shop doors sit two wrecked Oldsmobiles, reminders of bad days at the race track. The surrounding area is home to a few other race teams that, like Hagan's, decided to put roots down outside of Charlotte. Despite the race teams, the area is better known for its furniture, an oversized chair sits in a square downtown. Being separated by buildings, it's easy for the team to break along similar lines when it comes to arguing or finger pointing. For awhile, the guys in the body shop blamed the race preparation guys for the performances. At the same time, the guys in the race prep side blamed the fabricators for hanging the bodies on the cars wrong.

Though of late some had started to direct some criticism towards Labonte, for the most part no one openly blamed him throughout the team's troubled start. In racing, blaming a driver is something of a no-no. The driver is usually the last place anyone looks for a problem. Team members are usually blamed for not knowing enough or messing up when setting up the car. Rarely does someone ask if the driver actually knows what he's doing. And as Labonte had more time behind the wheel of the front-steer cars, his confidence as well as his knowledge of what he wanted from the car increased, making him less of a problem.

A short distance away, maybe six miles or so into Trinity, is the newly built racing shop owned by Terry Labonte. While not complete, the 29,000-square foot building is home to Labonte Racing and the base for Labonte's brother Bobby's Busch operation. Someday Labonte hopes to run his own team from the shop, though, until he can find a major sponsor, he'll be driving for Hagan.

Labonte rarely visited Hagan's shop during the week between races. For a race car driver that's not unusual. They are paid, and paid well, to drive the race cars and little more. Sterling Marlin also stayed away from the race team during the week. Instead, drivers routinely take care of other business on weekdays and show up to drive the cars on weekends. Labonte's absence early on, however, only increased ill-feelings between him and the team and perpetuated his "Ice Man" image. Even though going back to Hagan's was a homecoming of sorts, most of the day-to-day workers, the guys who worked on the cars Labonte raced, were not there when he and Hagan had their glory days. Despite the family reunion hubbub, he was a new driver to them. And, unfortunately, when the team was slipping in the standings, Labonte showed up even less at the shop.

Following Livengood's promotion to crew chief, Labonte started hanging around the shop more often. While he is friends with Loyd, the change brought him closer to the team than he had ever been. Indeed, after finishing in sixth place at Martinsville, he stopped by once a day in preparation for North Wilkesboro. Labonte knew that realistically the team's only solid chances of winning were on the short tracks. The speedways were a problem because of handling and the strength of the engines. But the short tracks were different. They provided more contact and demanded better driving skills. His finish at Martinsville was a sign that a win at North Wilkesboro was possible.

"I haven't been this pumped up all season," Labonte said before North Wilkesboro.

Labonte considers himself a fairly smart driver. "I'm as good as my equipment. If my equipment is good enough to win the race, I'm going to lead the race," he said. "If it's not good enough, I'm going to drive it to find out how to make it better and conserve the equipment. I'm a consistent driver."

With each race the team was increasing their knowledge of the basics of front-steer. Using their own experiences and anything they could pick up in conversations with friends on other teams, Hagan's team was getting better in preparing the cars before they got to the track. Early on they were way behind other teams when it came to most phases of the pre-track set-up, but in every instance they were progressing.

"Dewey has done an excellent job," Labonte said. "The cars are better prepared. The engines, well, he sees it now from a different side. Usually by the last practice we've got the car pretty good."

The .625 miles of asphalt that make up North Wilkesboro Speedway have been good to Terry Labonte over the years. He's been on the pole once, and took the checkered flag there twice. Team members also liked to race at North Wilkesboro because they could go home each night. No hotels, just an hour and a half drive back to Thomasville. They met each morning at the shop and drove in the company van to the raceway; when the day was over the routine was reversed. Coming at the end of the season, the trip to North Wilkesboro was welcome.

Before the team got to the track, they installed what would be the backup motor for the upcoming race in Charlotte. For most of the season they had been working on a new car for that speedway. They finished a week ago. Because Hagan's team had exhausted their seven test dates, Labonte's father and brother took the new car to Charlotte for testing. The track was rented under the name of fellow racer Irv Hoerr. Hoerr, an expert road racer, occasionally rented cars from Labonte to enter oval events. Hagan's team painted the new car blue and put No. 44 decals on the roof. As an added effect, the fabrication guys put Irv Hoerr's name above the car windows. Had Terry tested the car, the team would have been fined. None of Hagan's team went along for the test.

The car tested alright, though Terry said some minor changes were needed. However, his brother and father found that the motor in the car was strong.

Terry's first round qualifying run put him in seventeenth position. Due to the size of the field at North Wilkesboro, only the top fifteen are guaranteed starting positions. Nonetheless, he stood on his time for the second round and dropped only to nineteenth. Harry Gant won the pole and a shot at $200,000 in Unocal bonus money and the race purse, should he win the race. The Unocal bonus had more than doubled since Labonte had a shot at it back at Watkins Glen.

"That's about what we thought we'd run," Labonte said after qualifying. "This car is three years old. We'll definitely build another short-track car for next year."

Though they had hoped for better, the team was satisfied with the position. They also seemed more satisfied with the direction in which things were headed. Hagan's talk had brought more of a family atmosphere to the garage area. Everyone was getting along much better than in the past. The team members looked up to Livengood; Hupperich, now staying out of the mechanical side of the business, was getting along better with the team; and Labonte was taking a more active role in garage events.

As had been the case most of the season, Labonte reported that the car was a hair loose. Between practice runs early Saturday morning, the team changed springs and the sway bar. During a break, Labonte climbed in and adjusted the brake bias to cut down the grip of the rear brakes, and hopefully tighten the car up. Despite the changes, the car still didn't make it through the turns properly. Labonte returned to the garage for more adjustments.

Labonte was driving the same car he drove at Martinsville. Indeed, some of the damage from that race was still visible. It was inevitable that the car would be damaged at North Wilkesboro, making it senseless to repair the body. Only the motor was different.

While the team worked on the car, Harold Hughes tended to business in the truck. As a visitor walked over to the truck, Hughes warned the man against eating any brownies that might be in the truck later. A friend was expected to deliver a batch of brownies made with a laxative and he didn't want the visitor to get caught in his practical joke. Hughes pulled the same stunt a year ago with Sunoco race committee member Al Contino, Paul Mecca and a friend of the victims. Hughes resented the way that Mecca and Contino simply walked into the transporter acting like they owned it, and this was his way of teaching them a lesson.

Out on the track Labonte's practice laps were respectable, yet, he had trouble keeping the car in the turns. After each series of laps, he returned to the garages for further adjustments. When the team finished he would head back out, Dewey, Kelly, and Jesse trailing behind him. The effects of their work were immediately detectable, the results judged by a $30 stopwatch. Terry ran three laps and the car started to slow down, a tenth of a second each lap. Labonte pulled down pit road, his last lap four-tenths of a second slower than the first in this series. Even his best time was off the pace of the leaders.

"It ain't good," Livengood said to Hunt as they checked their stopwatches.

"Tires must be worn out," said Hunt.

After stopping on pit road to let Goodyear representatives check the tire temperatures, the team pushed the car into the garage. The car was making a strange noise. The rear wheels were not turning properly. Coke was the first to notice. He suspected a faulty rear end gear and, upon removal, his suspicions were confirmed. Coke headed to the phones to call for a new part, while Labonte looked to his friends on other teams for a replacement. "That's why it went from being one of the best race cars to being a piece of shit," Hunt said to Labonte.

They have just spent the better part of a day trying to get the car right, and it was actually the rear end that was causing the problem. No amount of changes to the springs or the wedge would have compensated for the problem. Yet, they are relieved that the problem was isolated before the race. The unanswered question is how will the car respond to a new rear end in the car?

Race day brings a typical fall day in late September. The early morning temperatures are cool as the new rear gear that Terry got from Junior Johnson is installed. By race time temperatures are expected to be up to a comfortable level.

Shortly before race time, ESPN reporter John Kernan stopped at the transporter to talk with Labonte.

"Terry, I need to get some notes. Last week when you were doing good they said 'what do you have on Labonte?' I said, 'he's doing well.'"

Both men laughed, though in a way it was sad. Running so far back in the pack, Labonte had fallen out of the spotlight. The media doesn't spend much time on the drivers in the rear. They're worth not much more than random notes or filler. Labonte filled Kernan in on recent events with the team and the reporter moved on.

The strategy for North Wilkesboro differed slightly from that used at Martinsville a week early. Instead of using a hunk of steel under the dashboard on the right side to get the car balanced out for inspections, two heavy right side wheels were acquired. The rims were much heavier than normal and made the car fit NASCAR's requirement of having no more than 55 percent of the total weight on the driver's side of the car. The team was playing a game in which the odds were in their favor. In the two races at North Wilkesboro in 1990, the caution flag came out within the first twenty laps, if not sooner. Once the caution dropped on this race, Labonte would duck into the pits. With the heavy wheels off the car, he would effectively have the same results as shifting the weight under the dash, with less risk of getting caught.

The plan backfires. The first caution does not come out until lap 96 and by then Labonte is down a lap, passed by fifty-one-year-old Harry Gant, who took the lead and started to break away from the field early. Around lap 40 Labonte says something over the radio that can't be heard back in the pits. Labonte's times are alright, though he wants some minor adjustments made to the car, including the removal of the heavy wheels.

"I just found a groove," he says during the caution. "It looked like everybody's car was getting loose."

"What did you say before?" Livengood asks.

"I said I can't believe this shit. I needed to make a chassis adjustment but I never got a flag."

"You're doing alright, just hang in there."

The stop takes 23.35 seconds. After the green flag drops, Labonte is turning laps as fast as race leader Gant. As the race continues, though, Labonte is having problems with consistency. Most of this is due to the tires on the car. The new tires the team is using are taking too long to come to him, while the scuffs aren't effective.

Terry pits on lap 220 under caution. The team scrambles to mount new tires and take two rounds of wedge out of the rear. Livengood and Billy Siler decide at the last possible moment to go with scuffs rather than stickers.

"I don't know, these scuffs might not work," Livengood says as Labonte exits the pits. "Terry, it's taking so damn long for these new ones to come to ya."

Labonte pushes his way up to fourteenth place by lap 230, though Harry Gant is still well ahead of the pack. Soon after there are a series of cautions. On lap 252, Labonte comes in for his last stop of the day. He comes in to the pits in fourteenth, and twenty-three seconds later returns to the track in fifteenth position. After twenty laps the car begins to slow a bit, but then picks back up. Labonte is holding his own until an accident on lap 360. Rather then pitting under the caution, Labonte stays on the track and moves up to tenth place. He will gamble that the race goes green the rest of the way.

"We didn't need that flag," Labonte says. The caution gave some teams a chance to put on new tires for the remaining forty laps. As a result, some of those cars would be faster than his when the race restarts.

"You got that right," Livengood answers. "You was doing a helluva job."

At the restart, Gant leads and holds on until lap 392, when a ten-cent o-ring in a brake line fails, leaving the driver without brakes. Dale Earnhardt, in the Goodwrench Chevrolet

Lumina, passes Gant to win the race. Labonte, passed by cars with new tires, comes home fourteenth, two laps off the pace.

"Good job, Terry, you ended up fourteenth. That ain't bad with what you had," Livengood says as Labonte drives to the garages.

"10-4, that's a lot better than I thought it'd be."

At the transporter, Labonte takes a seat on one of the two benches. He's tired and sweaty. There is no coasting, no letting up on the short tracks. The drivers take a beating as well as the cars. Livengood and other members follow, each carrying a piece of equipment from the pits.

"We had changed the rear end and adjusted the brakes," Labonte says after. "The last practice it was pushing real bad. The rear end was messed up and we thought it was the culprit. We just kinda adjusted ourselves out in left field."

Finishing fourteenth moves Labonte up one position to nineteenth in the Winston Cup battle and keeps the team alive in the Sunoco Challenge.

After dressing, Labonte starts to leave the raceway when he runs into spotter Danny Culler heading back to the truck.

"Do you belive Harry [Gant]?" Culler asks. "For $200,000 I would have put Earnhardt into the wall."

"I would have done it for less than that," Labonte says walking away.

twenty-five

Mashing the Gas

"Good job Terry. Thank you lord for being with us."
Dewey Livengood

Three days before the running of the Mello Yello 500 at the Charlotte Motor Speedway, the Sun Company, parent of Sun Refining and Marketing, announced it would undergo a major restructuring which included the elimination of some 900 employees. In announcing the decision, the company said it would take a $400 million charge against earnings in the third quarter.

The announcement was expected, and indeed, Bud Campbell had a role in the planned restructuring. Under the plan, employees were offered voluntary buyouts. If the 900 employee goal was not met through buyouts, layoffs were to follow.

Committee members Campbell and Plazer, both long-time employees of the oil giant, opted for the buyouts. Those on the committee not taking the buyouts became part of the restructuring. Some keeping similar jobs, others moving to other positions.

Sun's financial position reflected the general economy. Just like Sun, General Motors was going through its own economic troubles. As a result, the company made it official earlier that it was cutting back its factory sponsorship next season. Cut from the program would be the Buick teams, and Oldsmobile would drop more than half of the teams it backed for the 1991 campaign. Instead of providing support for a slew of teams, GM created a Motorsports Technology Group to oversee all of its racing programs.

The two separate events would have a profound impact on Hagan as he looked toward the future of his racing operation. Gone for the next season would be hundreds of thousands of dollars in manufacturer support from Oldsmobile and, perhaps more important, Sun's commitment to racing after the 1992 season was unclear. Hagan's strongest ally within Sun, Bud Campbell, agreed to take a package, his future overseeing the racing program uncertain. All areas of the program were under discussion within the company. While contractually committed to forking over $2.1 million to Hagan in 1992, there were no formal commitments for other support. Annually, the company had spent close to a million dollars promoting the racing program, but those expenses were eventually trimmed.

Only four races remained under his contract with Oldsmobile, yet Hagan was hopeful he could strike a deal with Chevrolet. He had won a championship with them in 1984, so he felt they might have some interest in the team.

"I'm waiting to see what Chevy thinks of my proposal," Hagan said standing in the garages at Charlotte. "If not then I'll go to Pontiac, then to Olds. If I've got to pay for it, I'll go with Chevy."

The odds of Hagan getting another manufacturer deal were small. His teams had not done real well in recent years, with Sterling Marlin's tenth-place finish in 1988 being the best.

More important, General Motors executives were trying to cut back, not shift teams to another division. Hagan had pretty much come to terms with the situation and advised the guys in the fabrication shop to start working on two superspeedway cars with Chevy Lumina bodies. While the change had an impact on his wallet, Hagan realized long before that Oldsmobile wasn't the top dog among GM's offerings. Chevrolet is where all the support is focused, and it showed on the track. Chevrolet had the most wins and had been dominant among the manufacturers.

"We'll have two cars made up for Daytona and Talladega," Hagan said. "And then as we crunch these [Oldsmobiles] up we'll change over."

The chassis for the cars would remain the same, just the sheet metal changed. Reskining the cars could take more than two weeks, each at a cost of over $10,000.

The team brought the newest car in the Hagan fleet to Charlotte. Hagan agreed to have the car built after Labonte's performance improved twofold the last time they built a new car. However, while the team had four days of testing with the first one, they were shut out with this car. The new car only had one test session, and that was with Bobby Labonte driving.

During practice earlier in the week Labonte said the car was loose. The car had a strong motor, maybe too strong, but with the car loose he couldn't test its limits.

Labonte's qualifying run put him in twenty-fourth position, twelfth row on the outside. Mark Martin won the pole by turning a lap at 176.499 mph. Labonte did his five miles per hour slower. "How's your car?" Hagan asked Labonte Saturday afternoon. The last practice session would be held shortly.

"It's got more motor than the car can handle," Terry answered. "It's almost there."

"Ya got one more hour to fix it."

Labonte laughed and walked away. His practice runs were at times a half second or more slower than some of the cars qualifying up front.

Hagan turned to Bud Campbell and Geoff Plazer, both in town for the race. Both committee members are avid race fans and many times made the races at their own expense. As part of Sun's attempt to cut costs, Campbell agreed that only one committee member would be designated as the company representative at each race. Sun only covered that person's expenses. The rest traveled on their own. Of the committee members only Al Contino rivaled Campbell and Plazer's attendance during the season.

The mood of the race committee was about the same as it had been for weeks. They were unhappy with the team's performance, though they could see some progress. Campbell admitted the team had moved ahead, and said Hagan had agreed to make more changes.

Shortly after the last practice on Saturday, Terry and Jesse Coke noticed that the rear end gear was slightly cocked, which might have been causing some of the handling problems Labonte complained about in practice. There, however, wasn't any time to fix it and practice. They would have to repair the car in the morning and hope it worked okay in the race.

Before the race started the track held about an hour's worth of entertainment, which included midget races and western music. The entertainment was brought to a close by a man jumping a car 300-feet over exploding buses. The man, of course, survived as they always do in entertainment like this. When the last piece of charred metal was carted away, the race began.

Labonte's car seems well enough for him to move up several positions at the start. During two early cautions he radios back that the car is fine, if not tight. By lap 18, Labonte has worked his way up to sixteenth. On lap 19 the race is under caution.

"I can't drive this thing," Labonte says.

Livengood shakes his head in disgust and looks at Hunt. They both shake their heads. They tried their best and now 19 laps into a 334-lap race their driver is saying he can't drive the car.

"We did the best we could. I don't know . . ." Livengood says, his voice trailing off before completing his thoughts.

Despite his complaints, Terry is able to keep the car under control. Though a lap down, he is running seventeenth at lap 100 and fifteenth on lap 130, when he gets a break. Going into turn three on lap 130, Labonte drives down onto the apron for a scheduled green flag pit stop. Coming out of four, nearing pit road, Ernie Irvan in the Kodak Chevrolet collides with another car sending both into the wall. Quickly, Labonte jerks his car off the apron leading to pit road and back onto the track. The smooth move keeps him from going another lap down in the pits as most of the rest of the field would do.

Labonte keeps his appointment in the pits on lap 131. During the stop his crew jams a piece of spring rubber in the right front spring to try and stiffen that wheel up some. Terry goes back out onto the track in fourth place.

"Terry, I don't know if we've got this car overwedged or not. You're wearing the right rear and left rear out. It's like we're ridin' on three wheels," Livengood says as track crews clean up debris from the wreck.

"You go off in the corner and it feels like the rear end's going to come around," Labonte says. "I started running a different groove and I thought it helped."

"Yeah, that was definitely better. Keep doing what you was doing."

Labonte wants to hear his lap times, something he hasn't asked for in a dozen races. At the start of the year, spotter Danny Culler would call out his times after each lap; however, when the situation on the track deteriorated, he stopped. Steve Loyd didn't want Labonte reminded of how slow he was going. But now Labonte is comfortable with his speeds. Hearing his lap times allows him to adjust to the track and find the fastest groove.

Though Labonte is able to stay up near the front of the pack, with each pit stop the car is handling worse. When the caution flag comes out on lap 234, Labonte heads for the pits even though his last stop came thirty-three laps earlier. Everyone is in agreement that the car needs more wedge. As Labonte enters pit road, Livengood counts how many men are going over the wall during the stop. He counts twice and comes up with seven both times, the NASCAR rule. When the men jump over the wall, Livengood checks again and then heads over himself to turn the ratchet adjusting the wedge.

A NASCAR inspector blocks Labonte's exit from the pits. Livengood had twice counted the number of men going the wall, but he forgot to include himself. The mistake cost Labonte fifteen seconds in the pit. After eleven laps at full speed, the caution flag is out again.

"Those tires any better?" Livengood asks.

"It's not the tires," Labonte says slightly disgusted.

"Well, each time we change 'em it gets worse."

"Okay, I'm gonna come in. Take that spring rubber out of the front and put in two rounds of wedge."

Labonte turns into the pits and the team goes to work. Donnie Crumley carries two tires to the right side of the car, makes sure they get near where the tire changers want them and moves to the rear of the car. There he inserts the ratchet through a hole in the rear window and gives it two full rotations to adjust the wedge. Around on the left side of the car, Kelly Hunt jacks up the car as Bryan Robertson pulls the front wheel off and reaches in for the rubber jammed in the springs. Pressure on the springs makes it difficult to pull out, though after a few tries he's got it. New tires mounted, Labonte's on his way.

He pits again under caution on lap 257 for tires and gas. Though his last stop was not that long ago, coming in now means that he will only have to stop for gas later. His closest competitor, Michael Waltrip in the Pennzoil Pontiac, is about half a lap behind Labonte.

"Let's go for it," Labonte says, and the team goes to work.

Labonte holds onto seventh position into the last laps of the race, though on lap 299 the car begins to slow. The culprit is a valve spring, and he is losing a cylinder. Only a few laps remain in the race, yet Labonte comes into the pits. Gasman Dan Gatewood jerks the gas can into the fuel spout and five seconds later Labonte exits the pits with about $18 worth of racing fuel. When he exits the pits, Waltrip is gaining on him. Though earlier he had let up on the car because of engine problems, he now mashes the gas again. With only two laps to go, Labonte is hoping the engine will hold. It does. Labonte finishes sixth while Geoff Bodine wins.

"Good job Terry. Thank you lord for being with us," Livengood says.

Labonte is in good spirits as he climbs from the car in front of the transporter. He is not overwhelmed with the car.

"We oughta call this one Lucy, 'cause it's so loose," he says laughing. "I felt the valve springs going. Then on the last two laps I saw the 30 car [Waltrip] so I stepped on it. I figured I could coast if it went. It was real survival. The last set of tires after we took that wedge out . . . if I almost wrecked once, I almost wrecked ten times.

For the second time in recent weeks Labonte is happy after a race. The car, while not handling well, was able to put him up front. With some attrition by the front runners, he was well in the mix.

"Damn a lot of cars fell out. We had a lucky finish. The car wasn't as nearly as good as we'd hoped for. It's taken us a long time to get the team in the right direction. We're not there yet, I'm not going to kid anyone. But we got it going in the right direction."

After the race, team members made the fifteen-minute drive to Hagan's Concord home for an annual party. Labonte's good finish helps make the event pleasant. Team members are happy because with three races remaining in the season, they are in fifth place in the Sunoco Challenge.

While Charlotte was a survival test, Labonte's run at Rockingham two weeks later brings back memories of the earlier part of the season. Though he starts twenty-second, Labonte gets off to a good start and has made it up to ninth place before a broken part in the suspension forces the team to take the car to the garages for repairs. He loses fourteen laps while the work takes place and finishes the race in twenty-eighth. However, the finish does move him up to eighteenth in the Winston Cup points race with two races to go.

twenty-six

Don't Mess with the Leaders

"I've learned there's a lot more to life than
race cars."
Bryan Robertson

At twenty-one, Bryan Robertson is the baby of the bunch. A year
ago the team was looking to hire someone to go to the race tracks
with the advance crew the year before; Robertson fit the requirements perfectly. He was young, unattached and willing to work
for a fairly low wage.

Being part of the advance team means being at the track
sometimes three days before the race and guarantees twenty-
nine weekends a year away from home, not counting miscella-
neous testing dates. While the race day crew usually gets to
spend Saturdays with their families, the advance team—the
crew chief, team manager, and a mechanic or two—is at the
track getting the car ready for the race.

For Robertson the job meant working seven days a week for a month straight or longer, depending on which point in the season it was. There's no such thing as a vacation during the season, and for the advance team a day off is something to look forward to. Indeed, early in the season, Robertson joked with others that he was going to work for one of the teams that regularly had trouble making races so he could have Sundays off.

Robertson stands just shy of six feet tall and carries his youth on a slim, but muscular, 180-pound frame. His arms bear the wounds of various accidents during the season, including three burn marks across his elbow where a hot pipe rolled by. His sharp facial features attract women, though he always appears embarrassed by the attention.

This is Robertson's first job in Winston Cup racing, although he did spend some time working for a man who built race cars. He's a good worker, though he needs encouragement from his managers. Encouragement for Robertson or his teammates was something not forthcoming when Steve Loyd was in charge. Always willing to learn, Robertson's good sense of humor also came in handy over the long season.

While he fit the job requirements perfectly, racing had started to wear on him by the time the NASCAR circuit rolled into Phoenix for the Pyroil 500. The hours on the road, and the nights away from home, had taken away some of his interest in the sport. He expected the large amount of work, but his outlook changed.

"Yeah, it was what I expected," he said standing near the car as the team prepared to push it through inspections at Phoenix. "But, I'll tell you, I've learned there's a lot more to life than race cars. I learned that about halfway through the season."

Robertson was angry early on at the way Loyd and Hupperich treated him. Nonetheless, Hupperich believed Robertson was a good worker. "He's got boy written on his back in big letters," Hupperich said once, endearingly. Livengood's promotion to crew chief thirteen races ago sat well with Robertson. "The place is better under Dewey," he said.

For many kids growing up near the Charlotte stock car racing community (Robertson grew up just a short drive from Hagan's shop), working on a Winston Cup team was a dream job. There are only a few dozen full-time teams operating, so landing a job in the business doesn't come easy. Robertson was one of the lucky ones able to break into the "circle."

"Everybody over there," he said pointing to the stands, "thinks this is a glamorous job. It is. We get to go a lot of places and meet a lot of people, but, all the time we're workin'."

The team got to Phoenix on Wednesday, two days before the track opened. It was not unusual for them to arrive early at a western site to do some sight-seeing and relax. Harold Hughes headed for Las Vegas, a short airplane ride away, while others went golfing and horseback riding.

Phoenix International Raceway is perhaps the most scenic speedway on the circuit. In the distance, large jagged-edged mountains form the horizon, while nearby are rolling hills. A large, pointed slope overlooks turns three and four. The air is clean and the weather comfortable for racing. On race day, fans will pay $12 to sit on the incline, which in past years has been infested with rattlesnakes. In fact, the raceway pays local residents to go onto the hill a couple days before the race to clear out the snakes.

The track opened Friday morning and the team went right to work. The race day crew was on their way, they would have Friday and Saturday for their sight-seeing portion of the trip.

It took nearly two and a half hours for the team to get the car through the first inspection. Team members stood with the car, pushing it forward when needed, passing the time talking and joking. The line of cars extended through the garage areas as all the cars attempting to make the race must first pass inspection. NASCAR inspectors tend to examine the car closer this first time around. Every angle of the body is checked against a sheet metal template, and the fuel cell is checked before the car is fully assembled.

The team rolled the Sunoco Ultra Oldsmobile into the inspection garage and NASCAR's crew of inspectors went to work. Everything was fine until one of the inspectors placed a template for the rear window on the car. There was an inch and a half gap between the template and the window edge. The inspectors prepared to fail the car while Livengood protested. Again the inspector mounted the template, however, when doing so, he realized he had the wrong one. The car fit correctly and the team moved on, though a little shaken.

"Damn, we'd be here till tomorrow getting that window right," Livengood said.

Livengood, Coke, Robertson, Hunt and Billy Siler pushed the car back into the garage. Practice was a half-hour away, with first round qualifying later in the day.

At 11 a.m., Labonte fired the engine and drove through the garage and out onto the track. It would be several laps before he put the car under pressure, before he really tested its handling. Seven laps later Labonte pressed the gas peddle, sending a gusher of racing fuel into the motor. His first lap went down as 30.08 seconds, the second as 29.47. A few more and he returned to the garages.

Labonte suggested the team change the drive shaft and the brakes. His Oldsmobile was tight coming off the corners, it could possibly need a larger right rear spring. "It might have too much wedge in it," he said. By the twenty-eighth race of the season, Labonte was more comfortable with front-steer cars. The team was also less afraid of the technology and had come to better understand it. However, it was still an accepted fact that the team needed someone with experience with front-steer cars for next season.

After several adjustments and tire changes, Labonte ran laps of 28.97, 28.88 and a few in the low 29s. Harry Gant had turned a lap at 28.64. A few changes and a couple of hours later Labonte turned a lap at 28.50 or roughly 126.3 mph, his fastest at the one-mile low banked track.

"I'll tell you what, right now it feels like a good race set-up," Labonte said.

Billy Siler rolled his eyes and looked at Dewey. The team worked hard, and they hadn't heard a lot of positive comments from Labonte about the car through most of the season. Labonte's admission came as a surprise.

Labonte guided the car back through the narrow path in the garage. About fifteen minutes remained before qualifying and the team wanted to change tires and prepare the car. Hupperich said there was another set, exactly like the ones Labonte just burned the track with, in the garage. They brought a bunch of left side tires with them from Thomasville and rights were going to be bought at the track. However, it hadn't been done. Hupperich was wrong, there were no right side tires left to put on the car. Livengood was angry. He yelled at Hupperich. Terry, Kelly and Bryan just shook their heads and went back to work. Hupperich left and returned with right side tires for the car, stumbling as he wheeled the handtruck over to the car.

Body heights were reset and the car was pushed through inspection again, and out to the track. Labonte stood in line waiting for his turn to qualify, watching the others zoom by. Labonte's car was eased forward, until the next time was his. When it was over his time of 28.83 was fast enough for twenty-eighth position. Had he equalled his fastest practice lap, he would have been thirteenth. Geoff Bodine captured the pole with one lap at 28.220 seconds, three mph faster than Labonte.

Labonte was one of the first back out onto the track after qualifying. There were still a few bugs to be worked out, mainly it was a bit too tight in the corners. Between his own laps on the speedway, Labonte kept track of driver Irv Hoerr, who was using one of Labonte's own cars. Practice came to a stop when Hoerr slammed the No. 44 Oldsmobile into the wall in turn two, the driver's side coming to rest on the wall.

"Can you see the car?" Labonte asked Hupperich standing on top of the transporter.

"Nah, not yet," answered Hupperich.

"This is the side most people don't get to see, Terry Labonte the car owner," Hupperich said to a visitor. "Everybody thinks the owners just sit there getting rich. You add of a few of these [accidents] and it's a lot different. We've put two in the boneyard this year."

Just then Labonte's crippled car was carried into the pits on a flatbed truck. Hoerr's racing at Phoenix was over, there would be no backup car this week.

Before practice ended, Labonte had Bryan and Kelly mount a metal pan under the front air dam. On relatively flat tracks like Phoenix the pan can add down force to the front and cuts drag on the rear. However, the risk is that it will loosen up the car. That's exactly what happened.

Practice ended and the team returned to their hotel twenty-five minutes away from the track. When they went back to the track on Saturday, the temperatures had dipped some, making the cars a little faster.

Sitting in twenty-eighth, Labonte knew he had to re-qualify, along with the other thirteen drivers that already said they were going back out. Labonte was the fourteenth car to requalify. Getting the signal from the NASCAR inspector, Labonte fired the engine and eased out of pit road and up into the turn. He had the remainder of the lap to get up to speed. By the time he got back around, the clock would be running. His car flew down the front stretch and into the turns, the rumble of the motor at full throttle vibrated the ground. Coming out of turn four he could see the checkered flag. The run was over. His time of 28.951 was well off of his time from the day before, moving him back not forward. Had he not gone back out he would have started thirtieth. Instead, he would start three rows further back in the thirty-fifth spot.

"Man, we shouldn't have requalified. It was too loose. We put that pan under there without tape. We shoulda taped it," Labonte said. "I wish we could draw for positions or clock us in practice. Well, I've started from the front row, I guess I can start from the back row. I'm getting good at passing people."

In practice afterward, Labonte said the car was too loose. Hunt and Robertson changed the two front springs and put a softer spring in the right rear. Labonte's laps were in the 29.40-29.50 range, and clearly not as fast as the front runners. In two days the car had gone from having a good race set-up to having no set-up at all.

While Labonte's on the track, Hunt is asked what could be done to loosen the car.

"Nothing, it's all here," he said pointing to his head. "The driver never questions himself."

As the sun started to set over turns one and two, time was running out in the last practice. Only three-quarters of an hour of track time remained and the car was no where near right. Labonte came in again. Bryan and Kelly went to work changing the sway bar and Jesse bumped the spoiler up some to put more pressure on the rear. When the clock ticked down to five minutes left, Labonte came in and instructed the team to remove the pan. It hadn't worked. The other times during the season that the team tried the pan it hadn't worked either.

The race teams were back at the track before the sun broke over turns three and four Sunday morning. Fans already dotted the hill looking over the track, there early to get the best spots. The season had almost come full circle. The weather was cooler and the smell of kerosene heaters filled the air again. The rushing sound they make was constant, the heat welcome.

Only the teams have made it to the garages this early. Sponsors and fans with garage passes will fill in late after battling traffic in the parking lot.

Off to the side of the garage, Billy Siler prepared the tires to mount on the car for the start. Jesse Coke was on his back under the car, well under way with his duties. Hunt and Robertson had begun their work as well. Outside in the pits, Dan Gatewood, Jim Coltrane and Mark Metcalfe, off from the show car job for a weekend, started to set up the pits. Livengood was preparing the engine. Over at the truck, Hupperich checked the radios while Hughes filled the coolers with ice and water. Donnie Crumley, working around the others, started to wax the car.

When he was done setting up the tires for the day, Siler joined Labonte at the drivers meeting, as he had done for most of the races since Livengood had been in charge. Drivers and crew chiefs collected in a roped off area in the garage. Fans packed in around them, hoping for a glimpse of their favorite drivers.

"Gentleman, we've got 312 laps to go today, lets do it the way we've been doing it all year and we'll get it over in a hurry," said Winston Cup Director Dick Beaty. Beaty ran through the rules and the pit road speeds for the day, then offered any other advice necessary. The race was significant because technically there were three drivers who had a shot at the Winston Cup Championship with a win at Phoenix—Dale Earnhardt, Davey Allison and Ricky Rudd. Beaty warned the drivers not to mess with any of the points leaders. "You hit one, by God, you'd better hit all of 'em."

Beaty continued, "If you're a lap down and the leader passes you, go ahead and race with him. If another comes along let him go on, you're not going to catch him.

"At the restarts, close it up. Keep it close on the pace car. Don't hit him. Don't just motor around like you're on a Saturday evening cruise."

The director reminded the drivers to think about how they would get out of the car in case of an emergency like fire. He wanted them to think about the steps they would take. "Gentleman, it scares the heck out of me when there's a fire and the guy's not getting out of that car."

After the drivers meeting, Labonte and Paul Mecca headed across the track to a hospitality tent rented by a local distributor. Located amongst a village of tents, the site was filled with retailers of Sun's lubricant products. As they entered the tent, a couple standing outside yelled Terry's name.

"Terry, you're my most favorite driver," said the wife.

"Terry, you held our little bitty boy after the last race at Riverside," the husband said as he stood next to Labonte for a picture. Labonte didn't seem to remember the Riverside incident, although he smiled like he did.

Labonte, uncomfortable himself, tried to make the couple feel at ease as the wife fumbled with the camera to take the picture. "I'm so nervous I forgot to turn this on," she said. The couple remained outside the tent, while Labonte went in. When he came out, they stopped him again for another autograph. He signed the card and walked quickly back to the safety of the garages.

A few hours later, the car went through inspection. As Metcalfe and Gatewood finished in the pits, Hunt walked over.

"Mark, what pit number is this? Hunt asked.

"Thirty-five," said Mark.

"We're supposed to be in twenty-five. The Skoal guys are up there talkin' to NASCAR right now, we're gonna have to move."

Hunt continued with the ruse, telling Metcalfe that the pit assignments made after qualifying were changed. Now they had to lug all of their equipment up pit road and set up all over again.

"Ain't we gonna look like the biggest jerks," Mark said.

A minute after saying that, Mark realized Hunt was putting him on and started chasing Hunt down pit road. Hunt took pleasure in practical jokes and had a knack for pulling them off.

Keeping a serious face though making ludicrous statements was an art Hunt had mastered. Metcalfe was his latest victim.

By race time, the hill overlooking turns three and four was full. Fans had scaled the incline and pitched tents and sun shields. The sun burned on the speedway, shadows almost straight from its angle.

As the cars snake through turn four for the start, they bunch together just like Beaty asked and the race is underway. Ten laps into the event, a bunch of cars collect on the front stretch in front of Labonte, but he is able to stay clear of the mess. Labonte comes in for tires, gas and to have some wedge taken out. In the pits, the crew bounds over the wall and to the right side of the car. As Bryan tightens the last lug on the front tire, Hunt releases the jack. Robertson makes a quick turn, and as he does the cartilage in his knee shreds. He crumples to the ground as the car bounces off the pavement. He gets up and limps around the front of the car to change the left side. He is in extreme pain, but he can't stop now. Once the stop is complete, it becomes apparent that, unable to put pressure on the leg, Bryan's day at Phoenix is over. Siler will change tires for the rest of the race.

The team has the set-up on the car a hair off going into the race, a problem amplified by inconsistent reactions to different sets of tires. The tire situation gets worse at the 100 lap point when Goodyear runs out of tires. Early cautions have caused teams to change tires more frequently than usual. Siler scrambles through the pits looking for a team with extra tires. Eventually, the team pitting next to Hagan's agrees to sell a set.

Through attrition and good driving, Labonte makes his way to the front portion of the field. He is running tenth at the 150 lap point in the race and thirteenth at lap 270.

"Terry, you're racin' the 5, the 10, the 15, the 26 and the 25," Livengood says.

"10-4."

"And the 3."

By lap 289, Labonte is gaining on Ricky Rudd in the No. 5 Tide Chevrolet. Labonte has the bright orange Lumina in his sights.

"Go get him, Terry. Ya got him, go get him," Livengood yells into the radio.

Livengood encourages Labonte to go after Rudd and gain another position. While he isn't going to win the race, it is the principle of the thing. Loyd had never coached Labonte on the track. Either he passed cars or he didn't. But, no matter where Labonte is running, near the end, Livengood would be pushing him.

"Go get the five. You got to beat the five to be in tenth place," Livengood says as the laps tick off.

Rudd finishes eleventh, Labonte twelfth.

"Well, you finished twelfth. You came a long way," Livengood says as the team starts to break down the pits.

"Damn it. I could out run him, but we ran the same line," Labonte says. "I almost had him. I caught up on the last lap but I couldn't get the bite. After qualifying where we did, this was remarkable. I was just holdin' on. We just weren't quite good enough."

It was the first time in the four-year history of the race at Phoenix that Labonte hadn't finished on the lead lap.

Now with the sun setting over their shoulders the team loads Labonte's ride onto the transporter. As the remainder of the equipment is loaded on, scorer Doris Livengood walks over with the day's results. They are eighteenth overall in the points standings

Looking over Herb Hupperich's shoulder, Donnie Crumley asks about the Sunoco Challenge. Hearing the results, his face lights up. They are tenth in the challenge. The team has won the bonus. There is only one race left in the season and Sunoco's deal includes an option to throw out the results of one race. No matter where they finish at Atlanta, they've won. Their hard work has paid off. They'd won something. The money would come in handy with Christmas just around the bend. Each crew member joked about how they would spend their new found wealth.

Everyone was happy, except Bryan Robertson. While Labonte was on the track wrapping up the challenge, he spent the day laying down in the medical center. The prognosis wasn't good. Doctors there told him they were 90 percent sure he would need an operation. Phoenix would be his last race of the season.

twenty-seven

The Finish Line

"After this miserable season, I'm glad it's over."
Harold Hughes

Ten months after the season started, NASCAR prepared for its final event, the Hardee's 500 at the Atlanta International Speedway. Some forty weeks had gone by and during that time twenty-eight races (not counting The Winston and the Winston Open) had been run on sixteen different race tracks across America. In that time, teams, fans, officials, sponsors, and other race related workers had traveled from Delaware to Daytona and from Richmond to Sonoma.

For some the last race of the season was a sad occasion. It would be the last race for teams with sponsors who won't be around next season. It would be the last race for some drivers. For others the last race brought with it a chance to start all over.

Hagan's shop was not immune to the emotions of a season ending. During the two weeks the team spent preparing for Atlanta, Steve Loyd resigned to become crew chief for a second team being formed by Roush Racing, owner of Mark Martin's ride. The move meant a fresh start for Loyd with a new crew at Roush's shop. While his crew at Hagan's was far from overwhelmed with Loyd's leadership, they were happy he was getting a second chance.

"He came in and told me he had another offer," Hupperich said. "I got up and shook his hand. Just because it didn't work out here doesn't mean he shouldn't get another chance somewhere else."

And Hagan rehired Pete Wright and Marc Fryar. Wright had worked for Hagan before, and Fryar worked on Labonte's Busch program.

The departure of Loyd made it possible for the return of former crew chief Pete Wright. Wright had worked for Hagan in the glory years and was good friends with Labonte. When Terry departed for Junior Johnson's team in 1986, Wright followed. Hagan Racing became the third team Wright worked for this season. An experienced chassis mechanic, Wright started the season with Johnson and jumped ship midway through the season to work for the Stavola Brothers, when Steve Wilson left Hagan to join the same team. Wright wanted to work for Hagan earlier in the year, but it posed a problem. Wright had taught Loyd the ropes and working for the person he taught would not have been healthy for either.

Wright brought another level of energy to the team, a higher one. Having been in the business so long, he was already friendly with much of the team, most important Labonte. Terry had respect for Wright, and the knowledge he had. Labonte would listen when Wright had suggestions. Where Livengood represented stability, Wright would be a driving force behind Labonte from here on. That became clear after just a few days on the job.

"He's not so much a wizard, but he'll give his opinion. What we need is a couple more like him," Labonte said. "If you look around, every team's got a leader, but they also have a couple just like him around."

Labonte immediately noticed an improvement in the team's work, having commented that the team did more in the first two hours at the track than they had during some entire weekends. He attributed the change to Wright.

While the last race brought some new talent to the team, the guys who spent the year struggling to get it together were glad the end was near. Their improvement on the track in recent weeks, the more enjoyable working atmosphere, and the winning of the Sunoco Challenge helped, but it had still been a long season. And two months down the road they would be back again, qualifying for Daytona.

"It's a breather," Hupperich said about the last race. "I'm looking forward to starting the second season."

"After this miserable season, I'm glad it's over," Hughes said. "But, I'm a lookin' forward to next year."

Labonte qualified seventeenth in the forty-car field, nearly four and a half miles slower than pole sitter Bill Elliott in the Coors Ford Thunderbird. It was good for the team not to have to go back and requalify. They could now spend Saturday, their final practice day of the 1991 season, working on the race set-up.

Qualifying three rows behind Elliott, in fifth position, sat Dale Earnhardt. Earnhardt's ninth place finish at Phoenix earlier in the month assured him of winning his fifth Winston Cup Championship by merely starting his engine on Sunday. Only one other driver, Richard Petty, has accumulated more points championships.

Though he didn't have to worry about requalifying, Labonte was not delighted with the way the car was handling. He complained that it was tight in the middle of the turns and coming out.

Friday night Hagan's team went out to dinner, together. Usually, the guys returned to their rooms and were on their own. If they went out, they splintered into smaller groups. However, as the season came to a conclusion, they were coming together.

Saturday morning, as second round qualifying took place on the track, the team took steps to modify the handling of Labonte's car. They changed the springs and then loosened the mounting brace holding the radiator in position. When it was free, Hunt walked over to the transporter about fifty feet away.

"Harold, we need the vacuum," Hunt said when he got there. "We need to vacuum the front, not the inside," he added with emphasis on the front.

Hughes moved to a back cabinet in the transporter and grabbed the box containing the vacuum, but not before adding in a few pieces of lead. He then walked to the garage where Hunt was waiting for him at the front of the car. Hunt set the box containing the vacuum on top of the motor. Going through the motions of vacuuming the front of the car, he checked to make sure no one was looking and slipped the lead into the front portion, in a position that violated NASCAR rules. They hoped the lead would put more pressure on the front of the car. A longer rear spoiler was also built to help control the car.

"Terry complained the car had a lot of lift in the front and the whole car," Hunt said. "He couldn't get into turn one."

For Hunt, Atlanta ended his eleventh season in Winston Cup racing, and he looked forward to a much needed rest. "I'm pretty much sick of this," he said. Though just after Thanksgiving he'll want to be back at it.

During the last practice session, Labonte drove onto the track and turned ten laps at top speed, generating lap times of 32.15 seconds through 32.53. He still wasn't comfortable with the car and came back in. Hunt took two rounds out, and Labonte went back to the track. His times weren't any better and the car still didn't feel right. He radioed back his concerns and the crew set up the scales to weigh the car. The numbers that flashed on the liquid crystal display angered Labonte. He was angry because the car had been set up wrong. He had spent a good portion of practice fighting a car that was out of whack. Labonte slammed the lid to the scales and walked away. There wasn't enough time to adequately fix the problem before practice ended. It was left for morning.

Unlike the others, the end of the race season was not as welcome to Billy Siler. A twenty-two-year racing veteran, Siler enjoyed racing, although to him it was a part-time affair. Throughout the season, Siler showed up at the tracks on the weekends to handle the tires. During the week, he ran his own tire business in North Carolina.

"Shit no," he said when asked about the end, minutes before the race was to start. "I don't know what to do with myself on Sundays. What is there to do but watch football, eat and get fat?"

Within the first four laps of the race, Labonte is on the radio saying the car is loose. The leader, Bill Elliott, is turning laps of 32.56, while Labonte's best are at 32.96 and growing slower. Though he is moving up a bit on the field, the handling of the car forces him into a high groove on the track.

Labonte pits under caution on lap 27 and the team takes out a rubber in the right rear spring and two rounds of bite. By lap 70 he has fallen to twenty-sixth. Then, as he comes out of turn two on the back side of the track, two cars collide, sending debris flying at his car. Something off the back of one of the cars crushes the front grill on Labonte's car. Under caution, Labonte comes into the pits where the team tapes up and pulls off parts of the front valence. At the same time, three rounds of wedge are taken out.

"Terry, the tires that came off showed about 15 degrees of push," Livengood says after the work is done.

"10-4," Labonte replies.

"That was a lot of changes."

"Yeah, I guess we just kinda overreacted," answers Labonte.

"Well, you said it was bad loose."

"That should help it, should probably fix it," Labonte says.

"You ain't got much of a valance either."

Terry fights the car much of the race. The handling problems the car had going into the race are magnified by the damage to the front of the car from the accident. No longer is his Oldsmobile efficiently cutting the wind. Instead, the damage slows the car down, sometimes a full second slower than the leaders.

The winner of the final event of the season is Mark Martin. Terry winds up in seventeenth, three laps off the pace.

Labonte drives his car through the garage entrance and over to the transporter parked nearby.

"Piece a shit race car," he says taking a cup of water from Paul Mecca. "I was hopin' I'd wreck it on the last lap so I wouldn't have to drive it next year." He is angry and at the same time relieved. The rollercoaster season is over and the team can now concentrate on rebuilding for next year.

"The car never really worked good the whole time we were here," he says. "Something hit the front and messed up the aerodynamics. We knew at the last practice we were going to be in trouble today. We're going to get these cars better. We're pretty much behind in aerodynamics. This car was an aerodynamic nightmare."

Labonte changes into his street clothes and moves to the rear of the transporter. The struggle is over.

"Usually at this point I'm in need of a break," Kim Labonte says as she prepares to leave the raceway with her husband for the last time this season. "It will be a relief to stop worrying, so to say."

With that, the Labonte family leaves the speedway. The transporter loaded, the rest of the team follows in groups according to their transportation home.

Labonte's finish put him in eighteenth position in the Winston Cup standings, 1,263 points behind Dale Earnhardt. Labonte completed the season on an upswing. At one point he was twenty-ninth in the standings.

Of a possible 9,766 laps run during the season, Labonte completed 79 percent or 7,748. His average starting position was twenty-second, while the average finish was twentieth. During the twenty-nine-race season, there was just one top five finish, eight top ten, and one pole, all worth $310,470 in prize money. The results were nothing to write home about. In fact, they were worse than his finish a season ago. However, the results were good enough to leave a flicker of encouragement for the next season.

Although Labonte ended his second consecutive season without a win, parts of his performance are likely to remain in the record books for some time. His record shattering pole-winning time at Watkins Glen may never be broken because the layout was changed after the death of J.D. McDuffie. It's unlikely cars will ever go that fast there again. And Labonte's passing of Michael Waltrip at Bristol in August will be around until 13,000 goes into the record books.

A week after the gates at Atlanta were locked, Labonte and the crew were in Richmond testing for the next season. Three weeks later, they tested at Daytona. There Labonte drove the same car he had parked at Daytona in July, this time at speeds a second and a half faster. The car had been reworked and carried a Chevrolet Lumina body. By the looks of things 1992 would be a good year.

Terry Labonte's 1991 NASCAR Winston Cup Performance Chart

DATE	EVENT	TRACK	ST POS	FIN POS	LAPS COMP	LAPS POSS	$$$ WON	POS PTS	STATUS
2/17	Daytona 500	Daytona	31	13	198	200	34,355	14	Running
2/24	Pontiac 400	Richmond	18	14	397	400	7,200	15	Running
3/ 3	Goodwrench 500	Rockingham	24	39	14	492	5,425	27	Accident
3/17	Motorcraft 500	Atlanta	32	39	256	328	6,385	29	Camshaft
4/ 7	TranSouth 500	Darlington	27	15	364	367	9,735	26	Running
4/14	Valleydale 500	Bristol	30	9	500	500	9,575	22	Running
4/21	First Union 400	N. Wilkesboro	30	31	207	400	5,000	24	Cyl. Head
4/28	Hanes 500	Martinsville	13	31	128	500	4,850	28	Overheat
5/ 5	Winston 500	Talladega	24	37	70	188	7,715	28	Accident
5/19	*Winston Open	Charlotte	3	9	133	134	8,000	28	Running
5/26	Coca Cola 600	Charlotte	13	10	399	400	21,750	27	Running
6/ 3	Budweiser 500	Dover	8	24	483	500	7,050	26	Running
6/ 9	Banquet 300	Sears Point	2	6	74	74	14,400	22	Running
6/16	Champion 400	Pocono	14	21	199	200	7,750	24	Running
6/23	Miller 400	Michigan	26	25	196	200	8,555	23	Running
7/ 6	Pepsi 400	Daytona	41	41	8	160	6,080	26	Vibration
7/21	#Miller 500	Pocono	23	15	178	179	9,550	26	Running
7/28	DieHard 500	Talladega	35	24	184	188	9,215	23	Running
8/11	Bud At The Glen	Watkins Glen	1	34	47	90	9,490	26	Engine
8/18	Champion 400	Michigan	25	17	198	200	10,500	25	Running
8/24	Bud 500	Bristol	28	9	493	500	9,225	23	Running
9/ 1	Heinz So. 500	Darlington	23	5	366	367	19,515	21	Running
9/ 8	Miller 400	Richmond	20	19	396	400	6,000	19	Running
9/15	Peak 500	Dover	23	26	302	500	6,850	20	Engine
9/22	Goody's 500	Martinsville	26	6	500	500	12,900	20	Running
9/29	Tyson 400	N. Wilkesboro	19	14	398	400	6,750	19	Running
10/ 6	Mello Yello 500	Charlotte	24	6	330	334	26,300	19	Running
10/20	A C Delco 500	Rockingham	22	28	471	492	6,850	18	Running
11/ 3	Pyroil 500	Phoenix	35	12	311	312	9,750	18	Running
11/17	Hardee's 500	Atlanta	17	15	324	328	9,750	18	Running

Average Starting Position:	22	Top 5 Finishes:	1
Average Finishing Position:	20	Top 10 Finishes:	8
Laps Completed/Total Possible Laps:	7748/9766	Pole Positions:	1
Percentage of Laps Completed:	79%	Outside Pole Position:	1
Total Money Won:	$310,470		

*Non-Winston Cup Point Event   #Rain Shortened from 200 Laps

Final 1991 Top 20 Winston Cup Point Standings

POS	DRIVER	POINTS	BEHIND
1.	Dale Earnhardt	4,287	— — — —
2.	Ricky Rudd	4,092	- 195
3.	Davey Allison	4,088	- 199
4.	Harry Gant	3,985	- 302
5.	Ernie Irvan	3,925	- 362
6.	Mark Martin	3,914	- 373
7.	Sterling Marlin	3,839	- 448
8.	Darrell Waltrip	3,711	- 576
9.	Ken Schrader	3,690	- 597
10.	Rusty Wallace	3,582	- 705
11.	Bill Elliott	3,535	- 752
12.	Morgan Shepherd	3,438	- 849
13.	Alan Kulwicki	3,354	- 933
14.	Geoff Bodine	3,277	-1,010
15.	Michael Waltrip	3,254	-1,033
16.	Hut Stricklin	3,199	-1,088
17.	Dale Jarrett	3,124	-1,163
18.	**Terry Labonte**	**3,024**	**-1,263**
19.	Brett Bodine	2,980	-1,307
20.	Joe Ruttman	2,938	-1,349

Index